André L. Simon's
Dictionary of WINES, SPIRITS and LIQUEURS

André L. Simon's

Dictionary of WINES, SPIRITS and LIQUEURS

Second edition

Edited and revised by
Lynne McFarland

Hutchinson

London Melbourne Sydney Auckland Johannesburg

Hutchinson & Co. (Publishers) Ltd

An imprint of the Hutchinson Publishing Group

17–21 Conway Street, London W1P 6JD

Hutchinson Group (Australia) Pty Ltd
30–32 Cremorne Street, Richmond South, Victoria 3121
PO Box 151, Broadway, New South Wales 2007

Hutchinson Group (NZ) Ltd
32–34 View Road, PO Box 40–086, Glenfield, Auckland 10

Hutchinson Group (SA) (Pty) Ltd
PO Box 337, Bergvlei 2012, South Africa

First published by Herbert Jenkins 1958
Reprinted 1961
Second edition published by Hutchinson 1983

Set in Linotron Helvetica by Input Typesetting Ltd,
London SW19 8DR

Printed in Great Britain by The Anchor Press Ltd
and bound by Wm Brendon & Son Ltd
both of Tiptree, Essex

British Library Cataloguing in Publication Data
Simon, André L.
    André Simon's dictionary of wines, spirits and
    liqueurs. – 2nd ed.
    1. Alcoholic beverages – Dictionaries
    I. Title   II. McFarland, Lynne
    641.2′0321   TP503

ISBN 0 09 150110 5 cased
        0 09 150111 3 paper

André L. Simon:
a short biography by his daughter

André Louis Simon was born in Paris on 28 February, 1877.

His father, an artist, died from a sunstroke while painting beside the Nile, when André was seventeen years of age. At the time, André was on a visit to England to improve his English, and he had been introduced to the Symons family, whose youngest daughter Edith, then aged fifteen, was later to become André's wife.

After completing his three years military service, André accepted the offer of a friend of his father's to join the Champagne firm of Pommery et Greno in Reims. Becoming bored with office life, André asked to be allowed to work in the cellars and there he developed great interest in the many facets of wine-making.

In 1900 he married, and in 1902 Pommery et Greno sent him to their London office. It was not long before he was giving free public lectures, illustrated by lantern slides, to help in the better understanding of wine.

It had always been André's desire to write, but he had a living to earn. On asking a friend for advice, the reply was 'do you spend every hour selling Champagne?' Therefore, in his spare time he wrote, and in 1905 his first book, *The Champagne Trade in England,* was published. Thereafter he wrote continuously until 1968, when his eyesight failed. He had had over a hundred books published. Although most of them were about wine, André also wrote some books on the combination of food and wine. During World War I, when André was assigned to the British Army as an interpreter, he found time to write about General Joffre, and an elementary Russian grammar. The whole edition of the grammar was sold to the War Office, and was issued to all men who went, or were being sent, to Archangel.

Returning to England after the war, André resumed selling Champagne until 1932, when he left Pommery et Greno.

In 1933, with A. J. Symons, he started the Wine and Food Society, carrying on alone after the early death of Symons. The aim of the Society was for the better understanding of food and wine, and the harmony and enjoyment of their being used together. André felt that the Society should have its own magazine, so he edited *The Wine and Food Quarterly* which was, and still is, sent to every member. The Society grew and is now known as the International Wine and Food Society, having many branches in America and around the world.

In 1961, when his wife became ill, André left the Society, but he was named as their Perpetual President. In 1963 André's wife died after sixty-three years of marriage. They had had a family of five children. André had felt the need for a complete change, and although eighty-six years of age, he decided to go alone, by sea, to visit for the first time the vineyards and the different branches of the Wine and Food Society in Australia and New Zealand. He celebrated his eighty-seventh birthday in Melbourne. On his return he wrote *The Wines, Vineyards and Vignerons of Australia.* The following year he sailed for South Africa, which he had visited many times during his Champagne-selling days. He was happy to see it again, and also to meet the Society's branch members whom he had not met before. He spent his eighty-eighth birthday in Cape Town.

On his return, André wrote *The Gazetteer of Wines,* the fruit of a lifetime's study and work. It had taken him two years to write, and he had just finished reading the proofs when his eyesight failed.

Not being able to write, or see to read the old books that he had collected through the years, was a great trial to him, but having been a religious man he accepted it with cheerfulness and patience.

André died on 5 September, 1970, aged ninety-three. The Queen had graciously awarded him the CBE, and the French Government had made him an Officier de la Légion d'Honneur. The Vintners' Company had made him an honorary member of their ancient company, the first non-Englishman to have been so honoured. It had been the Vintners' Company who had lent him their hall for those lectures he had given at the beginning of the century.

J. Rouyer Guillet

Editor's note

A common dream among editors is that one day they will light upon diaries that have never been read – it has happened occasionally, and fascinating books have been produced from them. Revising this book provided the same sort of privilege, and delving into André Simon's work I found there was almost as much between the lines as there was on them – facts and dreams abound, loves and hates, cherished memories, and stern judgements.

Inevitably in such a wide ranging work there were areas that were dealt with more deeply than others and also with more authority. In the revision I have only 'edited' Simon where there is a consensus among experts, and, of course, the updating process has necessitated change. Considerably more is known now about wines from outside Europe than was within the experience of experts at the time the book was compiled. It has been possible, therefore, to add a number of entries on Australia, on the American wine-producing states, and on South Africa.

It has been particularly interesting to research the English vineyards, and many are included. Italian wines have been thoroughly revised and many more grape varieties are mentioned.

Lynne McFarland

How to use the dictionary

Names are usually given in the spelling of the country's language, but where the English name is commonly used, for example in connection with Eastern European wines, then that spelling is used.

Experts differ as to the style of listing for the names of wines and estates; particularly names which include le, la, les, Château, Schloss, etc., cause the most inconsistencies. In this dictionary you will find, for example, Château Couhins is under 'Couhins, Ch.', and de la Roche, Ch. is under 'R'. On the other hand, Schloss Vollrads is under 'S'.

Cross-references are given wherever possible, and, in order to keep entries short, the country is not mentioned in an entry if it is possible to cross-reference to it. For example, an entry for a Sonoma County vineyard will be cross-referenced to California.

This book is not encyclopaedic, giving exhaustive information on each item. Instead it concentrates on giving good, factual, no-nonsense information on a range of wines, spirits and liqueurs. A browse through the pages will soon familiarize readers with the style.

Abbreviations

It would have been clumsy to repeat some words over and over again in a book already burdened by repetition. The following abbreviations have therefore been adopted:

AC or *app.*	Appellation Contrôlée
Ber.	Bereich
Ch.	Château
comm.	Commune(s)
Dpt.	Département(s)
Gr.	Grosslage
nr.	near
Mt.	Mount
r.	river
vyd.	vineyard
méth. champ.	méthode champenoise
5me, 4me, etc.	cinquième, quatrième, etc.

For definitions of these words see the individual alphabetical entry.

Aargau
Minor wine-producing district of northern **Switzerland.**

de l'Abbé–Gorsse-de-Gorsse, Ch.
Cru bourgeois of the **Haut-Médoc.**

Abboccato
Term for lightly sweet wines of **Italy.**

Abfüllung
German equivalent of **mise en bouteilles.**
See also **Erzeugerabfüllung.**

Abocado
Spanish term for a medium sweet wine.

Abrau-Dursso
Large wine-producing collective of the **USSR,** particularly for sparkling wine. *See* **Kaffia.**

Abricotine
French liqueur made from **Brandy** and small apricots with the tang of the kernel.

Abruzzo
Wine region of central **Italy** famous for **Montepulciano d'Abruzzo** and **Trebbiano d'Abruzzo.**

Absinthe
A distilled spirit flavoured with anise and wormwood, banned in most European countries because of its dangerous qualities but still said to be illegally manufactured and drunk in **Spain.** Largely replaced by **Anis** and **Pastis.**

Abtey
Gr. of the **Bingen** *Ber.*, **Rheinhessen.**

Abtswind
Village of **Franken,** *Gr.* **Schild (Abtswind),** producing some of the most reliable whites of the region.

AC
See **Appellation d'Origine Contrôlée.**

Acerbe
French term for sour or sharp wine; usually that made from insufficiently ripe grapes.

Acetic acid
The most prevalent of all undesirable acids in wine. Its presence arises mainly from the oxidation of **ethyl alcohol.** It is responsible for the sharp, sour taste of vinegar and **piqué** wines. Wines of low alcoholic strength are more prone to acetification.

Achaïa Clauss
One of the largest wine-producers of **Greece.** *See* **Demestica.**

Achkarrener
Red or white wine of the **Kaiserstühl-Tuniberg,** *Gr.* **Vulkanfelsen,** not often seen outside **Germany.**

Acids
Acids contribute to the fresh, tangy and fruity tastes in wine and also protect it from some harmful bacteria. **Tartaric acid** – the most important – and malic acid are both desirable in wine, **acetic acid** is among the most undesirable. Citric acid is present in small quantities and carbonic acid is present in some sparkling wines. **Acetic acid** is one of the group known as 'volatile' acids which are essential to the bouquet and retain quality but which give sharp vinegary tastes if present in excess of the 'fixed' acids, e.g. **tartaric.** *See* **Malolactic fermentation.**

11

Aconcagua Valley
An important wine-growing region of central **Chile**, where **Bordeaux** grapes produce some good wine.

Adega
The Portuguese equivalent of 'winery'.

Adelaide
Some wines are still made in the capital of **South Australia.**

Adelberg
Gr. of the **Bingen** *Ber.,* **Rheinhessen.**

Adgestone
Large English estate, Brading, **Isle of Wight.** Recent vintages have obtained recognition by the **EVA** and won the **Gore Browne Trophy.** Light, dry wines.

Advocaat
Thick, creamy yellow-coloured liqueur made from eggs, sugar and spirit – originally **Brandy.**

Afames
Brand name of one of the better dry red wines from **SODAP, Cyprus.**

Africa, North
The main wine-producing areas are **Algeria, Morocco, Tunisia.** North African wines were traditionally used for *coupage* – the bolstering of French wines after a bad harvest.

After-taste
The 'internal' bouquet that remains in the mouth and nose after the wine is swallowed.

Aghiorghitico
Greek red wine grape found especially in the Peloponnese.

Agker
State wine organization covering 125 farms in **Hungary,** including the **Tokay** estates.

Aglianico del Vulture
Superior dry red *DOC* wine from the slopes of Mt. Vultura, **Basilicata.**

d'Agly, Côtes
App. of the **Grand Roussillon** region.

Agrafe
The metal wire which holds in place the temporary cork used in the first bottling of **Champagne.**

Aguardente
Portuguese for **Brandy.**

Aguardiente
Spanish for *spirit.*

Ahr
Tributary of the Rhine, joining it near Bonn, and second smallest of the eleven specified regions after **Hessische-Bergstrasse.** Produces predominantly red wines.

Aigle
Village and district of the **Vaud** canton, producing some of the richer **Chablais** wines.

Aiguebelle
French liqueur said to have originated from the Cistercian monastery Notre Dame d'Aiguebelle founded in 1137. It may be flavoured with as many as fifty different herbs.

Aix-en-Provence
Centre for the red, white and *rosé VDQS* wines of **Provence,** e.g. *Coteaux d'Aix-en-Provence, Coteaux des Baux. See* **Palette.**

Akkerman
Important wine-producing district of
Moldavia, USSR.

Akvavit
Danish **Aquavit.**

Alba
Wine centre of **Piedmont.** *See* **Barbera d'Alba.**

Alba Flora
A white wine from Mallorca.

Albana
Italian white wine grape.

Albana di Romagna
DOC white wine from **Emilia-Romagna.** It
can be either **secco** or **amabile,** or
sparkling from the provinces of Forli,
Bologna and Ravenna.

Albani, Colli
South of Rome, in the **Lazio** region. The
vyds. produce generally dry, white wines
the best-known of which is **Frascati.**

Albariño
Spanish white grape found mainly in
Galicia.

Albariño del Palacio
White wine from Fefiñanes, Galicia.

Albariza
The white, chalky soil of the best **Sherry**
vyds. between **Jerez de la Frontera** and
Sanlucar, Andalucia.

Albillo
One of the minor **Jerez** grapes, used in
making **Sherry.**

Alcamo
Sicilian *DOC* wine – red or white.

Alcohol
When fermentation takes place the chief
products are **ethyl alcohol** and **carbon
dioxide. Ethyl alcohol,** which is present
in wine, beers, and spirits, is a colourless
liquid with a faint, pleasant smell and is
not a poison or a narcotic.

Alcoholic strength
The strength of an alcoholic liquor is
expressed either as a percentage of **proof**
(spirits) or as the percentage of alcohol by
volume (wines). In the UK, wine Excise
Duty is charged at different rates for
different strengths. *See* **Proof** and **Sikes.**

Aleatico
Italian **Muscat**-like grape. Also found in
Corsica and **California.**

Aleatico di Gradoli
Strong Italian *DOC* red wine from **Lazio,**
made from the **Aleatico** grape. There is
also the *DOC Aleatico di Puglia.*

Alella
Village and small demarcated region north
of Barcelona, **Catalonia,** and the name of
the mostly dry white wine from the
surrounding vyds.

Alexander Valley
Small high-quality vyd. district of **Sonoma
County.** Includes those of **Simi,
Souverain, Geyser Peak.**

Aleyor
Very dark red, almost black, table wine
from the vyds. of Mallorca.

Alf
Minor wine village of the **Zell-Mosel,** *Gr.*
Grafschaft.

Algeria
Once the major North African supplier of wines to **France** for blending, and to other countries under its own labels. The wine was frequently used to add colour, body and alcoholic content to the wines of the **Midi.**

Alicante
Demarcated region of **Spain,** producing heavy wines, high in alcohol.

Aligoté
One of the two permitted white **Burgundy** grapes – produces wines that are best drunk young. Also grown in the **Lorraine, Rumania** and the **USSR.**

Alkermès
French cordial. The red colour is from the dye obtained from insects of the cochineal genus found in the Mediterranean kermes oak.

Allasch
Type of Russian **Kümmel** now made in Holland.

Allesverloren
Large South African wine estate in **Malmesbury** specializing in red wines.

All Saints Winery
Large winery in north-east **Victoria,** producing a full range of wines.

Almadén
Big commercial winery, **California,** making a full range of wines and Sherries.

Almansa
Demarcated area west of **Alicante,** producing heavy wines, high in alcohol.

Aloxe-Corton
Important red wine-producing *comm.* of the **Côte de Beaune.** The *app.* of the lesser red wines after **Le Corton.**

Alsace
Province of north-east **France** now divided into two *Dpts.,* **Haut-Rhin** and **Bas-Rhin.** On labels the *app.* **Alsace** and **Vin d'Alsace** are followed by the name of the grape rather than place names. The Alsatian bottle is tall, thin and tapering. The best wines, made from **Noble** grapes, can carry the *app.* **Alsace Grand Cru.** A *Grand Vin* or *Réserve* must have at least 11° natural alcohol (**Gewürztraminer, Pinot Gris, Pinot Noir**) or 10° (**Riesling, Muscat**).

Alsenz
One of the tributaries of the **Nahe** valley. Its vyds. produce pleasant but not outstanding wines.

Alsheim
Quantity wine-producing village of the *Gr.* **Krötenbrunnen, Rheinhessen** – mostly whites.

Altar wine
The unadulterated fermented juice of fresh grapes used for sacramental purposes.

Altenahr
Village of the upper **Ahr** valley, *Gr.* **Klosterberg,** producing light red table wines.

Altenbamberg
Village in the **Nahe** region, *Gr.* **Burgweg,** producing red and white wines.

Alto
Stellenbosch estate producing full-bodied red wines.

Alto Adige
DOC area of the **Trentino-Alto Adige;** always associated on the label with the grape type, e.g. the local **Traminer** and **Schiava.**

Alto Douro
The upper valley of the **Douro.** Its vyds. produce the only wine which is entitled to the name **Port.**

Alupka
Pink dessert or 'white port' wines from the **Crimea.**

Alushta
Red wine of the Ukraine, **USSR.**

Alvarinho
Quality Portuguese white grape important in the production of **Vinho Verde.**

Amabile
Italian term denoting medium sweet wine.

Amador
North Californian county which specializes in wine from the **Zinfandel** grape.

Amarante
Sub-region of the **Vinhos Verdes.**

Amaretto
Italian apricot-flavoured liqueur.

Amarone
See **Recioto.**

Ambonnay
Grand cru of the **Champagne** region. The red wine is considered the peer of the red **Bouzy,** the best still red wine of **Champagne.**

Amelioration
A treatment or addition to grape juice or new wine to improve quality. *See* **vins Chaptalisés.**

America
See **USA.**

American vine stocks
These are of the genus **Vitis labrusca,** as opposed to the European **Vitis vinifera.** They were responsible for the spread of the dreaded **Phylloxera** in Europe at the end of the nineteenth century, but eventually produced disease-resistant root stocks on which it was, and is, possible for the European vines to be grafted, and from which disease-resistant **hybrids** have been produced.

Amer Picon
Pink-red French **Orange Bitters** served as an **apéritif.**

Amigne
Traditional white grape of the **Valais.**

Ammerschwihr
One of the more important wine-producing *comm.* of **Haut-Rhin, Alsace.**

Amoltern
Lesser white wine-producing village of the *Gr.* **Vulkanfelsen, Kaiserstuhl-Tuniberg** *Ber.*

Amontillado
Now the commercial word to describe a *medium Sherry.* Really a matured **Fino,** not as dry and with a little more alcohol.

Amoroso
A **Sherry** type. Softer, sweeter and slightly paler than an **Oloroso.**

Les Amoureuses
Premier cru from the **Chambolle-Musigny** *comm.* A red **Burgundy** of charm and distinction.

Ampelidaceae
Latin botanical family to which the grape vine belongs.

Ampelography
Scientific study of vines.

Amtliche Prüfungsnummer (AP)
The control number printed on the label of German **QbA** wines. The *AP* is assigned and recorded by the tasting authorities after rigorous tasting and laboratory tests to make sure the wine is as described on the label.

Añada
Spanish *wine of the year* kept for a time before blending in the **Sherry** process.

d'Ananas, Crème
Pineapple-flavoured liqueur.

Anapa
Wine district of the **USSR**, which gives its name to the *Anapa Riesling.*

Anbaugebiete
German for *region.* There are eleven specified quality wine-producing **Gebiete (QbA): Ahr, Baden, Franken, Hessiche Bergstrasse, Mittelrhein, Mosel-Saar-Ruwer, Nahe, Rheingau, Rheinhessen, Rheinpfalz, Württemberg;** and five for **Deutscher Tafelwein.**

Andalucia
Large wine-producing region of **Spain**, for **Sherry** in particular.

Andron-Blanquet, Ch.
Lesser *cru bourgeois* of the **Haut-Médoc, St. Estèphe** *comm.*

Añejado por
Spanish term meaning *aged by.*

Angelica
Basque liqueur of the **Chartreuse** type. Pale yellow, sweet and highly aromatic. Also a sweet white wine made in

California from grape juice where the fermentation is checked by the addition of spirit.

L'Angélus, Ch.
Grand cru classé, **Côtes Saint-Émilion.**

Angludet, Ch.
Cru exceptionnel of the **Cantenac-Margaux** *comm.*

Angostura
Popular brand of **bitters** from Trinidad, made mainly from **Rum** and herbs. Provides the 'pink' in pink gin.

Angoves
Family winery in **Adelaide** and the Murray Valley.

Aniseed (Anis)
Herb used in several countries to flavour proprietary liqueurs, e.g. **Anisette.**

Anisette
French aniseed liqueur.

Anjou
AC of the **Loire**, well known for its *rosés.* *See* **Rosé d'Anjou; Cabernet d' Anjou.** Also produces red and white wines. *See* **Coteaux de la Loir, Coteaux du Layon, Coteaux de l'Aubance.**

Annaberg
Renowned single vyd. of **Kallstadt,** *Gr.* **Feuerberg** in the **Rheinpfalz.**

Año
Spanish for *year.*

d'Anseillan, Ch.
Cru bourgeois of the **Haut-Médoc, Pauillac** *comm.*

Antika
Brand name of a Greek wine.

Antinori
Leading Italian wine family established in Florence, producing **Chianti** and **Orvieto.**

AP
See **Amtliche Prüfungsnummer.**

Apéritifs
French name for a variety of strong and often bitter drinks which are taken to stimulate appetite before meals. Today more loosely applied to any alcoholic drink taken before meals.

Apetlon
Village of the **Burgenland** region of **Austria** producing white wines, some of which are sweet.

Aphrodite
Brand name of one of the better medium dry white wines of **Cyprus.**

Apostles
Twelve large casks containing very old Rhine wine which are kept in the municipal cellars of the town of Bremen.

Appellation Communale
Third rank of *AC* wines of **Burgundy,** which show the *comm.* name on the label.

Appellation d'Origine Contrôlée (AC)
French legal guarantee of origin for quality wines controlled by the *Institut National des Appellations d'Origine des Vins et Eaux-de-Vie.* The law governs: the site of the vyd.; the grape varieties used; the quantity of wine produced per hectare; the minimum alcoholic strength; the method of planting, pruning, etc; and the vinification.
   In the **Burgundy** region the name of the vyd. is usually the name of the *appellation.*

Apple Brandy or Apple Jack
Colourless or pale straw-coloured spirit distilled from apples or cider and usually of high alcoholic strength, e.g. **Calvados** in Normandy. Apple Jack is the American name.

Âpre
French for *sharp,* referring to a wine with an excess of tannin.

Apremont
One of the lesser known but acceptable white wines of **Savoie.**

Apricot Brandy
National liqueur of **Hungary.** It is also made in **Austria, France,** Holland and **Australia.** Not to be confused with **Abricotine.**

Apulia
See **Puglia.**

Aquavit
Swedish spelling of the Danish **Akvavit.** A spirit distilled from grain or potatoes, or both, and usually flavoured with caraway seed. The name is a corruption of the Latin *Aqua-vitae* – water of life. *See* **Eau-de-Vie.**

Aquileia
DOC of **Friuli Venezia-Giulia,** from eleven *comm.* The label usually shows the grape variety.

Aragon
One of the more important wine-producing districts of northern Spain. *See* **Carineña.**

Arbois
Red, white and *rosé* district of the **Jura,** known for its **Vin jaune.**

d'Arche, Ch.
Large *2me cru* **Sauternes** estate. **Ch. d'Arche Lafaurie** is the unclassified bottling.

Arcins
Lesser *comm.* of the Haut-Médoc.

Ardine
French proprietary **Apricot Brandy.**

Arena
Characteristic sandy soil in the area around **Jerez** from which the lighter lower quality wines were produced. Hardly used now.

d'Arenberg
Family estate of **McLaren Vale, South Australia.**

Argentina
The wines of Argentina come mostly from the provinces of **Mendoza,** and **San Juan,** which produces a lot of **Sherry**-style wine and **Brandy.** There are red, white and *rosé* wines mostly of *ordinaire* quality, and some sparkling and dessert wines.

Les Argillières
Premier cru of the **Pommard** *comm.*, **Côte de Beaune.**

Arinto
The most important white grape from which the **Bucelas** wines are made.

Arkansas
Small wine-producing region of the **USA** with the vyds. mainly in the north of the state around **Altus.**

Armagnac
Brandy distilled from wine of the Gers *Dpt.*, **France.** The centres for Armagnac production are **Condom, Auch** and **Eauze.** The region is divided into **Haut-Armagnac, Ténarèze,** and **Bas-Armagnac,** the latter two districts producing the finest. Armagnac is distilled at a lower strength than **Cognac** and has a stronger flavour and 'scent'.

Aroma
Usually associated with the *nose* of a young wine as opposed to the *bouquet* of a more mature wine. Aromatic – fragrant, implying a rich aroma.

Arrack (Arak)
Fiery spirit distilled throughout the East and in Europe from rice, sugar-cane, dates, palm juice or other ingredients.

Arrières Côtes
Area to the west of the **Côte d'Or** producing second quality red and white Burgundies.

Arsac-Margaux
Comm. of the **Haut-Médoc** producing both red and white wines.

Arsinoë
One of the better-known brand names of dry white table wine from **Cyprus.**

Artichoke Brandy
French distillation from the Jerusalem artichoke. *See* **Cynar.**

Artisan
See **Cru.**

Les Arvelets
Premier cru of the **Pommard** *comm.,* **Côte de Beaune.**

Arvèze
Gentian-flavoured **apéritif** from the **Auvergne,** slightly sweeter than **Suze.**

Arvine
Old white grape of the **Valais** for dessert wines.

Asbach
Proprietary German **Brandy.**

Asciutto
Italian term for dry wine.

Assmannshausen
District of the **Rheingau** *Gr.* **Steil,** *Ber.* **Johannisberg;** known for its red wines.

Assumption Abbey
Brand name for wines of Brookside Cellars, San Bernardino, **California.**

Asti
Town of **Piedmont** surrounded by vyds. producing large quantities of both still and sparkling white wines of which the best known is **Asti Spumante.**

Asti Spumante
Sweet, sparkling *DOC* white wine from **Piedmont.**

Astringent
Dry, mouth-puckering sensation caused by high tannin content, often with high acidity content. Can disappear as the wine matures.

Asztalibor
Hungarian for **vin ordinaire.**

Aszú
Hungarian for the dried out grapes which produce the sweet **Tokay Eszencia** and **Tokay Aszú.**

Atholl-Brose
Name for a variety of Scottish drinks made by mixing **Whisky,** honey, cream, and fine oatmeal.

Atillafelsen
Gr. of the **Kaiserstuhl-Tuniberg** *Ber.*

Attica
Wine region around Athens, **Greece.** *See* **Retsina.**

de l'Aubance, Coteaux
AC of **Anjou** – rather sweet white wines from the banks of a tributary of the **Loire.**

Aube
Dpt. adjoining the **Marne** *Dpt.,* in the south of the **Champagne** region.

Aucerot
Minor white wine grape grown in the **Hunter Valley,** and used for blending.

Aude
One of the extensive wine-producing *Dpts.* in the south of **France.** Mostly red *ordinaire;* some white and sparkling wines. *See* **Corbières.**

Auenstein
Württemberg district, producing red and white wines but mainly **Schillerwein.**

Auflangen
Gr. of the **Nierstein** *Ber.*, **Rheinhessen.**

Auggen
Village of the *Gr.* **Burg Neuenfels,** *Ber.*
Markgräflerland, Baden.

Aume
Alsace cask; same size as the **Burgundy
Feuillette** – 114 litres.

Aurora
French-American **hybrid** planted
particularly in the **Finger Lakes** area of
New York State.

Aurum
Italian pale gold liqueur with a **Brandy** and
orange base and flavoured with herbs.

Ausbruch
Traditionally found on labels of sweet
wines from **Burgenland.** It is an old
German term for **Aszú.**

Auslese
German for *selected* referring to the best
and ripest grapes specially chosen at the
vintage. *See* **Beerenauslese,
Trockenbeerenauslese, Spätlese.**

Ausone, Ch.
Premier grand cru classé of **Saint-
Émilion.**

Ausonius
Fourth century Roman poet, born in
Bordeaux and property owner in **Saint-
Émilion. Ch. Ausone** is called after him.

Australia
The major wine-producing states are **New
South Wales, Victoria, South Australia**
and **Western Australia,** with pioneering
vyds. in Queensland and Tasmania.
Principal red grape varieties are **Cabernet-**

Sauvignon, Shiraz (the **Syrah** of France
and **Petite Sirah** of California) and
Grenache, with lesser quantities of
Malbec, Carignane, Cinsaut and **Pinot
Noir.** White grape varieties are **Rhine
Riesling, Sémillon, Clare Riesling** (a
South Australian grape thought to be a
clone of Sémillon), **Chardonnay,
Marsanne, Sauvignon Blanc** and
Traminer, with a number of other varieties
for dessert wines and Australian Sherries.

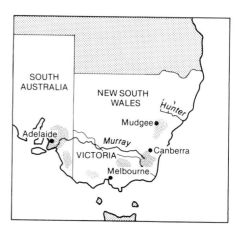

Austria
Vines are grown within the city of **Vienna,**
but the largest production comes from
Lower Austria, including the **Wachau,
Krems, Gumpoldskirchen, Falkenstein,
Langenlois** and **Klosterneuburg.** Other
vyd. areas are **Burgenland,** including
Neusiedlersee and **Eisenberg,** and
Steiermark. White wines predominate,
particularly those from **Grüner Veltliner.**
Other light, fresh wines from **Riesling,
Traminer, Muller-Thurgau** and **Muscat-
Ottonel.** Excellent dessert white wines
from the **Burgenland** from **Auslese** to
Trockenbeerenauslese quality. Reds
include **Schilcher** wine which can vary
from a *rosé* to dark red colour.

d'Auvergne, Côtes
Small *VDQS* district of **France** nr.
Clermont-Ferrand.

Auvernier
Village of the Neuchâtel district of

Switzerland, known for **Oeil de Perdrix,** made from **Pinot Noir.**

Auxerrois
Synonym in the **Lorraine** for the **Pinot Gris** and used especially for the local traditional **Vin gris.** Also in **Luxembourg.**

Auxey-Duresses
Comm. entitled to the *AC* **Côte de Beaune-Villages.** Red and white wines.

Aveleda
Brand of **Vinho Verde** from the **Minho** region, northern **Portugal.**

Avenay
Premier cru **Champagne,** from **Épernay.**

Avensan
Lesser *comm.* of the **Haut-Médoc.**

Avignon
Centre of the southern **Rhône** vyds.; **Châteauneuf-du-Pape,** etc.

Avize
Grand cru **Champagne,** and the most important township of the white grape district, known as the **Côte des Blancs,** east of **Épernay.**

Ayala
One of the large **Champagne**-producing Houses at **Ay.**

Ay-Champagne
Grand cru **Champagne** and a quaint old town on the right bank of the r. Marne almost opposite **Épernay.**

Ayl
Wine village on a slope of the **Saar** valley, **MSR.** The white wines are: *Ayler*

Herrenberg, Ayler Kupp, Ayler Scheidterberg.

Azay-le-Rideau
See **Touraine Azay-le-Rideau.**

Bacardi
A proprietary brand of white **Rum.** Bacardi Rum was originally produced in Cuba in the 1880s; since then it has been produced in Puerto Rico, Mexico, Brazil and the Bahama Islands.

Bacchus
American small black **hybrid** grape.

Bacharach
Ancient city and district of the **Mittelrhein** producing white wines.

Backsberg
Important large estate at **Paarl,** producing good red wines.

Baco Noir
French-American **hybrid** grape grown particularly in **New York State.** Also a newer variety of the **Armagnac** district.

Badacsoni Kéknyelü
One of the drier wines of the Mt. Badacsoni district of **Hungary.** Also produces the sweeter *Badacsoni Szürkebarát* and a *Badacsoni Riesling.*

Bad Dürkheim
Town of the **Rheinpfalz** producing quality white wines and some reds.

Baden
QbA region of south-west **Germany** from the Tauber r. in the north to Lake Constance nr. the Swiss border, producing red and white wines. The best come from the *Ber.* of **Kaiserstuhl-Tuniberg**. Other districts are **Bodensee, Markgräflerland, Breisgau, Ortenau, Badische Bergstrasse Kraichgau, Badisches Frankenland.**

Baden
Town and district south of **Vienna**.

Badische Bergstrasse Kraichgau
Ber. of **Baden, Germany**.

Badisches Frankenland
Ber. of **Baden, Germany**.

Bad Kreuznach
Wine centre of the **Nahe** valley and district name. Produces some of the best wine of the region.

Badstube
Gr. of the **Bernkastel** *Ber.*, **MSR**.

Bagaceira
Portuguese **Marc.**

Bahans, Ch.
The non-vintage second wine of **Ch. Haut-Brion, Graves de Bordeaux.**

Bailey's Bundarra Winery
Small family firm producing rich full reds (*Bundarra* **Hermitage**) and dessert wines, **Victoria.**

Bairrada
Undemarcated region of **Portugal**

producing quantities of good table wines and sparkling wines by the *méth. champ.*

Balance
See **Well-balanced.**

Balestard-la-Tonnelle, Ch.
One of the best-known *grands crus classés* of **Saint-Émilion.**

Balestey, Ch.
Minor estate of the **Cérons** *comm.*, **Graves de Bordeaux**, producing red and white wines.

Balling
Scale used in the **USA** for measuring the sugar content of unfermented grape juice.

Balthazar
Glass bottle large enough to hold sixteen ordinary bottles. It is mostly used for show purposes, especially in **Champagne.**

de Bananes, Crème
Sweet banana-flavoured liqueur.

Bandol
Well-known **Provence** *app.* – reds and rosés are better than the whites.

Banyuls
One of the best and better-known **Vins doux naturels** of the French **Pyrénées.**

Barack Pálinka
An unsweetened spirit distilled in **Hungary** from apricots.

Barbacarlo
Red wine, dry or semi-sweet, from the **Oltrepó Pavese, Lombardia, Italy.**

Barbaresco
Red *DOC* from **Piedmont**. Similar to but

lighter than **Barolo** and one of the best of the area.

de Barbe, Ch.
Well-known producer of red wines in the **Côtes de Bourg.**

Barbera
Italian black grape used especially in **Piedmont.** Gives full-blooded astringent wine in cool areas, softer wines in hot areas. Also grown in **California.**

Barbera d'Alba
Fragrant good maturing *DOC* red from **Piedmont.**

Barbera d'Asti
Dark red *DOC* of **Piedmont**; reputedly the best of the area.

Barbera del Monferrato
Dry, though can be slightly sweet, or sparkling *DOC* red from **Piedmont.**

Barberone
Californian red table wine from **Barbera** grapes.

Bardolino
DOC light red wine of **Veneto** from the vyds. of the eastern shore of Lake Garda.

Barea Velha
Fruity and rich Portuguese wine.

Baret, Ch.
Dry red or white **Graves** estate. *Comm.* **Villenave d' Ornon.**

Barolo
The best *DOC* red wine of **Piedmont.**

Barossa Pearl
Sparkling wine from the **Gramp** winery, **Barossa Valley.**

Barossa Valley
Large quality wine area of **South Australia** producing white wines, reds and dessert wines.

Barr
Comm. of **Alsace, Bas-Rhin** *Dpt.*

Barrel
English and American common term for a cask which can be any size. When used for US and Canadian spirits it contains 181.7 litres.

Barrica
Spanish and Portuguese for **Hogshead.**

Barril
Portuguese and Spanish for **Barrel.**

Barrique
French equivalent of **Hogshead** – contains 225 litres.

Barro
Spanish name for the mud or clay used to describe the second best soil around **Jerez.** Today rarely planted with vines.

Barsac
Important sweet wine-producing *comm.* of the **Gironde,** much larger than its great neighbour **Sauternes.** The wines are *AC* **Sauternes** as well as **Barsac;** sometimes both appear on the label.

Barton et Guestier
Well-known **Bordeaux** *négociant.*

Bas-Armagnac
See **Armagnac.**

Basilicata
Small wine-growing district of southern **Italy.** Only *DOC* wine is **Aglianico del Vulture.**

Bas-Médoc
Northern part of the **Médoc** now simply called that. Produces red and white wines generally less fine than those of the **Haut-Médoc** in the south of the **Bordeaux** region.

Bas-Rhin
See **Alsace.**

Basserman-Jordan, von
Old and important wine estate of the **Rheinpfalz.**

Bastia
The chief northern wine-producing centre of **Corsica,** noted for the *AC* **Patrimonio Rosé.**

Basto
Sub-producing region of the **Vinhos Verdes.**

Bastor-Lamontagne, Ch.
Cru bourgeois **Sauternes** estate, **Preignac** *comm.*

Batailley, Ch.
5me cru classé of the **Haut-Médoc, Pauillac** *comm.*

Le Bâtard-Montrachet
Name of a group of *grand cru* small vyds. partly in the *comm.* of **Puligny-Montrachet** and partly in **Chassagne-Montrachet,** which produce one of the best white Burgundies.

Bavaria
One of the more important wine-producing areas of **Germany;** its best vyds. are those of the **Rheinpfalz** and **Franken.**

B & B
See **Benedictine.**

Béarn
Small *VDQS* area of south-west **France,** east of Biarritz.

Beaujeu
Formerly the metropolis of the **Beaujolais** and still an important wine centre. Wines now have the *AC* **Beaujolais-Villages.** The *Hospice de Beaujeu* owns vyds. and produces a little white **Burgundy** – *Ch. de Chatelard.*

Beaujolais
Large wine-producing region south of the **Mâconnais** and the general *AC* of the region. Some of the best wines come from the vyds. that are geographically in the **Mâconnais.** There are nine named *crus* with their own *AC* in this northern part of the region.

Beaujolais de l'année
The current **Beaujolais** vintage.

Beaujolais Nouveau (Primeur)
Beaujolais drunk very young, often a few weeks after harvest (15 November is the earliest date, or 15 December for the named wines). The wine is young, fresh and has a lot of acidity.

Beaujolais Supérieur
This wine must have an alcoholic strength one degree more than **Beaujolais.**

Beaujolais-Villages
The highest *AC* covering thirty-six villages in the north of the **Beaujolais** region producing the stronger, fuller wines. There are nine named *crus:* **Fleurie, Brouilly, Morgon, Juliénas, Chénas, Saint-Amour, Moulin-à-Vent, Côte de Brouilly, Chiroubles.**

Beaulieu
Famous **Napa Valley** growers producing *de Latour Private Réserve Cabernet,* and white *Ch. Beaulieu;* also producing *rosé* and sparkling wines.

Beaulieu-sur-Layon
Comm. of **Anjou, Coteaux du Layon**
producing some fine sweet white wines
under their own *AC.*

Beaumont, Ch.
Grand cru bourgeois of the *Haut-Médoc;*
Cissac comm.

Beaumont-sur-Vesle
Champagne *grand cru,* canton de **Verzy.**

Beaune
The home of many important **Burgundy**
wine merchants and of some of the classic
Burgundies. Beaune has given its name to
the **Côte de Beaune,** immediately south
of the **Côte de Nuits,** a little beyond
Santenay, where the **Côte d'Or** ends.
The less distinguished wines may be sold
under the *app.* **Beaune-Villages.** *See also*
Hospices de Beaune.

de Beaune, Côte
The vyds. and general *AC* of the southern
half of the **Côte d'Or.** The **Corton** *comm.*
produces substantial reds, and
Montrachet, the famous dry but golden,
and slightly scented whites. Main areas
include: **Meursault; St. Aubin; Monthelie;**
Volnay; Aloxe-Corton; Pernand-
Vergelesses; Auxey-Duresses;
Pommard; Santenay; Savigny.

Beauregard, Ch.
One of the better **Pomerol** estates in the
south close to the **Saint-Émilion** district.

Beauroy
Premier cru **Chablis.**

Beauséjour-Fagouet, Ch.
Premier grand cru **Saint-Émilion.** The
other part of the estate is known as
Beauséjour Duffau-Lagarosse. Minor
growths are sold as *Ch. Picard.*

Beau-Site, Ch.
Grand cru bourgeois of the **Haut-Médoc,**
St. Estèphe *comm.*

Beau-Site-Haut-Vignoble
Cru bourgeois, **St. Estèphe** *comm.,* **Haut-**
Médoc.

Bechtheim
Minor wine-producing district of the
Rheinhessen, Wonnegau district.

Beerenauslese
German for one of the highest grades of
natural 'sweetness', referring to a fine
white wine made from the ripest berries
picked out from each bunch of the grapes
at the time of the vintage. *See* **Edelfäule,**
Trockenbeerenauslese, Auslese,
Spätlese.

Beerenlay
Gr. of the **Bernkastel** *Ber.,* **MSR.**

Beery
An undesirable smell caused by secondary
fermentation in the bottle. The wine is
basically unsound.

Beeswing
Fine floating crust peculiar to some old
bottled **Ports.**

Beilstein
Important **Schillerwein** producing locality
of **Württemberg.**

Beilstein
Minor wine-producing area of the **Mittel-**
mosel, MSR, in the section of the r.
known as the **Krampen.**

Bel-Air, Ch.
Premier grand cru classé, **Saint-Émilion.**
There are a number of chx. of the same
name in the **Bordeaux** region.

Bel-Air-Marquis d'Aligre, Ch.
Cru exceptionnel, **Soussans** *comm.,*
Haut-Médoc.

Belgrave, Ch.
5me grand cru classé of the **Haut-Médoc, St. Laurent** *comm.* Also *cru
bourgeois* of same *comm.* Different
property.

Beli-Pinot
Popular Yugoslavian version of the **Pinot
Blanc.**

Bellegrave, Ch.
Cru bourgeois of the **Listrac** *comm.,* **Haut-Médoc.**

Bellet
Provence wine from nr. Nice. Above
average wine, from a small *comm.*

Bellevue, Ch.
There are several chx. of this name in the
Gironde *Dpt.* – one a *bourgeois* growth of
the **Médoc,** one a *grand cru classé,*
Saint-Émilion, one in the **Blayais,** one in
the *comm.* of **Montagne Saint-Émilion,**
and one in the *comm.* of **La Brède,
Graves de Bordeaux.**

Bel-Orme-Tronquoy-de-Lalande, Ch.
Cru bourgeois of the **Haut-Médoc, Saint-Seurin-de-Cadourne** *comm.*

Ben Ean
Popular **Mosel**-type blended Australian
made wine by **Lindeman.**

Bénédictine
French liqueur which enjoys a world-wide
reputation. **Brandy**-based, flavoured with
herbs. Every true bottle carries the initials
DOM (Deo Optimo Maximo). **B & B** is the
brand name for a **Brandy** and Benedictine
mixture.

Benicarló
Very dark red wine of high alcoholic
strength, from Valencia, **Spain.**

Bensse, Ch.
Cru bourgeois of the **Médoc,**
Coopérative de Prignac.

Bentonite
Clay-like substance legally used as a
fining agent for clarifying wine, especially
white.

Berberana, Bodegas
Fruity full-bodied wines and some smooth
reservas of the **Rioja Alta, Spain.**

Bereich
A sub-region or district of an
Anbaugebiete.

Bergat, Ch.
Small *grand cru classé,* **Saint-Émilion.**

Bergerac
Centre of the best vyds. of the Dordogne
and the major *AC* of the area. Red, white
and *rosé* wines similar to those of
Bordeaux.

Bergheim
Important *comm.* of **Haut-Rhin, Alsace.**

Bergkelder, The
Major wine and spirit producers and
merchants at **Stellenbosch.** Main brands
include *Fleur du Cap, Grunberger,
Stellenryk.*

Bergkloster
Gr. of the **Wonnegau** *Ber.,* **Rheinhessen.**

Bergstrasse
See **Hessische Bergstrasse.**

Bergstrasse-Kraichau
See **Badische.**

Beringer
One of the older and larger **Napa Valley** wineries.

Berliquet, Ch.
Lesser growth **Parsac-Saint-Émilion.**

Bernkastel
One of the most famous and picturesque towns of the **Mittel-Mosel** and a sub-region of the **MSR.** Its vyds. produce much fine wine none better known than the *Bernkasteler Doktor* with its slightly smoky undertaste.

Berri Co-operative
The largest winery and producer in **Australia,** based at Berri in **South Australia.**

Bertani
Producer of quality **Veneto** wines.

Bertola
Sherry shippers owned by the **Rumasa** group.

Bertolli
One of the best-known producers of **Chianti Classico,** from nr. Siena.

Besigheim
Wine-producing area of the *Ber.* **Württembergisch Unterland, Württemberg.**

Best's
Established family winery at **Great Western,** central **Victoria,** producing a range of wines.

Beychevelle, Ch.
4me cru classé of the **Haut-Médoc, St. Julien** *comm.*

Beyer Leon
Established family business at **Eguisheim, Alsace.**

de Bèze, Clos
Grand cru and twin vyd. of **Chambertin.** The official *AC* is *Chambertin-Clos de Bèze.*

Bianco
Italian for *white.*

Bianco di Pitigliano
DOC Tuscan dry white wine.

Biddenden
One of the largest English estates and winery, **Kent.** Light dry whites.

Bienvenues-Bâtard-Montrachet
Grand cru white **Burgundy** vyd. at **Puligny-Montrachet, Côte de Beaune.**

Bijelo
Yugoslavian for *white.*

Bikavér
See **Egri Bikavér.**

Bilbainas, Bodegas
Large and well-known winery of the **Rioja Alta, Spain.**

Bin
The storage place of bottled wines from the moment they have been bottled until they are wanted.

Bingen
Important region and centre of the **Rheinhessen** wine trade.

Birkweiler
Wine-producing area of the **Südliche Weinstrasse** *Ber.,* **Rheinpfalz.**

Bischöfliches Weinguter
Major estate of the **MSR**, nr. **Trier**.

Bischofskreuz (Walsheim)
Gr. of the **Südliche Weinstrasse** *Ber.*,
Rheinpfalz.

Bissersheim
Small but ancient wine-producing locality
of the **Mittelhaardt, Rheinpfalz**.

Bite
Suggesting a substantial degree of acidity
in a wine and a noticeable amount of
tannin. A good factor in a young wine
which generally mellows with age.

Bitters
The generic name of a number of highly
flavoured pungent and bitter compounds
which are prepared by infusing spirits with
the roots, bark, fruits or leaves of trees
and plants, mostly from tropical or sub-
tropical countries. Bitters are used to
flavour drinks or to drink on their own as
an **apéritif** or **digestif**. They usually bear
the name of whatever flavour may be
outstanding, e.g. **Orange Bitters,** or the
brand name of the maker, e.g.
Angostura, Amer Picon, Fernet Branca.

Blackberry Cordial
A cordial compounded from spirit, crushed
blackberries and sugar.

Blackcurrant liqueur
A liqueur prepared from blackcurrants,
Brandy and sugar. *See* **Cassis**.

Black Rot
Fungus causing black patches on young
vine leaves, and on fruit, especially in
humid conditions.

Black Velvet
Equal parts of **Champagne** and a stout.

Blagny
Village and *app.* of the **Côte de Beaune**
nr. **Puligny-Montrachet**. Quality red
wines.

Blanc de Blancs
White sparkling **Champagne** made
exclusively from white **Pinot** grapes. Also
common name for some blended dry white
French wines.

Blanc de Noirs
White wine made from black grapes, e.g.
Champagne from **Pinot Noir**.

Blanc de Vougeot, Clos
The white wine area of the **Vougeot**
village and *comm.*, **Côte de Nuits**.

Blanc Fumé
The name for wines from the **Sauvignon
Blanc** grape in the **Pouilly-sur-Loire**
district. The *AC* is **Pouilly Fumé**.
Increasingly used in **California** as a
synonym for **Sauvignon Blanc**.

Blanchots
Grand cru vyd. of **Chablis**.

Blanco
Spanish for *white*.

Bland
Not complimentary; somewhat
characterless.

Blandy
Leading **Madeira** shippers famous for
Duke of Clarence Malmsey.

Blanquefort
Comm. of the **Haut-Médoc**.

Blanquette de Limoux
AC sparlking wines made by the *méth.
champ.* from Carcassonne, **Aude** *Dpt.*

Blatina
Native Yugoslavian red wine grape.

Blauburgunder
Name for the **Pinot Noir** grape in Austria, Switzerland, Czechoslovakia and **Italy.** In the **Baden** region of **Germany** it is the **Blauer Spätburgunder.**

Blauer Portugieser
German and Austrian red wine grape.

Blaufränkische
Red wine grape grown in **Austria, Hungary,** etc. *See* **Gamay.**

Blaye (Blayais)
The white wine district on the right bank of the **Gironde** in the east of the **Bordeaux** region. The white wines can also be **moelleux.**

de Blaye, Côtes
One of the *AC* for the ordinary wines, mostly white, of the **Blaye** district of **Bordeaux.** *Premières Côtes de Blaye* is the limited *AC* for the better reds of **Blaye,** e.g. *Ch. Barbe.*

Bleasdale
Family winery of **Langhorne Creek, South Australia,** producing good quality reds.

Blending
See **Cuvée.**

Blockesberg
Hungarian red table wine from Alderberg, nr. Budapest.

Blue Fining
Fining with potassium ferrocyanide to remove copper **casse.** It is not permitted in **France.**

Blue Nun
Brand name for **Liebfraumilch** from Sichel Söhne.

Boa Vista
One of the famous **Port**-wine estates of the **Alto-Douro,** owned by Offley.

Boberg
One of the controlled regions of origin in **Cape Province,** and designation for fortified wines only.

Boca
Dry red *DOC* from **Piedmont,** with a slight scent of violets.

Bocksbeutel (Boxbeutel)
Flat-sided glass flagon, often of dark green glass, in which most white wines of **Franken** are bottled.

Bockstein
Quality white wine from vyds. in **Ockfen,** *Gr.* **Scharzberg, MSR.**

Bodega
Spanish equivalent of **Chai** – a place where wine is stored.

Bodenheim
One of the more important towns of the **Rheinhessen, Nierstein** *Ber.*

Bodensee
Ber. of **Baden, Germany.**

Body
Corps in French. Complimentary term for a wine meaning that it has the right proportion of alcoholic strength and fruitiness.

Bogdanuša
White wine grape of **Dalmatia.**

Bolla
Famous producer of **Veneto** wines.

Bollinger
Leading *(Special Cuvée)* **Champagne** house at **Ay.**

Bols
Brand name of a popular Dutch **Gin,** and range of liqueurs.

Bommes
Sauternes *comm.* with some notable chx., e.g. **La Tour-Blanche; Peyraguey.**

Bonarda
Italian grape and a light red wine from the **Oltrepò Pavese, Lombardia, Piedmont, Emilia-Romagna.** Also grown in **Brazil** and **Argentina.**

Bonarda d'Asti
Semi-sweet sparkling red wine from **Piedmont.**

Bond
A cellar, store or vault, where wine and spirits are kept under Customs and Excise supervision until duty has been paid, when delivery will be granted.

Les Bonnes Mares
One of the larger and better vyds. of the **Côtes de Nuits,** partly in the *comm.* of **Morey-Saint-Denis,** partly in the *comm.* **Chambolle-Musigny** where it is one of two *grands crus* with **Musigny.**

Bonnezeaux
AC and one of the best sweet white wines of the **Coteaux du Layon, Anjou.**

Bönnigheim
Red wine-producing district, *Gr.* **Stromberg, Württemberg.**

Bontemps
Wooden pail or scoop formerly used to hold egg-white **finings** in **Bordeaux.** Now used in name of **Bordeaux** wine order.

Boonekamp
Dutch brand of **digestif** bitters.

Boordy Vineyards
Pioneers of **Hybrid** grapes in Maryland, **USA.**

Bór
Hungarian for *wine.*

Bordeaux
The metropolis of the **Gironde** *Dpt.,* and the largest quality wine-growing area in the world, centred on the three rs. Gironde, Dordogne and Garonne. **Bordeaux** is the *app.* for the less distinguished red and white wines of the Gironde. The quality wines are sold under the name of the *comm.* (**Margaux, St. Estèphe, Saint-Émilion,** etc.), and the best wines have the name of the ch.

Bordeaux Mixture
Copper-sulphate and quicklime mixed with water and sprayed on to vines to prevent downy-mildew.

Bordelesas
Spanish for the standard **Bordeaux** wine cask.

Borie-Manoux
Grower and *négociant* of **Bordeaux** – **Ch. Batailley, Trottevieille** and others.

Bosca
Italian wine producers known for their **Asti-Spumante** and **Vermouth.**

Le Boscq, Ch.
Minor growth of the **Haut-Médoc, St. Estèphe** *comm.*

Bota
See **Butt.**

Botelha
Portuguese for *bottle.*

Botella
Spanish for *bottle.*

Botrytis cinerea
Fungus which attacks the skins of ripe grapes, which is responsible, e.g., for the honeyed flavour of sweet dessert wines such as **Sauternes,** and the **Tokay** wines. Called **Pourriture Noble** in French, **Edelfäule** in German, and **Noble Rot** in English. The fungus penetrates the skin of the grape without breaking it. The grape begins to wither and the juice becomes concentrated.

Botticino
DOC red wine from **Brescia, Lombardia.**

Bottles
The earliest bottles were made of skins sewn together or from the bladder of an animal. Modern wine bottles are made of glass composed chiefly of silica, soda and lime in varying proportions.

Bottlescrew
The first name given to the **corkscrew** in **England.**

Bottle sickness
A kind of distemper to which wines may be subject to from three to six months after being bottled; time is usually a remedy.

Bouchard Ainé
Famous **Burgundy** grower and *négociant.*

Bouchard Père et Fils
Burgundy shipper for two-and-a-half

centuries with vyds. mainly in the **Côte de Beaune.**

Bouché
French for bottled wine, sealed with a cork.

Bouchet
Saint-Émilion and **Pomerol** name for the **Cabernet** grape.

Bouchon
French for *cork.*

Bouchon de tirage
The temporary cork used to protect the **Champagne** before **dégorgement.**

Bouchonné
French term for a corked wine; that is, a wine tainted by a musty or otherwise defective cork.

Bougros
Grand cru **Chablis** vyd.

Bouquet
French for the fragrance of wine. Used in association with mature wines. **Aroma** is used for youthful or lesser wines.

Bourbon
American **Whiskey** distilled, originally, in Kentucky, primarily from fermented corn.

Le Bourdieu, Ch.
Cru bourgeois from the **Vertheuil** *comm.,* **Bas-Médoc.**

de Bourg, Côtes
The *AC* of the **Bourg** district *(bourgeois)* on the east bank of the Gironde and Garonne.

Bourgogne
French for **Burgundy.** The fourth rank of
AC wine in the region which comes from
the less quality vyds. and sometimes from
within the great *comm.*

Bourgogne Aligoté
The *app.* for **Burgundy** whites which may
be used for wine made entirely from
Aligoté grapes from any part of the
region.

Bourgogne Grand Ordinaire
The lowest *app.* for **Burgundy** wines. Red,
white or *rosé.*

Bourgogne Passe-Tout-Grains
Light **Burgundy** red or *rosé* wine made
from not less than a third **Pinot Noir,**
blended with **Gamay.**

Bourgueil
Considered to be the most important *AC*
red wine of **Touraine** in the *Loire* valley.
The best is from the vyds. of **Saint-
Nicolas-de-Bourgueil.**

Bouscaut, Ch.
Grand cru classé **Graves, Cadaujac**
comm.

du Bousquet, Ch.
Premier cru bourgeois, **Bourg** estate.

Bouvier
Red grape variety grown in **Austria,**
Yugoslavia and **Hungary.**

Bouzy
Grand cru canton d'**Ay-Champagne,**
famous for its still red **Champagne.**

Boyd-Cantenac, Ch.
3me cru classé of the **Haut-Médoc,**
entitled to the **Margaux** *app.* Made with
Ch. Pouget.

Brachetto d'Acqui
DOC sparkling red from **Piedmont.**

Brackenheim
Small wine-producing area of
Württemberg – mostly red wine.

Braga
One of the six demarcated sub-regions of
the **Vinhos Verdes.**

Branaire-Ducru, Ch.
4me cru classé of the **St. Julien** *comm.,*
Haut-Médoc.

Branco
Portuguese for *white.*

Brand
Winery of Coonawarra, **South Australia,**
producing a range of quality table wines.

Brandy
A potable spirit distilled from wine, any
wine, anywhere. See **Armagnac** and
Cognac.

Brane-Cantenac, Ch.
2me cru classé of the **Haut-Médoc,**
Cantenac-Margaux *comm.*

Brauneberg
Village nr. **Bernkastel, MSR,** producing
well-known wines, e.g. *Brauneberger
Juffer.*

Brazil
Increasing plantings of mainly **hybrid**
grapes for wines for domestic
consumption.

Breaky Bottom
Small but well-known English vyd. of
Lewes, **Sussex.**

La Brède
Comm. of the **Graves de Bordeaux** region.

Brédif, Marc
Important grower with cellars at **Rochecorbon,** in the **Vouvray** region.

Breed
The quality of a fine wine which is the most difficult to describe. It concerns the effects of soil, climate and wine-making skill reflected in the fragrance, the bouquet, the body and the after-taste.

Breede River Valley
One of the controlled regions of origin of **Cape Province.**

Breisach
Town of the **Kaiserstuhl, Baden;** the home of one of the largest co-operative wineries in Europe, the *Zentralkellerei Badischer Winzergenossenschaften.*

Breisgau
Minor district of **Baden, Germany.**

Brentano, Freiherr von
Small family estate of the **Rheingau,** in **Winkel.**

Bressandes, Les
Premier cru vyd. of the **Côte de Beaune** with the right to the **Corton** *app.*

Bretzenheim
One of the lesser growths of the **Nahe** valley, in the **Kreuznach district.**

Breuil, Ch, du
Bourgeois growth of the **Haut-Médoc, Cissac** *comm.*

Brézé
Comm. nr. **Saumur, Anjou.** Its white wines are highly prized locally.

Briedel
Village of the **Bernkastel** district, **MSR.**

Brights
Canada's biggest winery, in Ontario, using French-American **hybrids** and some European vines.

Brillette, Ch.
Cru bourgeois of the **Moulis** *comm.,* **Haut-Médoc.**

Bristol Cream
Brand name of a dessert **Sherry** of fine quality from **Harveys.**

Bristol Milk
Brand name of a dessert **Sherry** from **Harveys.**

British wine
Wine made from imported, dehydrated grape **must** that comes from other countries, which is reconstituted by the addition of water and refermentation. Until recently most British wines were fortified local versions of **'Sherry'** and **'Port'.** Now some light wines are also being made. Not to be confused with English wines which are natural table wines made from grapes grown in the British Isles.

Broadfield
Vyd. at **Bodenham, Herefordshire.**

Brochon
Town of the **Côte de Nuits** producing wines under the name **Gevrey-Chambertin.**

Brolio Chianti
The most famous **Chianti Classico** estate, where the **Governo System** was created.

Brouilly
One of the nine *crus* of **Beaujolais,** and

the southernmost. Produces some of the lightest *cru* **Beaujolais** wines.

Brouilly, Côte de
The centre of the larger **Brouilly** area, and producing the best of its wines. Ranked as one of the nine *crus* in its own right.

Broustet, Ch.
2me cru of **Sauternes.**

Bruce, David
Small luxury winery of Santa Cruz, **California,** with rich, quality wines.

Bruisyard
Fairly new English vyd. at Saxmundham, **Suffolk,** capable of large production.

Brunello di Montalcino
Rich full-bodied *DOC* Tuscan wine. Called **Riserva** after five years. Has been called an 'Aristocrat of Italian wines'.

Brut
French for *unsweetened* wine, especially very dry **Champagne.** Drier than *dry* or *extra dry.*

Bruttig
Small village of the **Zell-Mosel, MSR.**

Bual (Boal)
Sweet **Madeira** wine from the grape of that name.

Bucelas
Small demarcated region of southern **Portugal** producing delicate aromatic dry white wines.

Bucherburger
One of the few red wines of **Switzerland.**

Buckholz
Village of the **Breisgau** district, **Baden.**

Buck's Fizz
Name of a drink made from equal parts **Champagne** and natural orange juice.

Buena Vista
Producers of some of the best and best-known Californian table wines of the **Sonoma** district.

Buhl, von
Top quality family estate in the **Mittelhaardt, Rheinpfalz.**

Bukettraube
German **hybrid** white grape grown in **South Africa.**

Bulgaria
Large quantities of wine are produced for export, the best of which are red and are mainly marketed indicating the grape name.

Bulk Process
See **Charmat.**

Bullay
Village of the **Zell-Mosel, MSR,** producing white wines.

Bull's Blood
See **Egri Bikavér.**

Bundesweinprämierung
Top German wine award. Bottles carry a gold, silver or bronze 'medal'.

Burckheim
Red wine district of **Baden, Germany.**

Burgenland
Austrian wine region in the south-east producing white, sweet and some red wines.

Burger
White German grape, also grown in
California, and the name of the white
wine from **Burg** in the **Bernkastel** *Ber.,*
MSR.

Bürgerspital zum Heiligen Geist
Famous estate at **Würzburg** producing
full, dry wines.

Burg Hammelburg
Gr. of the **Maindreieck** *Ber.,* **Franken.**

Burg Hammerstein
Gr. of the **Rheinburgengau** *Ber.,*
Mittelrhein.

Burg Lichteneck
Gr. of the **Breisgau** *Ber.,* **Baden,**
Germany.

Burg Neuenfels
Gr. of the **Markgräflerland** *Ber.,* Baden,
Germany.

Burg Rheinfels
Gr. of the **Rheinburgengau** *Ber.,*
Mittelrhein.

Burg Rodenstein
Gr. of the **Wonnegau,** *Ber.,* **Rheinhessen.**

Burgsponheim
Village of the **Nahe** valley, in the **Schloss**
Böckelheim region.

Burgundy
The province which contains some of
France's greatest red and white wine
districts. It is divided into five wine regions:
Côte d'Or (Côte de Beaune and **Côte**
de Nuits), Chablis, Côte Chalonnais,
Mâconnais, and **Beaujolais.**

Burgweg
Gr. of the **Schloss Böckelheim** *Ber.,*
Nahe.

Burgweg
Gr. of the **Johannisberg** *Ber.,* **Rheingau.**

Burgweg (Iphofen)
Gr. of the **Steigerwald** *Ber.,* **Franken.**

Burg Zähringen
Gr. of the **Breisgau** *Ber.,* **Baden.**

Buring, Leo
Established white wine specialists of
Barossa, owned by **Lindeman.**

Burkheim
Village of the **Kaiserstuhl-Tuniberg** *Ber.,*
Baden.

Bürklin-Wolf
Important family estate of the **Palatinate,**
Rheinpfalz.

Burrweiler
Minor wine-producing area of the
Südliche-Weinstrasse, Rheinpfalz.

Bushmills Whiskey
Irish Whiskey with a particular smoky
flavour, and name of the country's oldest
distillery in the northern part of Eire.

Butt
The English name of the Spanish **Bota,**
the standard **Sherry** cask containing 108
gallons/490.7 litres. *See* **Hogshead.**

Buxy
Town and *premier cru* vyd. area of the
Côte Chalonnaise, in the **Montagny**
comm.

Buzau
Wine-producing district of **Wallachia, Rumania.**

de Buzet, Cotês
Recent *AC* red **Bordeaux**-like wines from **Lot-et-Garonne** *Dpt.*

Byrrh
A wine-based French **apéritif,** flavoured with quinine.

La Cabanne, Ch.
Bourgeois cru of the **Soussans-Margaux** *comm.,* **Haut-Médoc.**

Cabannieux, Ch.
Small white *cru bourgeois,* **Graves de Bordeaux, Portets** *comm.*

Cabernet d'Anjou
AC rosé wine made from the **Cabernet** grape and therefore fruitier than the **Rosé d'Anjou,** from the **Saumur** vyds., **Loire** valley.

Cabernet de Saumur
AC **Anjou** *rosé.*

Cabernet di Pramaggiore
DOC red wine of **Veneto.**

Cabernet-Franc
Red grape variety planted with **Cabernet-Sauvignon** in **Bordeaux.** Also grown in the **Loire** and elsewhere.

Cabernet Sauvignon
Classic red grape variety of **Bordeaux** responsible for the finest clarets, and also for quality red wines of **California, Australia, Chile, South Africa** and Eastern Europe.

Cabinet
See **Kabinettwein.**

Cabrières
VDQS of the **Coteaux du Languedoc.**

Cacao, Crème de
Sweet cocoa-flavoured liqueur.

Cadarca
Rumanian red grape. **Kadarka** in **Hungary.**

Cadet-Bon, Ch.
Small *grand cru classé* estate of **Saint-Émilion.**

Cadet-Piola, Ch.
Grand cru classé of **Saint-Émilion.**

Cadillac
AC area of the **Côtes de Bordeaux** – semi-sweet white wines.

Cahors
Chief city and name of the very dark red *AC* from the vyds. of the **Lot** *Dpt.* Also synonym for the **Malbec** grape variety.

Caillou, Ch.
2me cru **Sauternes, Barsac** *comm.* Mainly sweet wines.

Le Caillou, Ch.
Less important vyd. of **Pomerol.**

Cairanne
Village and *comm.* entitled to the *app.*
Côtes du Rhône-Villages.

Calabria
Ordinaire wine-producing province of
southern **Italy.** One *DOC* wine, **Cirò.**

Calcinaia
Quality **Chianti Classico** estate.

Caldaro
DOC red wine from the vyds. facing lake
Caldero in the **Trentino Alto-Adige.** The
Austrian name is **Kaltererseewein.**

California
Rapidly emerging as one of the premier
wine regions of the world. Top quality
white wines from **Chardonnay, Semillon,
Sauvignon Blanc** and **Johannisberg
Riesling** grapes, and reds from **Cabernet
Sauvignon, Zinfandel** and **Pinot Noir**
grapes. Prime growing areas include:
Napa Valley; Sonoma and **Russian River
Valley** to the north of San Francisco Bay;
Santa Clara, Monterey, San Luis Obispo
and **Santa Ynez Valley** to the south.
Inland the vast **San Joaquin Valley**
produces vast quantities of inexpensive
wine and wine for distilling into **Brandy.**
Some premium wine from this area from
selected sites.

Calisay
Catalan digestive liqueur which is strongly
herbal.

Calissano
Established producer of **Asti Spumante** in
Piedmont.

Callaway
Small southern Californian (Riverside
County) winery.

Calon-Ségur, Ch.
3me cru classé of the **St. Estèphe**
comm., **Haut-Médoc.**

Caloric Punsch
The most popular 'tonic' liqueur in
Scandinavian countries. It is made by
different methods but **Rum** is always the
base.

Caluso Passito
DOC sweet white wine made from over-
ripe grapes at Cana Vesano, **Piedmont.**

Calvados
The name of one of the Normandy *Dpt.*
and also of a potent spirit distilled (twice)
from the pulp and juices of apples.

Calvet
Growers and *négociants* in **Bordeaux** and
Burgundy.

Cama de Lobos
One of the best vyds. of **Madeira.**

Camensac, Ch.
5me cru classé of the **Haut-Médoc, Saint-Laurent** *comm.*

Campania
Wine-producing province around Naples, **Italy,** famous for **Lacrima Christi.**

Campari
One of the most popular Italian red, bitter **apéritifs.**

Canada
Viticulture in Canada is severely hampered by the hard winters but there are established vyds. in Ontario. *See* **Brights; Chateau Gai.**

Canary Islands
The wine of Palma was popular in England during the seventeenth century under the name of *Canary Sack.* The islands make much less wine today.

Cannonau di Sardegna
One of **Sardinia's** better red or rosé *DOC* wines and the name of a local grape.

Canon, Ch.
Well-known *premier grand cru* **Saint-Émilion.** There is also a *Ch. Canon* in the **Fronsac** district producing red **Bordeaux** of *bourgeois* quality.

Canon-Fronsac, Côtes (and Côtes de Fronsac)
The two *AC* for wines of the southern **Fronsac** *comm.* **Bordeaux,** nr. **Pomerol.**

Canon-la-Gaffelière, Ch.
Grand cru classé of **Saint-Émilion.**

Cantebou-Couhins, Ch.
Originally part of **Ch. Couhins.** Mostly white **Graves.**

Cantegril, Ch.
Minor growth of **Sauternes, Barsac** *comm.* There is also a *Clos Cantegril* in the Cabanac *comm.,* **Graves** – dry white *ordinaire.*

Canteloup, Ch.
Bourgeois cru of the **Haut-Médoc, St. Estèphe** *comm.*

Cantemerle, Ch.
5me cru classé of the **Macau** *comm.,* **Haut-Médoc.**

Cantenac
A *comm.* of **Margaux, Haut-Médoc.** Most are sold under the **Margaux** *app.*

Cantenac-Brown, Ch.
3me cru classé **Cantenac-Margaux** *comm.,* **Haut-Médoc.**

Cantina
Italian for **cellar** or *winery.*

Cantina Sociale
Italian co-operative of growers.

Capbern, Ch.
Cru bourgeois of the **St. Estèphe** *comm.,* **Haut-Médoc.**

Cap Corse
French **apéritif** made from the red wines of **Corsica** and flavoured with quinine and herbs.

Cap-de-Mourlin, Ch.
Grand cru classé **Saint-Émilion,** the property of the Capdemourlin family for the past five centuries.

Capena, Bianco
DOC white wine of **Lazio.**

Cape Province
The only major wine-producing area of
South Africa. The Wine and Spirit Board
has demarcated 'districts of origin' of
which the major ones are: **Robertson,
Paarl, Stellenbosch, Constantia,
Durbanville, Tulbagh, Swellendam,
Swartland** and **Worcester.** Their
equivalent of **Appellation Contrôlée**
results in a coding on the **capsule** label
showing the grape (green band), the place
(blue band) and date of vintage (red
band).

Capiteux
French for *heady* as applied to a wine not
necessarily of high strength but aromatic
and more likely to 'go to the head'.

Capri
The wines from the Italian island of Capri
and from the mainland opposite Capri.

Capsule
The metal or plastic cap which protects the
cork of bottled wines.

Carafe
An open-topped glass (or earthenware) jug
in which, e.g., table wines are sometimes
served in restaurants.

de Caralt, Cavas Conde
Sparkling wines made by the *méth.
champ.* in **Catalonia.**

Caramel
Slightly burnt, toffee-like flavour which can
have a literal origin in the case of certain
spirits. It is a characteristic flavour of
Madeira and **Marsala.**

Carbonated wine
Wine that has been made sparkling by the
addition of carbon dioxide under pressure.
The cheapest version. *See also* **Méthode
Champenoise** and **Cuve Close.**

Carbon dioxide
Carbonic acid gas. A product of

fermentation which normally escapes as
gas, but is dissolved into bottled fermented
sparkling wine. *See* **Méthode
Champenoise.**

Carbonnieux, Ch.
Classified white **Graves** of the **Léognan**
comm.

Carcavellos
Small demarcated area of **Portugal,** nr.
Lisbon, producing white wines.

Cardinal Villemaurine, Ch.
One of the better unclassified growths of
Saint-Émilion.

Carema
One of the better red wines of **Piedmont;**
velvety and strong. The grapes come from
the **Valle d'Aosta** vyds.

Carignan
Red **Rhône** grape variety. Prolific in
California, North Africa, Spain and
Cyprus. There is a *Carignan Blanc.*

Cariñena
Demarcated region of **Aragon,** and
producer of table wines.

de Carles, Ch.
Vyd. of the **Côtes de Fronsac,** Saillans
comm.

Carlos I
Brand of Spanish **Brandy** produced by
Demecq.

Carlowitz
Old name, once well known, for a
Yugoslav red wine.

Carmenère
Lesser red grape variety of **Bordeaux,**
now rarely seen.

Carmes-Haut-Brion, Ch.
Lesser-known vyds. of **Graves de
Bordeaux, Pessac** *comm.*

Carmignano
DOC Tuscan red from north-west of
Florence.

Carneros Creek
Napa Valley winery.

Caronne-Sainte-Gemme, Ch.
Cru bourgeois estate of the **Haut-Médoc,**
St. Laurent *comm.*

Carpano
An Italian proprietary **Vermouth.**

Carr Taylor Vineyards
English vyds. nr. Hastings, **Sussex,**
producing a range of dry and medium dry
white wines from **Reichensteiner, Müller-
Thurgau,** Gutenborne and Kerner Huxel.

Carruades
The name of that part of the **Ch. Lafite**
vyds. which occupies the higher ground.
The wine is called *Carruades de Ch.
Lafite.*

du Cartillon, Ch.
Cru bourgeois of the **Lamarque** *comm.,*
Haut-Médoc.

Casa Fondata Nel
Italian for *firm established in.*

Casaleiro
A brand of **Vinho Verde.**

Casal Garcia
Popular brand of **Vinho Verde.**

Casal Mendes
A brand of **Vinho Verde.**

Cask
The generic name for containers made of
assembled and coopered staves of wood.
The casks, mostly used for storing wine,
are, in English: **Barrel, Butt, Hogshead,
Pipe** and Tun.

Casse
French term for certain disorders in wine,
causing cloudiness or darkening.

Cassis
French for the name of the Burgundian
liqueur made from blackcurrants. It is the
essential ingredient in **Kir.**

Cassis
The wine-producing *comm.* of the
Bouches-du-Rhône *Dpt.* nr. to
Marseilles. It produces table wines, the
best of which is a dry white.

Castel Danielis
Brand name of one of the best dry Greek
wines.

Castel del Monte
DOC red, white and *rosé* wines from
Puglia.

Castillo de Tiebas
Recognized wines from Las Campañas,
Spain.

Castillo Ygay
Fine red **Rioja** from **Marqués de
Murrieta.**

Catalonia
Large table and sparkling wine-producing
region of **Spain** with many guaranteed
wines.

Catawba
An indigenous American grape, grown in
New York State, to produce **foxy** wines.

Cava
Spanish name for sparkling wines made by the *méth. champ.*

Cave
French for **cellar.**

Cave cooperative
French for a winery run by a co-operative of growers.

Cavendish Manor
Estate in **Suffolk** producing dry white wine, mainly from **Müller-Thurgau,** that has won several awards.

Caviste
French for *cellarman.*

Cavit
Trento co-operative, **Italy.**

Cellar
An underground storing place for wine; it is from the French *cellier,* which is an overground store for wine. Cellars in which wine is kept for any length of time should be airy and scrupulously clean. It does not matter if they are damp as this encourages moulds which are not harmful to the wine and which discourage cork weevils which bore dry corks and do irreparable harm. Wine is kept in cellars because the temperature is more likely to be constant.

Cellatica
DOC red wine from the province of **Brescia, Lombardia.**

Cenicero
Wine village of the **Rioja Alta, Spain.**

Centerbe
Italian **digestif** which claims to be flavoured by a hundred herbs.

Centilitre
One-hundredth part of a litre.

Central Coast
Large quality Californian wine-producing area from **Santa Clara** on the southern tip of San Francisco Bay down to Monterey County. Many important wineries, among them **Almaden,** David Bruce, **Paul Masson, Mirassou, Ridge, Chalone,** and the **Monterey Vineyard.**

Cepa
Spanish for *a grape variety.*

Cépage
French for *a grape variety.*

Cerasella
Popular Italian **Cherry Brandy** liqueur.

Cérons
The last *comm.* of the **Graves** region before coming to **Barsac.** It has its own *app.* and the wines are slightly less sweet than those of **Barsac** and **Sauternes.**

Certan-de-May, Ch.
Quality **Pomerol** wine. Once part of the **Vieux Ch. Certan** estate. Usually known as just Ch. Certan.

Certan-Giraud, Ch.
Tiny **Pomerol** estate nr. **Vieux Ch. Certan** estate. Also *Ch. Certan Marzelle.*

Chablais
District of the **Vaud** canton, **Switzerland,** producing white wines. *See* **Aigle, Yvorne, Lavaux.**

Chablis
Small town of the **Yonne** *Dpt.* and one of the major French wine districts. The famous **Chablis** white wines are sold under four different *AC* according to

Chacoli

strength and quality: *Chablis Grand Cru* or
*Grands Chablis; Chablis Premier Cru;
Chablis;* and *Petit Chablis*, in descending
order.

Chacoli
Sharp white Basque wine, **Spain.**

Chagny
Town in the north of the **Côte
Chalonnaise**, in the **Mercurey** district.

Chai
The **Bordeaux** name for the above ground
store for wine before bottling.

Chaintré
Comm. of the **Mâconnais** producing
Pouilly-Fuissé.

de la Chaize, Ch.
Well-known **Burgundy** estate of the
Brouilly *comm.*

Chalone
Small, premium, hill-top vyd. in Monterey
County, south of San Francisco,
California.

Chalonnaise, Côte
The continuation of the **Côte de Beaune.**
The vyds. take their name from Chalon-
sur-Saône. The best of the wines can be
compared with those of the **Côte de
Beaune.**

Chalons-sur-Marne
The metropolis of the **Marne** *Dpt.* and one
of the more important centres of the
Champagne trade.

Chalons-sur-Saône
An industrial town on the r. Saône above
Mâcon and the metropolis of the **Côte
Chalonnaise.**

Chambertin
One of the *grands crus* of the **Gevrey-
Chambertin** *comm.* **Côtes de Nuits,**
considered to make one of the world's
great red wines. The tiny area is split
between a number of growers. *See* **de
Bèze.**

Chambéry
One of the old cities of **Savoie;** its vyds.
produce mostly white wines, but it is better
known for white, quality **Vermouth.** The
pink version is known as *Chambéryzette*,
and flavoured with strawberries.

Chambolle-Musigny
Large and famous *comm.* of the **Côte de
Nuits,** containing **Les Musigny** and **Les
Bonnes-Mares,** its top vyds.

Chambré
French word for bringing up the
temperature of a red table wine to the
temperature of the dining-room from the
cellar. It definitely does not mean 'warmed
up' and care must be taken as today
eating places are too hot for this process
to be taken literally.

Champagne
The most famous of all sparkling wines.
Made from **Pinot Noir, Pinot Meunier** and
Pinot Chardonnay grapes grown in
delimited areas of the **Marne** valley,
around **Reims** and **Épernay,** in the north-
east of **France.** Though black grapes are
used, they are pressed quickly and the
skins removed to avoid colouration of the
juice, which is then blended and
processed by the *méth. champ.*

Champaña
Spanish for **Champagne.**

Champenois, Coteaux
AC for still **Champagne.**

Champigny
See **Saumur Champigny.**

42

Chanson, Père et Fils
Burgundy shippers and major vyd. owners at **Beaune.**

Chante Alouette
Famous white **Hermitage** vyd. of the northern **Côtes du Rhône.**

Chantepleure
A tube for removing wine from a cask, in **Anjou.**

La Chapelle
Well-known and important vyd. of **Hermitage.**

Chapelle-Chambertin
Red **Burgundy** vyd. at **Gevrey-Chambertin, Côte de Nuits.**

Chapelle Madeleine, Ch.
Tiny *grand cru classé* vyd. of **Saint-Émilion.**

du Chapitre, Clos
French name for vyds. associated with collegiate churches.

Chapoutier
Important growers of the **Côtes du Rhône,** with cellars at Tain l'Hermitage.

Chappellet
Small hillside winery of the **Napa Valley** producing good table wines.

Chaptalisés, vins
Wines which have been assisted at the vintage time by the addition of sugar to **must** to raise the alcoholic strength of the wine after fermentation. The whole of the added sugar is eventually fermented so that it does not impart any degree of sweetness to the wine. The process gets its name from the inventor Jean Antoine Chaptal. It is illegal in **California,** and requires government permission in **Bordeaux.**

Charbono
Little seen red wine grape of **California.**

Chardonnay
Classic grape variety of fine white **Burgundy,** and the white grape of **Champagne,** which when made from pure Chardonnay is sometimes called **Blanc des Blancs.** It is the best white grape of **California** and is also grown in **Australia, South Africa, Spain, Bulgaria, Rumania** and elsewhere.

Charlemagne
See **Corton-Charlemagne.**

Charmat
The inventor of the bulk system **(Cuve close)** of making sparkling wine. Still wine is pumped into a closed tank and artificially aged by raising its temperature; the fermentation and bottling are then done in one continuous process, retaining the sparkle in the wine produced by **carbon dioxide.**

Charmes- and Mazoyères-Chambertin
Two *grands crus* vyds. of the **Côte de Nuits** in the **Chambertin** *comm.*

Charnu
French for fleshy, in the sense of a wine that is *full-bodied.*

Chartreuse
One of the most famous of all French liqueurs made by the Carthusian monks of La Grande Chartreuse, nr. Grenoble. It is made in two colours, the green is of higher alcoholic strength than the yellow.

Chassagne-Montrachet
Comm. of the **Côte de Beaune** producing a small quantity of fine red **Burgundy** not

typical to the area. It is famous for the dry golden, white **Montrachet** wines.

Chasselas
French name of one of the best white eating grapes and a widely grown, early ripening, wine-making grape. *See* **Gutedel** and **Fendant.**

Chasse-Spleen, Ch.
Cru exceptionnel of the **Moulis** *comm.,* **Haut-Médoc.**

Château
French word for a wine-producing estate, mainly **Bordeaux.**

Château-bottled
A wine which has been bottled where it was made, which is recorded on the label, e.g. **Mise en bouteille au château.** The château bottling is an indication of authenticity.

Château-Chalon
This *app.* is applied to the **Vin jaune** of four *comm.* nr. **Arbois.** A curious wine that resembles **Sherry.**

Chateau Gai
European and **hybrid** wines from an Ontario winery, **Canada.**

Château-Grillet
Very fine, very small, white wine vyd. within **Condrieu, Rhône,** but with its own *app.*

Châteaumeillant
Small area of the **Loire.** *VDQS* from nr. **Sancerre.**

Chateau Montelena
Small winery of the **Napa Valley.**

Châteauneuf-du-Pape
One of the most famous wines of the

Côtes du Rhône *app.* Traditionally thirteen grapes are blended to make the red wine which is richly flavoured, heady and strong in alcohol.

Chateau St. Jean
Small high-quality winery of **Sonoma, California,** specializing in white wines.

Chateau Tahbilk
Historic estate in central **Victoria,** producing recognized wines.

Châtillon en Diois
Recent *AC* **Rhône, Drôme** district; red and *rosé* wines.

de Chaunac
French-American **hybrid** grape, grown mainly in **Canada** and **New York State,** producing full-bodied dark red wine.

Chautauqua
Biggest grape-growing district of the east coast of the **USA.**

Chavignol
Village with famous vyd. *Les Monts Damnés,* **Sancerre.**

Chelois
French-American **hybrid** red wine grape grown in **New York State** to produce dry red, slightly **foxy** wines.

Chénas
One of the nine *crus* of **Beaujolais.** A small area to the north of **Moulin-à-Vent,** and one of the fuller wines of the area.

Chenin Blanc
White grape variety of **Vouvray** and other **Loire** wines where it is called **Pineau de la Loire.** Very popular in **South Africa** and also grown in many other countries.

Chenôve
Minor wine town of the **Fixin** *comm.,*
Côte de Nuits.

Cherry Brandy
A liqueur distilled from the juice of ripe
cherries fermented with some crushed
cherry stones which give the distinctive
bitter almond finish.

Cherry Heering
Popular and not over sweet Danish brand
of cherry liqueur.

Cheste
Demarcated area of **Catalonia, Spain,**
producing dark red wines high in alcohol.

Cheval-Blanc, Ch.
Premier grand cru classé **Saint-Émilion,**
and probably the best wine of **Saint-**
Émilion.

de Chevalier, Domaine
Grand cru classé of **Graves Léognan**
comm. Red and white wines.

Le Chevalier-Montrachet
Vyd. of the **Puligny-Montrachet** *comm.,*
producing some of the great white
Burgundies.

Cheverny
VDQS white wine district of the **Loire**
valley.

Chianti
Large area of **Toscana** producing wine
sold as Chianti, or superior grades. The
DOC red wine area covers the following
Chianti sub-regions which are entitled to
use the name Chianti – **Classico,**
Montalbano, **Rufinà,** Fiorentini, Senesi,
Aretini, Pisane. It is drunk young, or
Vecchio or as **Riserva.**

Chianti Classico
Central sub-region of **Chianti,** between

Florence and Siena, producing the finest
Chianti wines. Signified by a black rooster
emblem. **Riservas** are aged in **oak** for a
minimum of three years.

Chianti Putto
High quality wine produced outside the
Chianti Classico area. It is distinguished
by a pink and white cherub on the neck
label.

Chiaretto
Italian *DOC rosé,* from Riviera del Garda,
Lombardia.

Chichée
Small town in the south of the **Chablis**
premier cru region.

Chignin
White table wine from the vyds. of Chignin,
south of **Chambéry, Savoie.**

Chigny-les-Rosés
Champagne *cru* of the canton de **Verzy,**
Arrondissement de **Reims.**

Chile
The vyds. produce some of the best wines
of **South America** and the largest quantity
after **Argentina.**

Chilford Hundred
Large English estate at Cambridge
producing dry, fruity wines.

Chilsdown
Established and developing vyd. nr.
Chichester, **Sussex,** producing crisp, dry
white wine from **Müller-Thurgau** and
Reichensteiner.

Chinon
Red, white and *rosé AC* of **Touraine.**
Thought, with **Bourgueil,** to be the best
red of the **Loire.**

Chiroubles
One of the nine classic *grands crus* of the **Beaujolais.**

Chopine
French for *pint.*

Chorey-lès-Beaune
Comm. of the **Côte de Beaune** producing mostly lesser quality red wine.

Chouilly
Champagne *cru* from the canton **d'Épernay.**

Christian Brothers
Big **Napa Valley** winery; also in **San Joaquin.** The establishment also makes **Brandy.**

Chusclan
A light red or *rosé* wine from the **Tavel** vyds. under the *AC* **Côtes du Rhône-Villages.**

Cinque-Terre
DOC of **Liguria.** Fruity white wines made nr. La Spezia.

Cinquième cru (5me)
In the **Mèdoc,** the fifth and last of the five *cru classés,* eighteen chx.

Cinsaut
Red grape variety of the southern **Côtes du Rhône.**

Cinzano, Francesco
Producers of Italian **Vermouth** and **Asti-Spumante,** based at Turin, **Piedmont.**

Cirò
Italian *DOC* red and white from **Calabria.**

Cissac
Small *comm.* and *cru bourgeois* of the **Haut-Médoc.**

Citran-Clauzel, Ch.
One of the better-known *cru bourgeois* of the **Haut-Médoc,** Avensan *comm.*

Clairet
Formerly a light blend of red and white **Bordeaux** wines. Now a light red wine usually drunk cool and young. The term 'claret' is derived from it.

Clairette
White grape of the south of **France.**

Clairette de Die
A semi-sparkling white wine from the **Drôme** district, **Côtes du Rhône.**

Clairette de Languedoc
Best-known white wine of the **Midi, Hérault** *Dpt.*

La Clape
VDQS wine of the **Midi.**

Claret
The name by which the red wines of **Bordeaux** have been known in England since the twelfth century. When used for wines from regions outside **Bordeaux** it must be qualified, e.g. Spanish Claret. *See* **Bordeaux.**

Clarete
Spanish and Portuguese name for lighter reds.

Clare-Watervale
Wine area in the north of **South Australia.**

Clarity
Clearness; absolute limpidity.

Classico
Central part or heart of an Italian wine region probably producing the best and most typical wine of that *DOC.*

Classification of 1855
See **Médoc.**

Clavelin
Wide, rather square bottle used only for the *AC* **Vins jaunes,** e.g. **Château-Chalon.**

Clean
See **Franc de Gout.**

Clerc-Milon-Rothschild, Ch.
5me cru classé, **Pauillac** *comm.,* **Haut-Médoc.**

Clevner
See **Klevner.**

Climat
A strictly delimited plot of land in **Burgundy,** a vyd. or even an individual field. The equivalent of the *cru* in **Bordeaux.**

Climate
Of all the climatic conditions the most harmful is frost, and some newer vines have been developed with more frost resistance. Heat is only damaging in real extremes around 110°C. Hail can scar leaves and strip the vines of late harvested grapes. Wind in some regions breaks shoots and withers leaves.

Climens, Ch.
Famous substantial *premier cru* estate, **Barsac** *comm.,* **Sauternes.** Sweet white wines.

Clinet, Ch.
Principal growth of **Pomerol.**

Cliquot
See **Veuve-Cliquot.**

Clos
The prefix to French vyds. which are, or once were, enclosed by a wall or fence. Mainly associated with the **Burgundy** region, but many examples elsewhere in **France.**

La Closerie du Grand Poujeaux, Ch.
Bourgeois growth of the **Haut-Médoc, Moulis** *Comm.*

La Clotte, Ch.
Small *grand cru classé* of **Saint-Émilion.**

Cloying
Tasting term for a sweet, heavy wine which lacks acidity and crispness.

Coarse
Tasting term for wines of rough texture and possibly indifferently made.

Coastal Region
Designated wine area of **Cape Province.** Takes in five areas including **Stellenbosch** and **Paarl.**

Cobblers
The American name for iced and sweetened summer drinks made up with various wines or spirits and usually decorated with fruit or foliage.

Cochem
One of the more important towns of the **Zell-Mosel, MSR.**

Cochylis
One of the worst scourges of European vyds. The Cochylis moth lays its eggs in the wood of the vine and the grubs eventually attack one berry after another in each bunch of grapes.

Cockburn
Famous British-owned **Port** shippers.

Codorníu, SA
Largest Spanish sparkling wine makers, using the *méth. champ.,* based in San Sadurni de Noya, **Catalonia.**

Cognac
The name of an old French city on the r. Charente and the name of the **Brandy** distilled from white wine made in a strictly delimited area of which Cognac is the centre. The very best come from what are called the **Grande Champagne** vyds.; the next best from those of the **Petite Champagne,** and the next from those of the Borderies. Many vyds. to the west, north and east of Cognac produce white wines from which **Brandy** is distilled, which is genuine Cognac but not of the same quality. Cognac must be left to grow and mellow in the cask.

Cointreau
One of the best-known French liqueurs. The orange-flavoured, colourless liqueur, produced nr. Angers, is related to the Dutch **Curaçao.**

Colares
Small demarcated region of **Portugal,** nr. Lisbon, now almost disappeared.

Colheita
Portuguese for **vintage.**

Collage
French for **fining.**

Colli
Italian for hills. Commonly used in wine area names.

Colli Albani
Soft, fruity *DOC* white from **Lazio.**

Colli Bolognesi
Red or white *DOC* dry or semi-sweet wine from **Emilia-Romagna.**

Colli Euganei
Italian *DOC* wine area of **Veneto,** producing quantity table wines for Venice.

Collio (Goriziano)
DOC for ten wines from the **Friuli-Venezia Giulia.**

Colli Orientali del Friuli
DOC covering twelve wines from **Friuli-Venezia Giulia.**

Collioure
AC naturally sweet red wine of **Banyuls** in the **Roussillon** district.

Colmar
Alsace town and wine trade centre. The scene of an annual wine fair.

Colombard
See **French Colombard.**

Colour
Wines have a characteristic colour which often is considerably different at stages in the maturing process. It comes from pigments in the grape skins.

Comblanchien
Wine village of **Burgundy.** Mostly red wines entitled to the *AC* **Côte de Nuits-Villages.**

Commandaria
The great luscious dessert wine of **Cyprus** and one of the longest lasting in the world.

La Commanderie, Ch.
Principal growth of **Pomerol.**

Commune
French for *parish*. A wine village and its surrounding vyds.

Compãnia Vinicola del Norte de España (CVNE)
Producers of some of the best red and dry whites of the **Rioja Alta.**

Concannon
Livermore winery producing a famous **Sauvignon Blanc** and **Semillon.** Also some good reds.

Concord
American native vinestock producing dark red wine with a distinctive **foxy** aroma and taste – especially in **New York State.**

Conde de Santar
Full-bodied estate grown wine of the **Dão** region, **Portugal.**

Condrieu
Small town and *app.* of the **Rhône** producing highly regarded white wines.

Conegliano
Area north of Venice producing dry white and red table wines.

La Conseillante
First growth, **Pomerol.** Close to the **Cheval-Blanc** estate but not as good.

Consejo Regulador
Official Spanish body for control of quality and promoter of **Denominación de Origen.**

Constantia
The oldest and most famous of the designated wine-producing areas of **Cape Province,** and an estate, now owned by the Government: **Groot Constantia.** Constantia wines were once considered to be among the world's finest dessert wines.

Consumo
See **Vinho de consumo.**

Contratto
Italian wine producers at **Canelli, Piedmont.**

Coolers
American name for a number of long drinks, always served in a tall glass with ice.

Cooked
Tasting term meaning a heavy, sweet, but not unpleasant, smell indicating the use of sugar or concentrated **must** during **vinification.**

Cooking wine
Wine that has deteriorated below drinking standard but is still suitable for cooking.

Coonawara
Famous red wine area in the south of **South Australia,** producing some of **Australia's** finest red wines especially from **Cabernet Sauvignon.**

Cooper
A maker and repairer of casks.

Cooperage
Cooper's work, and the fee charged by a cooper.

Co-operative
Winery run by a co-operative of growers.

Cora
Italian wine and **Vermouth** producers at Turin.

Corbières
VDQS red from a large area of the **Aude** *Dpt.*

Corbin, Ch.
Grand cru classé, **Saint-Émilion.**

Corbin Michotte, Ch.
Grand cru classé, **Saint-Émilion.**

Cordial Médoc
French reddish-brown claret-based herb liqueur from **Bordeaux.**

Cordials
Sweetened and variously flavoured spirits which owe their name to their real or supposed stimulating action upon the heart.

Cordier, Ets. D.
Growers and *négociants* in **Bordeaux.** Chx. include *Chx. Gruaud Larose, Talbot, Meyney.*

Corgoloin
Burgundy village entitled to the *AC* **Côte de Nuits-Villages.**

Cori
A group of *DOC* red and white wines from **Lazio,** to the south-east of Rome.

Corkage
Charge made by a restaurant for allowing customers to bring in and drink their own wine.

Corks
Bottle-stoppers made of cork bark, the only substance known which will keep wine in a bottle without shutting off the oxygen of the air completely, and without giving the wine any taste or smell.

Corkscrew
Implement for drawing the cork from a bottle.

Corky (commonly 'corked')
A wine spoilt by a mouldy or otherwise objectionable smell and taste due to a defective cork. *See* **Bouchonné.**

Cornas
Red **Rhône** *app.* producing wine that matures well over a long period.

Corsé
French term for a wine of rather high alcoholic strength and full body.

Corsica (Corse)
The largest of the French islands in the Mediterranean which produces strong red, white and *rosé* wines, e.g. *AC* **Patrimonio, Ajaccio.**

Cortaillod
The best of the few red table wines of the **Neuchâtel** canton, **Switzerland.**

Cortese
Italian white wine grape.

Cortese di Gavi
DOC dry white from **Piedmont.**

Le Corton
Finest vyds. of **Aloxe-Corton** *comm.,* **Côte de Beaune.** Renowned.

Corton-Charlemagne
Famous *grand cru* **Burgundy** vyd. mainly in **Aloxe-Corton,** partly in **Pernand-Vergelesses,** and the *AC* for the white wine of **Aloxe-Corton.**

Corton-Grancey, Ch.
Label name for red **Burgundy** by Louis Latour from their **Aloxe-Corton** estate.

Corvo
Sicilian red and white wines from a winery owned by the State.

Cos d'Estournel, Ch.
2me cru classé of the **Haut-Médoc, St. Estèphe** *comm.*

Cosecha
Spanish for **vintage.**

Cos Labory, Ch.
5me cru classé of the **Haut-Médoc, St. Estèphe** *comm.*

Cossart Gordon
Leading established **Madeira** shippers.

Costières-du-Gard
VDQS red and *rosé* wine district of the **Midi.**

La Côte
White wine district on the western bank of Lake Geneva.

de Côtes, vins
Wines from hillside vyds. in **France.** *See* **Colli.**

Coteşti
Red and white table wines from the **Focşani** district of **Rumania.**

Cotnari
Famous Rumanian natural white dessert wine.

Couderc
General name for French **hybrid** vines developed by Georges Couderc.

Coufran, Ch.
Bourgeois cru of the **Haut-Médoc; Saint-Seurin de Cadourne** *comm.*

Couhins, Ch.
Classified white wine ch. of the **Graves, Villenave d'Ornon** *comm.*

Coulée de Serrant
Small vyd. at Savennières, **Anjou,** producing a light and naturally rich white wine. One of the few non-sweet **Loire** whites which develops with bottle-age.

Coulure
Physical disease of the vine causing flowers or berries to drop.

Coupé
French for *cut,* in the sense of a wine blended with another. It also means watered wine.

Courbu
Local white wine grape of **Jurançon.**

La Couronne, Ch.
Cru exceptionnel of the **Pauillac** *comm.,* **Haut-Médoc.** Part of **Haut-Batailley.**

Coutelin-Merville, Ch.
Bourgeois growth of the **Haut-Médoc, St. Estèphe** comm.

Coutet, Ch.
There are two chx. of this name in the **Gironde.** One is a *grand cru classé* of **Saint-Émilion** and the other a *premier cru* **Barsac.**

Couvent des Jacobins
Unclassified but high quality vyd. of **Saint-Émilion.**

Cradle
A wicker or wire basket designed to hold a wine bottle at an angle suitable for pouring without disturbing the sediment.

Cramant
Grand cru comm. of the **Côte des Blancs, Avize.**

Cranmore
Vyd. at Yarmouth, **Isle of Wight.**

Creaming
See **Crémant.**

Cream Sherry
A pale sweet **Sherry** made by sweetening mature **Olorosos.**

Crémant
French term meaning 'creaming' that denotes a lightly sparkling wine due to the lower carbon dioxide content.

Crémant de Loire
Good quality sparkling wine from **Anjou.**

Crème
When applied to liqueurs, mostly French ones, *crème* denotes a more than usual degree of sweetness. It is followed by the name of the fruit or plant responsible for its informing flavour.

Crépy
AC dry white wine of **Savoie.**

Cresta Blanca
Livermore winery on the north coast of **California** owned by the *Guild* co-operative.

Criadera
Spanish for the nursery cellar for young Sherries before the **Solera.**

Criado y embotellado por. . .
Spanish for *grown and bottled by. . . .*

Crimea
Important wine-growing region of the **USSR.** *See* **Saperavi.**

Criots-Bâtard-Montrachet
White wine vyd. in **Chassagne-Montrachet** area, **Côte de Beaune.** Rarest of the **Montrachet** whites.

Crisp
A desirable refreshing feature of some white wines, through the right level of acidity.

Crni
Yugoslavian for *black* and the name of a red wine grape.

Le Crock, ch.
Cru bourgeois of the **Haut-Médoc**, made with **Ch. Fatin, St. Estèphe** *comm.*

Crofts
Old established firm of **Port** shippers. Also now producing **Sherry.**

La Croix, Ch.
One of the top **Pomerol** chx.

La Croix-de-Gay
A good class **Pomerol** from one of the larger estates.

Croizet-Bages
5me cru **Pauillac, Haut-Médoc.**

Croque Michotte, Ch,
Grand cru classé, **Saint-Émilion.**

Crown Lane
Vyd. at Ardleigh, nr. Colchester, **Essex.**

Crown of Crowns
See **Langenbach.**

Crozes-Hermitage
Important *AC* **Rhône, Drôme** district – marginally less distinguished than its neighbour, **Hermitage.** Red and white wines.

Cru
French for *growth.*

Cru artisan
Médoc term for rank below *cru bourgeois*
– no longer used.

Cru bourgeois
Fourth rank of **Médoc** wines below the
five *crus classés*.

Cru bourgeois supérieur
The third rank of the **Médoc** growth
below the five *crus classés*.

Cru classé
One of the first five classified growths of
the **Médoc**, or any classed growth of
another district.

Cru exceptionnel
Second rank of **Médoc** growths below
the five *crus classés*.

Cru Paysan
Médoc name for rank below *cru artisan* –
no longer used.

Cruse et Fils, Frères
Growers and *négociants* in **Bordeaux**.

Crust
Fairly hard sediment, chiefly **tartrates,**
which red Ports cast off as they age in the
bottle and which should adhere to the
glass of the bottle when the wine is
decanted with care.

Crusted or Crusting Port
A vintage-type, full-bodied red **Port,**
bottled early and matured in the bottle.
When the wine is bottled and binned for
the first time, a splash of whitewash over
the **punt** of the bottle makes it easy to tell
subsequently how the bottle was first laid
down, hence where the crust will form. If
the wine is moved from cellar to cellar it
must always be binned again with the
splash uppermost.

Csopaki Furmint
One of the better white table wines of
Hungary; it is made from **Furmint** grapes
grown in some of the Csopak vyds. of the
Balaton district.

Cuaranta y Tres
Spanish, yellow, herb-based liqueur.

Cubzac
See **St. André de Cubzac.**

Cumières
Canton d'**Ay, Champagne** *cru,*
Arrondissement de **Reims.**

Cups
Summer drinks prepared in large jugs and
made up of any kind of wine watered
down by ice, soda or seltzer with the
addition of some spirit, one or two sweet
liqueurs and sprigs of mint or borage,
some cucumber-rind and grapes.

Curaçao
The most popular of all Dutch liqueurs. It
was first made in Amsterdam from
Oranges, **Brandy** and sugar. There are
now many brands from a number of
countries.

Curé-Bon-La-Madeleine, Ch.
Grand cru classé of **Saint-Émilion.**

Cusenier
Famous **Brandy** and liqueur house based
in Paris.

Cussac
One of the minor *comm.* of the **Haut-
Médoc.** Its vines are entitled to be sold
under the better-known name of the
adjoining *comm.* of **St. Julien.**

Cut
See **Coupé.**

Cuva
Large cask of the **Rioja** region in northern **Spain.** It contains 25,000 litres (5500 gallons).

Cuvaison
French term for the vatting process of fermenting **must** with the skins to give colour and **tannin** to red wine – it may be two–three days or two–three weeks. Also the name of a small new winery in the **Napa Valley.**

Cuve
French for *vat.*

Cuve Close
French for *closed vat* and the method of making sparkling wine where second fermentation takes place in closed tanks.

Cuvée
French for vatting, or a blend of wines.

Cviček
A dark *rosé* from the Slovenia region of **Yugoslavia.**

Cynar
An Italian bitter **apéritif** made from Jerusalem artichokes. *See* **Artichoke Brandy.**

Cyprus
In recent years the wine industry has undergone expert reorganization and Cyprus now exports quantities of 'Sherry', good red wines and some white.

Czechoslovakia
Although viticulture has an ancient history the country does not produce enough wine to satisfy local demand and quantities are imported. The provinces of Slovakia and Moravia produce the most wine, Bohemia almost none, and most is made by the State.

Dackenheim
Village of the **Rheinpfalz, Mittelhaardt** *Ber.*

Daises
The name given to iced long drinks or coolers of a somewhat superior kind, usually served in goblets and decorated with various fruits, flowers and leaves.

Dalmatia
That part of **Yugoslavia** facing the Eastern Adriatic; it is chiefly noted for its cherry liqueur, or **Maraschino.**

Dalsheim (Florscheim)
Village of the **Wonnegau** *Ber.* of the **Rheinhessen.**

Dame-Jeanne
French name for *demijohn,* the large glass bottle covered with wicker with a capacity of 5–45 litres. In **Bordeaux** it is the **Marie Jeanne,** a bottle equivalent to 2.5 litres.

Damery
Champagne *cru* from canton d'**Épernay,** Arrondissement **Épernay.**

Dampierre
Leading *comm.* of the **Coteaux de Saumur.** Mainly white wine.

Damson Gin
A once popular English cordial, **Gin**-flavoured with dark Damson plums.

Danglade, L. & Fils
Well-known shipper of **Saint-Émilion** and **Pomerol.**

Danziger Goldwasser
A colourless liqueur originally made at Danzig, with plain spirit as the base, flavoured with caraway and **aniseed.** Its chief feature is a number of small gold-leaf specks which are tasteless and harmless and float about when the *Goldwasser* is shaken and poured out. Also **Silberwasser** with silver flakes.

Dão
Demaracated region producing some of the best red and white wines of **Portugal.** Located south of the **Douro** valley.

Dassault, Ch.
Grand cru classé, **Saint-Émilion.**

Daubhaus
Gr. of the **Johannisberg** *Ber.*, **Rheingau.**

Dauzac-Lynch, Ch.
5me cru classé of the **Haut-Médoc, Labarde-Margaux** *comm.*

Dealul-Mare
Important modern red wine vyd. of Rumania.

Débourbage
French term for leaving the **must** to stand before starting the fermentation, in order to let impurities settle to the bottom of the vat. The clean **must** is then drawn off. This is now often done by introducing a sterilizing gas, e.g. sulphur dioxide.

Debröi Hárslevelü
One of the better white table wines of **Hungary.**

Decant
Whether a wine should be decanted or not is a matter of opinion. A white wine, young or old, may equally well be served either straight from its bottle or from an elegant decanter. An old bottled red wine with sediment, is best when served after it has been carefully decanted so that none of the sediment passes into the decanter.

Decanter
An elegant glass vessel with a stopper used to serve decanted wines or spirits.

Dégorgement
The **Champagne** process of getting rid of all the sediment resulting from the second fermentation of the wine before it is finally bottled.

Dégustation
French for *tasting.*

Deidesheim
Old town of the **Mittelhaardt, Rheinpfalz**, producing some of the best wines of the district.

Delaforce
Well-known **Port** shippers.

Delas Frères
Established **Rhône** wine growers and merchants at Tournon.

Delaware
Native American white grape variety, grown in the eastern States.

Delor, A., et Cie.
Bordeaux shippers, now owned by Allied Breweries.

Demerara
Dark, heavy West Indian **Rum.**

Demestica
Brand of red or white dry Greek table wine from the firm **Achaïa-Clauss.**

Demi-barrique
Half a **Bordeaux barrique,** 112 litres.

Demijohn
See **Dame-Jeanne.**

Demi-sec
French for *semi-dry;* means sweet on a
Champagne label.

Denominação de Origem
In **Portugal** similar to *AC.* The principal
named regions are **Vinhos Verdes, Dão,
Colares, Bucelas, Carcavelos,** and
Moscatel de Setubal.

Denominación de Origen
Applicable to wines from delimited areas in
Spain, similar to *AC,* and produced
according to controlled regulations.

Denominazione di Origine Controllata
See **DOC.**

Département
French for a sub-division or province, like
the English county. There are ninety, of
which about two-thirds are wine-producing.
Abbreviated *Dpt.* throughout this book.

Dépôt
French for the sediment or deposit which
wine casts off during fermentation and in
the process of maturing.

Dernau
Village of the **Ahr** valley.

Desmirail, Ch.
Once a *3me cru* of the **Haut-Médoc,
Margaux** *comm.* Now part of the **Ch.
Palmer** estate.

Dessert wines
Sweet wines, often **fortified,** which take

their name from being considered ideal for
serving with, or after, desserts.

Detzem
Village nr. Trier in the **Mittel-Mosel, MSR.**

Deutelsberg
Gr. of the **Johannisberg** *Ber., ***Rheingau.**

Deutscher Tafelwein
The lowest rank of purely German wine
from five official districts: **Main, Mosel,
Neckas, Oberrhein, Rhein,** and from
approved grape varieties. The label must
show the name of the bottler. The simple
designation **Tafelwein** indicates that the
wine has been blended with wines from
other EEC countries.

Deutz and Geldermann
One of the smaller **Champagne** houses
producing quality wine: *Cuvée William
Deutz.*

Deuxième cru (2me)
The second of the five *crus classés* of the
Médoc.

Dézaley
Well-known village of **Lavaux, Vaud**
canton, producing white Swiss wines.

Dhron
One of the better white wines of the
Mittel-Mosel, Bernkastel district, from
Neumagen-Dhron.

Diabetiker Wein
Wine suitable for diabetics because of the
minimal quantity of residual sugar – very
dry wine.

Diedesfeld
Village of the **Mittelhaardt** *Gr. Neustadt
an der Weinstrasse, Ortsteil, Diedesfeld,*
Rheinpfalz.

Dienheim
Village of the *Gr. Guldernmorgen* of the
Rheinhessen, nr. **Oppenheim,** producing
white wines.

Dietlingen
Village of the **Badische-Bergstrasse** *Ber.*
of **Baden,** producing red and white wines.

Digestif
Liqueur-style drink usually taken after
rather than before **(apéritif)** a meal.

Dimiat
White Bulgarian grape.

Dingać
Rich red **Plavac** red from the Dalmatian
coast region of **Yugoslavia.**

Dionysus
Greek wine god.

Dirmstein
Village of the *Gr.* **Rheinpfalz** *Ber.,*
Mittelhaardt.

Disgorging
See **Dégorgement.**

Distillation
The process of making a spirit by heating
an alcoholic liquid to high temperatures
so that the vapours that rise can be
condensed back to form a liquid of higher
alcoholic content. *See* **Pot Still; Patent
Still.**

Dittelsheim-Hessloch
Parish of the **Wonnegau** *Ber.,*
Rheinhessen.

Dizy
Champagne *cru* of canton d'**Ay,**
Arrondissement de **Reims.**

DOC
Denominazione di Origine Controllata – in
Italy indicates controlled denomination of
origin. To qualify for *DOC* status the
producer has to satisfy the authorities on a
number of matters including minimum
alcoholic content. There are currently
about 200 *DOC* wines. It is the equivalent
of the French **Appellation d'Origine
Contrôlée.** There is a higher grade
designation for a small number of highest
quality wines: *Denominazione di Origine
Controllata e Garantita,* which was
introduced after the *DOC* laws.

Doce
Portuguese for *sweet wine.*

Doisy-Daëne, Ch.
2me cru **Sauternes, Haut Barsac**
producing sweet and dry **Sauternes.**

Doisy-Dubroca, Ch.
Second growth **Sauternes** in 1855
classification. Now part of **Ch. Climens.**

Doisy-Védrines, Ch.
2me cru **Sauternes, Haut Barsac.** Also
producing some red **Bordeaux.**

Dolce
Italian for *sweet.*

Dolcetto
Italian red wine grape.

Dolcetto d'Acqui
Red *DOC* from **Piedmont.**

Dolcetto d'Alba
Good *DOC* red from **Piedmont.**

Dolcetto d'Asti
Red *DOC* from **Piedmont.**

Dôle
Swiss red table wine from the **Valais,**
made from the Dôle or **Gamay** grape.

Domain Chandon
Napa Valley winery belonging to **Moët et
Chandon.**

Domaine
French for estate or property; a collection
of vyds. in one ownership, whether
adjoining or not. In **Burgundy,** *Domaine-
bottled* means grown and bottled on the
estate. In other parts of **France** it is the
equivalent to *Château* or *Clos.*

Domblick
Gr. of the **Wonnegau** *Ber.,* **Rheinhessen.**

Domdechaney
The best-known vyd. of **Hockheim** *Ber.,*
Johannisberg, *Gr.* **Daubhaus,** at the
southern limit of the **Rheingau,** producing
fruity wines.

Domecq
Large famous family owned **Sherry** house
at **Jerez;** also producing considerable
amounts of Spanish **Brandy.**

Domecq Domain
Red **Rioja** from the **Rioja Alta.**

Domherr
Gr. of the **Nierstein** *Ber.,* **Rheinhessen.**

La Dominique, Ch.
Graves de Saint-Émilion. Principal
growth vyd. next to **Ch. Cheval-Blanc.**

Dom Pérignon
See **Pérignon, Dom.**

Domtal (Domthal)
German vyd. name meaning *valley of the*
cathedral. **Gutes Domtal:** *Gr.* of the
Rheinhessen.

Donnaz
DOC brilliant garnet red wine of the **Valle
d'Aosta,** with a slight hint of almonds.

Donnici
DOC red and *rosé* wine from **Calabria.**

Dopff and Irion
Growers and shippers of fine Alsatian
wines at **Riquewihr, Alsace.**

Dopff 'Au Moulin'
Important wine-producing family at
Riquewihr, Alsace.

Dorin
Name by which wine from **Chasselas**
grapes is known in the **Vaud** canton,
Switzerland.

Dorsheim
Village of the **Nahe** valley, *Ber.,*
Kreuznach.

Dosage
The topping up of **Champagne** bottles
after **dégorgement** with identical
Champagne and cane sugar solution
(liqueur d'expédition) according to the
degree of sweetness required.

Doudet Naudin
Merchant and *négociant* of **Savigny-les-
Beaune.**

Douro
From a wine point of view, the most
famous r. of the Iberian peninsula. During
its run from **Spain** in a general east-to-
west direction through **Portugal,** it is
divided into the **Alto Douro** and the
Lower Douro ending at **Oporto.** The
valley produces **Port** and table wines.

Dourthe Frères
Established **Bordeaux** merchant.

Doux
French term for sweet wine.

Dow
Well-known name of **Port** shippers.

Drambuie
A Scottish liqueur made from a blend of
Whisky, herbs and honey.

Drayton
Hunter Valley estate producing **Shiraz**
reds and **Semillon** whites.

Dromersheim
Village of the **Bingen** *Ber.,* **Rheinhessen**
with some of the oldest wine-producing
vyds.

Dry
A wine that has been fully fermented, so
no sugar remains. **Champagne** described
as dry is not excessively sweet but it will,
as a rule, have been slightly sweetened.

Dry Monopole
Brand name of the non-vintage **Heidsieck
and Co. Champagne.**

Duboeuf, Georges
Reputed **Beaujolais** merchant at
Romanèche-Thorins.

Dubonnet
Proprietary French **apéritif;** red with a
sweetened wine base with quinine and
herbs added. There is also a white variety
manufactured mainly for the **USA.**

Ducru-Beaucaillou, Ch.
Important *2me cru classé* of the **Haut-
Médoc, St. Julien** *comm.*

Duff Gordon
Sherry shippers famous for the
Amontillado: *El Cid.*

Duhart-Millon Rothschild, Ch.
4me cru classé of the **Haut-Médoc,
Pauillac** *comm.*

Dulce
Spanish for *sweet,* especially in connection
with wine.

Dumb
When used of wine it means *undeveloped.*

Dur
French for hard or rasping; usually used
for wines with an excess of **tannin.**

du Duras, Côtes
Red and white wines from the *Dpt.* Lot and
Garonne to the south-east of **Bordeaux.**

Durbach
Village of **Baden,** in the **Ortenau** district,
from which comes some of the best
Baden wines, both red and white.

Durbanville
Demarcated wine region of **Cape
Province,** closely linked with **Constantia.**

Durfort-Vivens, Ch.
Small *2me cru classé* of the **Haut-
Médoc, Margaux** *comm.*

Durif
Little-known red **Rhône** grape, also
grown in **Victoria** and **California.**

Dürkheim
See **Bad Dürkheim.**

Durnstein
Austrian village of the **Wachau,** well

known for its white wines of the same name.

Dutruch-Grand-Poujeaux, Ch.
Bourgeois cru of the **Haut-Médoc, Moulis** *comm.*

Duttweiler
Village of the **Mittelhaardt, Rheinpfalz.**

E

Earthy
Characteristic of certain wines derived from the soil.

Eau-de-Vie
Water of life *(Aqua-vitae)* the first name given to spirit distilled from wine. In particular the spirit produced by distilling the **marc** in **Champagne,** e.g. *Eau-de-Vie de Marc,* or the clear spirits derived from distilling different fruit mashes.

Ebringen
Village of the **Markgräflerland** *Ber.,* **Baden.**

Les Échezeaux
The name of the largest *climat* in the **Flagey,** *comm.* **Côte de Nuits,** which with the smaller **Grands Échezeaux** produces fine wines of *grand cru* quality. The wines can also carry the **Vosne-Romanée** *app.*

Echt
German for *unsugared.* Found on early labels as one of the descriptions of a

natural wine. Also in spirits can denote 'matured'.

Edelfäule
German equivalent of **Pourriture Noble;** an over-ripe stage of white grapes affected by **Botrytis cinerea** from which the finer, naturally sweet dessert wines are made.

Edelweiss
Proprietary Italian liqueur, pale gold in colour, flavoured with herbs and sweetened with crystallized sugar on a twig standing in the bottle.

Edelzwicker
AC for **Alsace** white wine from a blend of two or more of the seven permitted **Noble** grape varieties. *Zwicker* is not an *AC* and is a mixture of ordinary grapes (but can also include **Noble** varieties).

Edenkoben
Village of the **Südliche Weinstrasse** *Ber.* of the **Rheinpfalz,** which produces one of the better wines of the area.

Edesheim
Village of the **Südliche Weinstrasse** *Ber.* of the **Rheinpfalz.**

Ediger-Eller
Village of the **Zell-Mosel, MSR.**

Eger
Wine centre of the Mátraalya district of **Hungary.** *See* **Egri Bikavér.**

Eggnog
An old-fashioned 'pick-me-up', consisting of hot milk with an egg beaten in it, sweetened to taste, braced also to taste with **Rum** or **Brandy,** or both, and usually with a grating of nutmeg.

de l'Église, Domaine (or Couvent)
Small, central **Pomerol** estate said to be the oldest of the *comm.*

L'Église Clinet, Ch.
One of the leading **Pomerol** growths.

Égrappage
French term for the process of separating the grapes from their stalks before the pressing.

Égrappoir
The French name for the revolving colander which separates the ripe grapes from their stalks.

Egri Bikavér
Hungarian red table wine from the **Eger** vyds., known as *Bull's Blood.*

Egri Kadarka
Hungarian red grape and wine from the **Eger** vyds.

Egri Leanyka
Delicate white grape and wine from the **Eger** district of **Hungary.**

Eguisheim
Important **Alsace** wine *comm.* of **Haut-Rhin, Alsace**

Ehrenfelser
White wine grape – German **hybrid** developed by crossing **Riesling** with **Silvaner.**

Einzellage
German name for an *individual vyd.*

Eiswein
German for ice wine **(QmP)** made from grapes that have frozen on the vine. The grape juice is separated from the ice and is, therefore, exceptionally full of flavour.

Eitelsbach
Village of the **Saar-Ruwer,** nr. **Trier,** with an outstanding vyd. that originally belonged to the Carthusians: *Karthäuserhofberg.*

Elba
Mediterranean island off the coast of Tuscany, producing dry red and white *DOC* wines.

Elbling
High yielding white wine grape which produces rather characterless white wines. Still planted in some areas of **Germany.**

Elderberry
Fruit of the elder tree. Traditionally used by home wine-makers to produce elderberry wine.

Elixirs (bitters)
Herb-flavoured liqueurs or potions such as: **Pommeranzen, Angostura, Boonekamp, Longae Vitae.**

Eller
Village of the **Zell-Mosel, MSR,** nr. **Cochem.**

Ellerstadt
Town of the **Mittelhaardt, Rheinpfalz.**

Elliott
Established **Hunter Valley** estate.

Ellmendingen
Village of the **Badische Bergstrasse Kraichgau** *Ber.,* **Baden.**

Elmham Park
Established English estate at Dereham, **Norfolk,** producing a grapy, dry, crisp white wine from **Müller-Thurgau.**

Eltville
Town of the *Gr.* **Steinmächer** that produces some of the best white wines of the **Rheingau.**

Elvira
Little planted white **hybrid** grape of North America grown in some eastern states.

Emerald Riesling
White Californian **hybrid** grape from a cross of **Riesling** with **Muscadelle.** Very German in style.

Emilia-Romagna
Wine region of central-northern **Italy.** **Lambrusco** is its best-known wine.

EMU
Bulk shippers of **South Australia.**

L'Enclos, Ch.
Respected **Pomerol** estate.

Endingen
Village of the **Kaiserstuhl-Tuniberg** *Ber.,* **Baden,** producing both red and white wines.

Enfant-Jésus
Vyd. owned by **Bouchard Père,** which is part of the *premier cru* vyds. of **Les Grèves, Côte de Beaune.**

Enfer d'Arvier
DOC light mountain red from part of the *comm.* of **Arvier** in **Valle d'Aosta.**

Engaraffado na Origem
Portuguese for *estate-bottled.*

England
Wine production has been revived in recent years and there are vyds. in the following counties: Avon; Bedfordshire; Berkshire; Cambridgeshire; Cornwall; Derbyshire; Devonshire; Dyfed; Essex; Glamorgan; Gloucestershire; Hampshire and the Isle of Wight; Herefordshire; Hertfordshire; Kent; Leicestershire; Northants; Oxfordshire; Somerset; Suffolk; Surrey; Sussex; Wiltshire; Worcestershire; and also in the Channel Islands.
Grapes include: **Seibel; Müller-Thurgau; Pinot Noir; Pinot Meunier; Seyval Blanc; Huxelrebe; Muscat** and some **Cabernet.** England is not able to ask for EEC wine status until ten years of production have been scrutinized. *See* **EVA.**
English wine is made only from grapes grown in Britain and is not to be confused with British wine which is made from reconstituted grape **must** imported in dehydrated form from other countries.

English Vineyards Association
See **EVA.**

Enkirch
Small village of the **Mittel-Mosel, MSR.**

Enology
See **Oenology.**

Entre-Deux-Mers
AC district of the **Bordeaux** region between the Garonne and Dordogne rs. Average quality dry, and some sweet, white wines. Red wines are sold as *AC* **Bordeaux** or **Bordeaux Supérieur.**

Entre-Deux-Mers Haut Benauge
White **Bordeaux** *app.* covering a group of *comm.* in the south of the overall area.

Épenots (Épeneaux)
Premier cru vyd. in the **Pommard** *comm.*

Épernay
Important **Champagne** town and Arrondissement of the **Côte des Blancs.** Headquarters of many of the big houses including **Moët, Perrier-Jouett, Pol Roger.**

Épesses
Wine-producing village of the **Vaud** canton, **Switzerland.** Good dry white wine.

Épineuil
Village of the **Yonne** *Dpt.* nr. Tonnerre, known for **Vin gris.**

Erbach
Town of the **Rheingau,** *Gr.* **Deutelsberg,** with vyds. producing full-bodied wines including the famous **Markobrunn.**

Erbaluce di Caluso
DOC white wine of **Piedmont.**

Erdelega
Small vyd. at Ardleigh, **Essex.**

Erden
Village of the **Mosel** valley nr. **Bernkastel.**

Erlach
Village of the **Ortenau** *Ber., Gr.* **Fürsteneck.**

Erlenbach
A minor wine-producing village of the **Württembergisches Unterland** *Ber.,* **Württemburg.**

Erntebringer
Gr. of the **Johannisberg** *Ber.,* **Rheingau.**

Erpolzheim
Village of the **Mittelhaardt Deutsche Weinstrasse,** district of the **Rheinpfalz.**

Erzeugerabfüllung
German for *estate-bottled.* Equivalent of **Mise en bouteilles au château par le propriétaire.**

Eschenauer, Louis
Bordeaux merchants and owners of **Ch. Smith-Haut-Lafitte,** and others.

Escherndorf
One of the most importand towns of the **Franken** region, *Gr.* **Kirchberg,** producing full-bodied dry white wines.

Espumante
Portuguese for *sparkling.*

Espumoso
Spanish for *sparkling.*

Essence, Eszencia
Pure **Furmint** grape juice. *See* **Tokay.**

Essingen
Village of the **Südliche Weinstrasse** *Ber.,* **Rheinpfalz.**

Esslingen
Small town of the **Neckar** valley, **Remstal-Stuttgart** *Ber.,* **Württemberg.** Its vyds. produce some red wine but mostly **Schillerwein.** The first German sparkling wine was made here.

Estate-bottled
Bottled by the grower on the estate – **Mise en bouteilles au château par le propriétaire.**

Estate wine
Wine made from grapes grown on a Cape estate in **South Africa.** It only applies to a controlled number of estates.

Esterhazy
Austrian family with vyds. nr. Eisenstadt, producing luscious white wines.

Est!-Est!!-Est!!!
Famous *DOC* white wine from **Montefiascone, Lazio.**

d'Estournel
See **Cos d'Estournel.**

Estufa
Portuguese name for the hot chamber in which the young wines are lodged and 'cooked' in the **Madeira** process.

Etna
Sicilian red white and *rosé DOC* wines from around Mt. Etna.

L'Étoile
One of the best *AC* **Vins Jaunes** from the **Jura.**

L'Étoile-Pourret, Ch.
Principal growth of **Saint-Émilion,** part of **Ch. La Grâce-Dieu.**

Ettenheim
Village of the **Breisgau** *Ber.,* **Baden.**

EVA
English Vineyards Association. Wines that receive the EVA Gold Seal of approval have undergone certain laboratory tests and been approved by a panel of experts. Methods of judging are similar to the French and German for quality wine designation and one of the Association's objectives is to encourage high standards of wine production in **England.**

L'Évangile, Ch.
First quality **Pomerol** vyd.

Ewiges Leben
Gr. of the **Maindreieck** *Ber.,* **Franken.**

Extra sec
Dry **Champagne.**

d'Eyguem, Ch.
Bordeaux from the **Côtes de Bourg.** Mostly red wine.

Ezerjó
Hungarian white grape and the name of a golden, full-bodied wine from the **Mór** *comm.* nr. **Budapest.**

Faber
Hybrid white wine grape developed in **Germany.**

Faisca
Brand of slightly carbonated *rosé* produced by J. M. de Fonseca, **Portugal.**

Faiveley
Growers and *négociants* at **Nuits St. Georges.**

Falerio dei Colli Ascolani
DOC dry white from the **Marches, Italy.**

Falerno
Historically famous Italian red and white dry wine from **Campania.**

Fara
One of the fine but lesser-known *DOC* red wines of Novara, **Piedmont.**

de Fargues, Ch.
Sauternes from the *comm. of* **Fargues, Bordeaux.** Under the same ownership as **Yquem.**

Faro
Red table wine from Messina, **Sicily.**

Fass
German for *cask.*

Fat
Of wine, full-bodied, soft and high in natural glycerol.

Fatin, Ch.
See **Ch. Le Crack.**

Faugères
Comm. of the **Hérault** producing red and white wines entitled to the *VDQS app.* **Coteaux de Languedoc.**

Faye d'Anjou
AC comm. **Coteaux du Layon, Anjou.**

Fein-Feinste
German for **fine/finest.** Now illegal for use on labels.

Feints
'Heads' and 'Tails', or first and last parts of spirits distilled in a **still;** of poorer quality than the rest, and returned for re-distillation.

Fellbach
Village of the *Gr.* **Weinsteige, Remstal. Stuttgart** district of **Württemberg.**

Felstar
One of the older and established English estates, Felsted, **Essex.** Dry and medium dry white wines, some sparkling *(méth. champ.),* and **muscat** and *rosé* and light red wines from **Müller-Thurgau, Chardonnay, Seyval Blanc, Madeleine Angevine** and **Sylvaner, Scheurebe, Pinot Noir** and **Meunier.**

Fendant
Swiss name for the French white **Chasselas** grape, and the name of the famous dry, white wine of the **Valais.**

Fermentation
The process whereby the yeast which forms on the skin of the grapes as they ripen, acts on the sugars in the grape juice. As the **must** ferments the sugar is converted mainly into *ethyl alcohol* and carbon dioxide.

Fernet Branca
A well-known brand of Italian **bitters.** Also made in **France.**

Ferran, Ch.
Bourgeois cru of **Mantillac, Graves de Bordeaux.**

de Ferrand, Ch.
Good unclassified **Saint-Émilion,** *comm.* **St.-Hippolyte,** with a large output. Also the name of a large **Pomerol** estate.

Ferrande, Ch.
White wine estate of the **Castres** *comm.,* **Graves de Bordeaux.**

Ferrari
Trentino-Alto Adige sparkling wine firm *(méth. champ.).*

Ferreira
Portuguese owned growers and shippers of the **Douro.**

Ferrerinha
Brand name of good, light red wine produced by **Ferreira, Portugal.**

Ferrière, Ch.
Lesser-known *3me cru classé* of the **Haut-Médoc, Margaux** *comm.*

Fetească
Rumanian white grape, in Bulgaria – Fetiaska; in the **USSR** – Fetyaska.

Fetzer
Californian winery at **Mendocino.**

Feuerberg (Bad Dürkheim)
Gr. of the **Mittelhaardt** *Ber.*, **Rheinpfalz.**

Feuillette
French for half a **pièce.** In **Beaujolais** 108 litres; in **Burgundy** 114 litres. In **Bordeaux,** half a **barrique,** 112 litres. In **Chablis** a standard cask of 132 litres.

Feytit-Clinet, Ch.
Small red **Bordeaux** estate of **Pomerol.**

Fiasco
Italian straw-covered *flask* which holds about 1 litre of wine. Usually associated with **Chianti.**

Ficklin
Small winery of the **San Joaquin** valley producing the best port wine and quantities of table wines.

de Fieuzal, Ch.
Grand cru classé for red wines of the **Léognan** *comm.*, **Graves de Bordeaux.**

Figeac, Ch.
Premier cru classé, **Graves Saint-Émilion.**

Filfar
A **Cyprus** liqueur, flavoured with oranges.

Filhot, Ch.
Large *2me cru* **Sauternes** estate.

Fillette
French slang term for a half-bottle of wine, especially in **Anjou.**

Filtering
Passing wine through a paper or other filter to capture suspended impurities prior to bottling.

Fine
Common French name for a **Cognac Brandy**; *Fine Champagne* is a blend of *Grande Champagne* and *Petite Champagne Cognacs.*

Fine de Bourgogne
A **Brandy (marc)** from **Burgundy** made from a distillation of the material left after the grapes have been pressed.

Fine Champagne
Not **Champagne** but the name of a **Cognac Brandy** which should be made only from wine of the *Grande Champagne* and *Petite Champagne* vyds.

Fine Maison
The staple **Brandy** of the house (hotel or restaurant), seldom very fine but usually a reasonable **Cognac.**

des Fines Roches, Ch.
Large estate of **Châteauneuf-du-Pape, Rhône.**

Finesse
French term for elegance or class in a wine.

Finger Lakes
Most important wine-growing region of **New York State,** famous for its sparkling wines.

Fining
The process of clarifying wine of any suspended particles by using an agent such as protein or gelatine. The agent falls through the liquid collecting the impurities. See **Collage.**

Finish
The lingering after-taste a wine leaves in the mouth.

Fino
The driest of all Sherries. The real *fino* is

dry without any bitterness, and delicate without being thin.

Fior d'Alpi
Italian liqueur, aromatic and very sweet, which is usually bottled with a twig covered with crystallized sugar inside it.

Fitou
AC red wine area; a sub-district of **Corbières, Aude** *Dpt.*

Fixes
A variety of iced summer drinks compounded in many different ways.

Fixin
One of the smaller wine-producing *comm.* of the **Côte de Nuits.** The best vyds. are **Clos de la Perrière,** and **Clos du Chapitre.**

Fizz
Slang term for any beverage which is effervescent, more particularly **Champagne.**

Fizzes
American 'long' drinks made up of various kinds of spirits and some sugar or syrup, well shaken with plenty of ice, then strained and served in tall glasses topped up with soda.

Flagey-Échezeaux
Village in the north of the **Côte de Nuits,** adjoining the famous **Romanée-Conti.** Its vyds. also produce some superlative red wines. *See* **Échezeaux.**

Flétri
Swiss name for the withered grapes used for sweet wine.

Fleurie
A village of the Beaujolais district and one of the nine named *crus.*

La Fleur-Milon, Ch.
Bourgeois growth of the **Haut-Médoc, Pauillac** *comm.*

La Fleur-Pétrus, Ch.
First quality **Pomerol;** neighbour of **Ch. Pétrus.**

Flietre
The name for the **Syrah** grape in the **Drôme.**

Flinty
Certain white wine grapes grown on certain soils have a hint of gun-flint in the bouquet and flavour.

Flips
Winter drinks made up of hot ale, wine or spirits, sweetened to taste, with an egg beaten in and some nutmeg coated on top at the time of serving.

Flor
Spanish for the yeast **Mycoderma vini,** which forms a white skin on some wines in casks and changes them slowly to **Sherry.**

Flora
Californian **hybrid** white grape developed by crossing **Gewürztraminer** with **Semillon.**

Flûte
Tall French **Champagne** glass. Also the tall and thin bottle for Alsatian and Rhine wines made of clear glass.

Focşani
Large wine region in the east of **Rumania.**

Folle Blanche
Widely grown second class white wine grape of **France,** particularly for **Brandy.** Produces well in **California.** Also called **Gros Plant,** and **Picpoul.**

Fombrauge, Ch.
Established unclassified **Saint-Émilion** growth, **St. Christophe des Bardes** *comm.*

Fonbadet, Ch.
Cru bourgeois of the **Pauillac** *comm.*, **Haut-Médoc.**

Fonplégade, Ch.
Grand cru classé of **Saint-Émilion.**

Fonréaud, Ch.
Cru bourgeois of the **Listrac** *comm.*, **Haut-Médoc.**

Fonroque, Ch.
Grand cru classé of **Saint-Émilion.**

Fonseca
One of the best **Port** shippers.

Fontanafredda
Major Italian wine producers of **Piedmont.**

Foppiano
Old Californian winery of **Sonoma** County.

Forbidden Fruit
An American liqueur with a citrus fruit basis; it is sold in an ornate globular bottle.

du Forez, Côtes
VDQS wine from the **Loire.**

Forst
A leading wine village of the **Mittelhaardt, Rheinpfalz,** producing light wines with a rich bouquet.

Fortia, Ch.
Important property of **Châteauneuf-du-Pape.** The father of the owner of the property Baron Le Roy de Boiseaumarié was the originator of the *AC* system.

Fortified
Usually wine to which grape spirit has been added to increase the alcoholic strength and to stop fermentation. The term is illegal in the **USA.**

Les Forts de Latour
Second wine of **Ch. Latour, Pauillac** *comm.*

Foudre
French name for the 1000 litre casks of **Alsace;** known as *Fuder* in German.

Fourcas-Dupré, Ch.
Better-known *cru bourgeois* of the **Listrac** *comm.*, **Haut-Médoc.**

Fourcas-Hosten, Ch.
Better-known *cru bourgeois* of the **Listrac** *comm.*, **Haut-Médoc.**

Fourchaume
Premier cru **Chablis.**

Les Fourneaux
Premier cru **Chablis.**

Fournier, Charles
Chief wine-maker of **Veuve-Cliquot** until 1934 when he emigrated to America to run **Gold Seal** vyds. at Hammondsport, **New York State.**

Fourtet, Clos
Premier grand cru classé of **Saint-Émilion.**

Foxy
The pronounced earthy bouquet and flavour of the wine from most native American vine varieties *(Vitis labrusca).*

Fracia
Red wine of **Lombardia,** *DOC* **Valtellina.**

Fragrant
See **Aroma.**

Frais
French for *fresh* or *cool.*

de Fraise, Crème
Strawberry-flavoured liqueur. Also known as *Fraisia.*

de Framboise, Crème
French fruit liqueur with a raspberry base.

Franc de Goût
French for the clean, refreshing taste of a wine.

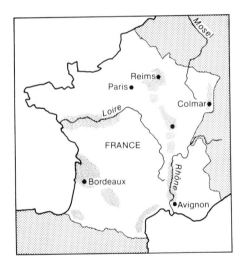

France
The country from which come the world's greatest wines. The main wine regions are **Bordeaux, Burgundy, Loire, Alsace, Champagne, Rhône,** and the **Midi.** *See also* **VDQS, AC, Vins de Pays.**

Franciacorta
Red or white, still or sparkling, *DOC* wine of **Brescia** province, **Lombardia.**

Franc Mayne, Ch.
Small *grand cru classé* vyd., of **Saint-Émilion.**

Frank, Dr Konstantin
Founder of the **Vinifera Winery, New York State.**

Franken (Franconia)
Important German **(QbA)** wine region producing reliable dry wines and the famous **Stein** wines in their **Bocksbeutels.** Districts are **Bodensee, Maindreieck, Mainviereck, Steigerwald.**

Franzia
Large family winery, **San Joaquin** valley.

Frappé
French term for serving a drink on broken ice, or for wine served ice-cold.

Frascati
One of the showplaces of the Roman Hills which produces the famous *DOC* white wines.

Freemark Abbey
Small high quality winery, **Napa Valley.**

Freezomint
Popular brand of French **Crème de Menthe** made by Cusenier, **Paris.**

Freiburg-im-Breisgau
The wine centre of the **Markgräflerland** district, **Baden.**

Freinsheim
Lovely village of the **Mittelhaardt, Rheinpfalz,** producing a quantity of all quality wines.

Freisa
Italian white grape.

Freisa d'Asti and Freisa di Chiera
Two delightfully fruity red **Piedmont** wines from the **Freisa** grape. Some are sold with a slight sparkle.

French Colombard
White wine grape producing semi-dry wines in **California, South Africa** and **New Zealand.**

Frescobaldi
Established wine producers, especially **Chianti Putto,** at Florence, **Toscana.**

Friedelsheim
Village of the **Mittelhaardt** district, **Rheinpfalz.**

Friesenheim
Village of the **Breisgau** district, *Gr.* **Schutter-Lindenberg, Baden.**

Friularo
Italian black grape grown in **Veneto** province; also the name of the local red table wine.

Friuli-Venezia Giulia
One of the smaller Italian wine-growing regions, in the very north-east of **Italy.** Six *DOC* wines.

Frizzante
Italian equivalent of **pétillant.**

Fronsac
Area covering seven *comm.* on the east side of the **Gironde** and of the **Bordeaux** region. There are two *app.* **Côtes de Fronsac,** and **Canon-Fronsac.**

de Fronsac, Côtes
One of the *AC* for the red wines of the **Fronsac** *comm.* of **Bordeaux.**

Frontignan
Sweet dessert wine made from white **muscat** grapes in the vyds. of the **Languedoc.** It is tawny in colour and acquires a **rancio** flavour after some years in the bottle.

Frost
See **Climate.**

Frühburgunder
German grape variety from the **Ahr** valley.

Fruity
The attractive fresh quality of a wine derived from good ripe grapes.

Fruska Gorka
Centre of vast vyds. on the banks of the Danube, Vojvodina, **Yugoslavia.**

Fuder
German **Mosel** cask containing 100 litres – *see* **Foudre.**

Fuissé
Small *comm.* of **Saône-et-Loire;** its vyds. adjoin those of **Pouilly** and the wine is usually sold as **Pouilly-Fuissé.**

Full or full-bodied
A wine high in alcohol and extract, which 'fills' the mouth.

Fumé Blanc
See **Blanc Fumé.**

Funchal
The capital of the island of **Madeira** and centre of the **Madeira** wine trade.

Fundador
Brand of Spanish **Brandy,** made by **Domecq.**

Furmint
A distinctive white grape from which quality Hungarian wines are made such as *Balatonfüred Fürmint.* It is also the chief grape of **Tokay** wines. See **Sipon.**

Fürsteneck
Gr. of the **Ortenau** *Ber.,* **Baden.**

G

La Gaffelière-Naudes, Ch.
Premier grand cru, **Côtes Saint-Émilion.**

Gaglioppo
Italian red wine grape, mainly found in
Calabria and **Sicily.**

Gaillac
AC wine area of the **Tarn** *Dpt.* which
produces quantities of table wines, red,
white and *rosé* as well as sparkling
wines, e.g. *Clairette de Gaillac.*

Galliano
Popular Italian herb-flavoured liqueur.

Gallo, E & J
Huge Californian winery, said to be the
world's largest; **San Joaquin** valley.

Gallon
Standard British measure and still common
today, although metrication was introduced
in 1975, equivalent to 4.546 litres. In the
USA equivalent to 3.785 litres.

Gamay
The most extensively cultivated grape of
Beaujolais. Also grown in the **Loire** and in
Switzerland, Savoie, and **California.**

Gamay Beaujolais
Red wine grape of **California**; a variety of
Pinot Noir.

Gambellara
DOC dry or semi-sweet white wine of
Veneto.

Gambingay
Vyd. of Sandy, **Bedfordshire.**

Gamza
Common red grape of **Bulgaria.**

Gancia
Italian wine producers based nr. Asti,
Piedmont, famous for **Asti Spumante** and
Vermouth.

Gard
Quantity producing *Dpt.* in south-west
France – some *VDQS* wines. *See*
Costières.

La Garde, Ch.
Bourgeois cru red **Graves. Martillac**
comm.

de Garde, vin
Wine good enough to lay down, or which
should be laid down to mature.

Garganega
Italian white wine grape used in the
production of **Soave** and **Gambellara;**
Veneto.

Garnacho
Rioja red wine grape (called *Tinto
Aragones* in parts of **Italy**).

Garrafeira
Private cellar – indication of the best
quality, matured Portuguese wine.

Gatão
Popular brand of **Vinho Verde.**

Gattinara
Full-bodied *DOC* red from **Piedmont.**

Gau-Algesheim
Village of the **Rheinhessen,** *Gr.* **Abtey,**
Bingen *Ber.*

Gau-Bischofsheim
Village of the **Rheinhessen.**

Les Gaudichots
Premier cru red **Burgundy** vyd. in the
Vosne-Romanée *comm.*

Le Gay, Ch.
A **Pomerol** estate of some reputation.

Gazin, Ch.
Small red wine vyd. of the **Léognan**
comm. **Graves;** and the name of the
larger, better-known *premier cru* vyd. of
Pomerol.

Gebiete
See **Anbaugebiete.**

Gedeonseck
Gr. of the **Rheinburgengau** *Ber.,*
Mittelrhein.

Geisenheim
Township of the **Rheingau** and the home
of **Germany's** leading wine school, the
Hessische Forschungsanstalt für Wein –
Obst- & Gartenbau.

Geisweiler et Fils
One of the biggest merchant houses of
Burgundy with cellars at **Nuits St.
Georges, Hautes-Côtes de Nuits,** and
the **Côte Chalonnaise.**

Genesis Green
English vyd. at Wickhambrook, **Suffolk.**

Geneva
See **Jonge Jenever** and **Oude Jenever.**

Gensingen
Village of the **Rheinhessen** in the Sankt
Rochuskapelle district.

Gentil
Alsace name for the **Riesling** grape.

Germany
Viticulture was introduced in the valley of
the **Rhine** by the Romans. Mainly white
wines are produced and little of the red is
known abroad. It is divided into quality
wine regions **(Anbaugebiete): Rheingau,
Rheinhessen, Hessische Bergstrasse,
Ahr, Nahe, Mosel-Saar-Ruwer, Baden,
Franken, Mittelrhein, Württemberg,
Rheinpfalz;** and corresponding **Deutscher
Tafelwein** regions: **Rhein, Mosel, Main,
Neckar** and **Oberrhein,** though no
indication of the area is given. *Deutscher*
means that the wine is entirely German. If
labelled just *Tafelwein* it could include
wine from other EEC countries.
   The wines of the *Gebiete* are graded
into **QbA** and **QmP** which appear on the
labels. *See also* **AP.**

Geropica
See **Jeropica.**

Gevrey-Chambertin
One of the greatest *comm.* of the **Côte de
Nuits** with two famous *grand cru* vyds.
Chambertin and **Clos de Bèze.**

Gewächs
German for *the growth of* followed on the label by the name of the person or concern owning the vyd. *See also* **Kreszenz.**

Gewürztraminer
A distinctive spicy white **Traminer** grape of **Alsace,** used a little in the **Rheinpfalz.** Successful in **California,** and in the **Tulbach** region of **Cape Province** and in **South Australia.**

Ghemme
Fine *DOC* dry red wine of **Piedmont.**

Giennois, Coteaux
VDQS of the **Loire** valley.

Gigondas
Ancient vyds. and famous **Rhône** *AC,* **Vaucluse** district. Mainly red, similar to **Châteauneuf-du-Pape.** Some *rosé.*

Gilbey, S. A.
Long established British **Bordeaux** merchants and owners of **Ch. Loudenne.**

Gimmeldingen
Township of the *Gr.* **Meerspinne,** *Ber.* **Mittelhaardt, Rheinpfalz.**

Gin
A spirit distilled from grain and flavoured mainly with juniper berries. There are two main sorts of English gins, *London Dry Gin* and *Plymouth Gin;* the latter is usually more aromatic than the former but less so than **Hollands.** Gin is often distilled to a three times higher strength than other spirits. This is particularly so in the **USA** where the basis of *Gin* is practically pure alcohol, that is, a spirit out of which everything has been distilled; this means that it matters little from what it is distilled. In the final distillation process the juniper and other flavourings are added to create the characteristic flavour. Gin is used extensively as a base for cocktails.

Ginestet
Established French **Bordeaux** *négociants* and former owners of **Ch. Margaux.**

Ginger Ale
A carbonated mineral water to which essence of ginger, colouring and sugar have been added.

Ginger Beer
An effervescent drink made by fermenting ginger, cream of tartar, and sugar, with yeast and water, and bottling before the fermentation is completed.

Ginger Wine
A warming English beverage wine generally made with water, sugar, lemon-rind, ginger, yeast, raisins, and frequently fortified with spirit.

Gipfel
Gr. of the **Obermosel** *Ber.,* **MSR.**

Girò di Cagliari
DOC of **Sardegna** producing strong, naturally sweet red wines.

Gironde
The waterway formed by the junction of the rs. Garonne and Dordogne, below **Bordeaux.**

Giscours, Ch.
3me cru classé of the **Haut-Médoc,** *AC* **Margaux.**

Givry
Small town and *comm.* of the **Côte Chalonnaise.** Its vyds. produce red wines comparable to those of the **Côte de Beaune.**

du Glacier, vin
Wines of **Valais, Switzerland,** stored for a

long period at high altitudes. Hardly seen today.

Glana, Ch. du
Cru bourgeois of **St. Julien, Haut-Médoc.**

Glayva
Scottish proprietary, honey, **Whisky**-based liqueur, flavoured with herbs and spices.

Glen Mist
Scottish proprietary **Whisky,** herb and honey liqueur.

Gloria, Ch.
High quality *cru bourgeois* of **St. Julien** *comm.,* **Haut-Médoc.**

Goldbäumchen
Gr. of the **Zell-Mosel, MSR.**

Gold Seal
Very large **New York State** winery now owned by **Seagram.** *See* **Fournier.** Brand name *Henri Marchant.*

Goldwasser
See **Danziges Goldwasser.**

Gombaude-Guillot, Ch.
Lesser-known **Pomerol** vyd.

Gönci
Small Hungarian **Tokay** casks.

Gönnheim
Village of the **Rheinpfalz, Mittelhaardt** district.

Gonzalez Byass
Famous *Sherry* shippers including *Tio Pepe, Elegante Dry Fino,* and *San Domingo Pale Cream.*

Gore-Browne
This family, who started the famous **Beaulieu Abbey** vyd., give their name to an annual trophy for the best English wine.

Goron
Ordinary wine red of the **Valais, Switzerland.**

Gotteshilfe
Gr. of the **Wonnegau** *Ber.,* **Rheinhessen.**

Gottesthal
Gr. of the **Johannisberg** *Ber.,* **Rheingau.**

Goût
French for *taste.* When applied to wine, *Goût* is used in such expressions as the following: *Goût de ferment* – still fermenting, not ready to drink; *Goût français* – a very sweet **Champagne;** *Goût de pierre à fusil* – a flinty and not unpleasant after-taste; *Goût de piqué* – pricked, on the way to the vinegar tub; *Goût de terroir* – taste derived from the soil. *See also* **Franc de Goût.**

Governo System
Method of **vinification** used in **Tuscany** to make **Chianti Classico** and other Chiantis. **Must** from sun-dried grapes is added to young wine causing further fermentation which increases the glycerin content and freshness.

Graach
Town of the **Mittel-Mosel.** The vyds. produce some well-known white wines.

La Grâce-Dieu, Ch.
Minor red **Bordeaux** from **Saint-Émilion.**

Graciano
Spanish red grape, important in the **Rioja.**

Gradi
Italian for *degrees,* e.g. of alcohol.

Grafenstück (Bockenheim)
Gr. of the **Mittelhaardt** *Ber.,* **Rheinpfalz.**

Grafschaft
Gr. of the **Zell-Mosel, MSR.**

Graham
Famous rich vintage **Port,** and other styles.

Gramp
Family concern of the **Barossa** valley now owned by **Orlando** and **Reckitt and Colman,** producing large quantities of wines from a variety of grapes, including a quality **Rhine Riesling.**

Grand-Barrail-Lamarzelle-Figeac, Ch.
Substantial *grand cru classé* of **Graves Saint-Émilion.**

Grand Clos
Red wine vyd. of **Bourgueil.**

Grand-Corbin, Ch.
Grand cru classé of **Graves Saint-Émilion.**

Grand-Corbin-Despagne, Ch.
Grand cru classé of **Graves Saint-Émilion.**

Grand cru
French for *great growth.* In **Burgundy** it means a top growth with its own *AC.* The label carries only the vyd. name. It is also the name of a small vinery in **Sonoma** County.

Grande Champagne
See **Cognac.**

Grande réserve or Grand vin
Simply means a late harvested vintage with a minimum 11° alcohol in **Alsace.**

La Grande-Rue
Vyd. of the **Vosne-Romanée** area of the **Côtes de Nuits.**

Les Grandes-Murailles, Ch.
Grand cru classé of **Saint-Émilion.**

Grand Marnier
Popular French liqueur with an orange flavour and a **Cognac Brandy** basis. It is made in two styles: *Cordon Rouge,* which is drier; and *Cordon Jaune,* which is both sweeter and of lower alcoholic strength.

Grand-Mayne, Ch.
Grand cru classé of **Saint-Émilion,** sometimes sold as **Ch. Cassevert** when not up to *grand cru* standard.

Grand-Pontet, Ch.
Grand cru classé, of **Côtes Saint-Émilion.**

Grand-Puy-Ducasse, Ch.
5me cru classé of the **Haut-Médoc, Pauillac** *comm.*

Grand-Puy-Lacoste, Ch.
5me cru classé of the **Haut-Médoc,** Pauillac *comm.* Larger and more important than Ducasse.

Grand Roussillon
Wine region of southern **France** which includes **Côtes du Roussillon, Banyuls, Côtes d'Agly, Maury** and **Rivesaltes.** The sweet and fortified wines are of outstanding character.

Grand-St. Julien, Ch. du
Cru bourgeois, **St. Julien.**

Les Grands Échezaux
See **Échezaux.**

Granjo
A Portuguese naturally sweet white wine of the **Sauternes**-type.

Grão Vasco
Reliable brand of red and white **Dão.**

Grape
The fruit of the vine. *See* **Aghiorghitico, Albana, Albariño, Albillo, Aleatico, Aligoté, Alvarinho, Amigne, Arinto, Arvine, Aurora, Bacchus, Baco Noir, Barbera, Beli-Pinot, Blanc Fumé, Blatina, Blauburgunder, Blauer Portugieser, Blaufränkische, Bogdanuša, Bonarda, Bouchet, Bouvier, Bual, Bukettraube, Cabernet-Franc, Cabernet Sauvignon, Cadarca, Carignan, Carménère, Catawba, Cepa, Charbono, Chardonnay, Chasselas, de Chaunac, Chelois, Chenin Blanc, Cinsaut, Clairette, Colombard, Concord, Cortese, Couderc, Courbu, Delaware, Ehrenfelser, Elbling, Elvira, Emerald Riesling, Ezerjó, Faber, Fendant, Flietre, Flora, Folle Blanche, Freisa, French Colombard, Friularo, Frühburgunder, Furmint, Gaglioppo, Gamay, Gamza, Garganega, Garnacho, Gentil, Gewürztraminer, Graciano, Grasa di Cotnari, Graševina, Grauerburgunder, Greco, Grenache, Grey Riesling, Grignolino, Groslot, Gros Manseng, Gros Plant, Grüner-Veltliner, Gutedel, Hárslevelü, Huxelrebe, Hybrid, Isabella, Italian Riesling, Johannisberg, Kadarka, Kékfrankos, Kéknyelü, Kerner, Klevner, Knipperlé, Lagrein, Laski Rizling, Leanyka, Liatico, Limberger, Listan, Malbec, Mali Plavać, Malmsey, Malvasia, Malvoisie, Mandilari, Maraština, Marsanne, Mavroudi, Mavrud, Mazuelo, Médoc Noir, Melon d'Artois, Merlot, Misket, Mission, Molinara, Monica, Morio-Muscat, Morre's Diamond, Moscato, Mourvèdre, Mullerebe, Müller-Thurgau, Muscadelle, Muscadet, Muscat, Muscat d'Alsace, Muskotály, Nagyburgundi, Napa Gamay, Nebbiolo, Neuberger, Niagara, Nigrara, Noir de Pressac, Oesterreichischer, Olasz Riesling, País, Palomino, Pamid, Pedro Ximenez, Petit Manseng, Petite Syrah, Petit Verdot, Phileri, Picardan, Picpoul, Pineau des Charentes, Pineau de la Loire, Pinot Blanc, Pinot Grigio, Pinot Gris, Pinot Noire, Pinotage, Pinot Chardonnay, Pinot Meunier, Portugieser, Posip, Primitivo, Prokupac, Ranina, Ravat, Rczaziteli, Reichensteiner, Renski Rizling, Riesling, Rivaner, Roditis, Romeiko, Rotgipfler, Roussanne, Ruby Cabernet, Ruländer, St.-Laurent, Sangiovese, Saperavi, Sauvignon Blanc, Savagnin, Savatiano, Scheurebe, Schiava, Scuppernong, Seibel, Sémillon, Seyval Blanc, Shiraz, Sipon, Spätburgunder, Spätrot, Steen, Sylvaner, Syrah, Szürkebarát, Tannat, Tempranillo, Teran, Terlano, Tocai, Tokaier, Tokay d'Alsace, Traminer, Tramini, Trebbiano, Trollinger, Ugni Blanc, Varietal, Verdelho, Verdicchio, Verdisi, Vernaccia, Viognier, Vitis Labrusca, Wälschriesling, Weisser Riesling, Xynisteri, Zierfändler, Žilavka, Zinfandel, Zoldszilvani.**

Grapey
A rich, **Muscatelle**-like aroma produced by certain grape varieties such as **Scheurebe.**

Grappa
Italian **Marc.** It is drunk fairly young and is usually unaged. The name is also used in **California.**

Grasa di Cotnari
Rumanian equivalent of the Hungarian **Furmint,** from the **Grasa** grape.

Graševina
Yugoslavian for **Wälchsriesling,** the most common Yugoslavian **Riesling** grape.

Gratiesti
White dessert wine of Moldavia, **USSR.**

Grauerburgunder
Another name for the **Pinot Gris.**

Grave del Friuli
Red or white *DOC* wines from **Friuli-Venezia Giulia.**

Graves
This district, which lies immediately to the west and south of **Bordeaux,** is known chiefly for its dry to medium sweet, white wines. Red **Graves** are also produced which are of high quality, e.g. **Ch. Haut-Brion, Ch. Haut-Bailly, Ch. La Mission-Haut-Brion, Domaine de Chevalier.** Important communes are **Pessac, Léognan, Villenave d'Ornon, Martillac, Mérignac.**

Graves (de) Saint-Émilion
The name given to a small district of the **Saint-Émilion** vyds., the soil of which differs from that of others in **Saint-Émilion,** being more gravelly. The finest wine is that of **Ch. Cheval-Blanc.**

Graves de Vayres
The *AC* district for white **Bordeaux** wines, part of **Entre-Deux-Mers.**

La Grave Trigant de Boisset, Ch.
An average light **Pomerol.**

Les Gravières
Premier cru red **Burgundy** vyd. of **Santenay, Côte de Beaune.**

Great Western
See **Pleasant Valley.**

Greco
Italian white wine grape.

Greco di Gerace
One of the better wines of **Calabria.** Sweet, golden and flowery.

Greco di Tufo
DOC dry white wine from **Campania.**

Greece
Most of the large quantities of grapes grown are exported. From the rest about half of the domestically drunk wine is flavoured with a resin **(Retsina).** More unresinated wine is being made and there are some luxury dessert wines including the famous *Mavrodaphne.*

Green wine
Unripe, raw and young.

Grenache
Major red wine grape grown mainly in the south of **France, Spain, California** and **Cyprus.** It produces light, fruity red and *rosé* wines.

Grenadine
Bright red sweetening syrup in cocktails, which is usually free from alcohol.

Gressier Grand Poujeaux
Cru bourgeois of the **Moulis** *comm.,* **Haut-Médoc.**

Grey Riesling
American white grape. No relation to the German **Riesling.**

Grignolino
Native grape of **Piedmont** and grown in **California.** Good for young reds and *rosés.*

Grignolino d'Asti
DOC red wine of **Piedmont.**

Grignolino de Monferrato Casalese
Light bodied red wine of **Piedmont.**

Grinzing
A Viennese suburb famous for **Heurige** wines.

Griottes-Chambertin
Fine *grand cru* vyd. of **Gevrey-**

Chambertin *comm.* with a very small production.

Grk
Local Dalmatian grape, **Yugoslavia,** producing a dry, almost **Sherry-**type wine.

Groot Constantia
Old and famous **Cape Province** estate.

Groslot
Minor red grape grown in the **Loire** valley for ordinary red wines and **Rosé d'Anjou.**

Gros Manseng
Local white grape of the **Jurançon** area of south-west **France.**

Gros Plant
Loire valley name for the **Folle Blanche** grape, where it is used in the production of the *VDQS* white wine *Gros Plant du Pays Nantais.*

Grosslage
German name for one group of single vyds. within each *Ber.*

Gruaud-Larose, Ch.
Well-known *2me cru* of the **Haut-Médoc, St. Julien** *comm.*

Grumello
DOC red wine from the **Valtellina** vyds., **Lombardia.**

Grüner-Veltliner
Principal white wine grape of **Austria**, also grown in **Hungary, Yugoslavia** and in **Württemberg, Germany.**

Guebwiller
Comm. of **Haut-Rhin, Alsace.**

Guerry, Ch.
Côtes de Bourg estate.

Guignolet
French **Cherry Brandy** from Angers.

Guild Wineries and Distilleries
Big co-operative of **San Joaquin,** producing quantities of table and dessert wines.

Guiraud, Ch.
Premier cru **Sauternes.**

Güldenmorgen
Gr. of the **Nierstein** *Ber.,* **Rheinhessen.**

Gumpoldskirch
Village south of Vienna which produces one of **Austria's** best-known wines – **Gumpoldskirchener.**

Gundersheim
Village of the **Wonnegau** district, **Rheinhessen.**

Guntersblum
One of the best-known areas of the **Krötenbrunnen** district, **Rheinhessen.**

Guntrum, Louis
Important family producer in **Nierstein** in the **Rheinhessen.**

Gurdzhaani
Good quality light white wine of Georgia, **USSR.**

Gutedel
German name for the **Chasselas** grape grown for the production of ordinary white wines, particularly in **Baden, Alsace** and **Switzerland** (where it is called **Fendant**). Grapes can be red or white but the wine is always white.

Gutes Domtal
Important *Gr.* of the **Nierstein** *Ber.,* **Rheinhessen.**

Guttenberg (Schweigen)
Gr. of the **Südliche Weinstrasse** *Ber.*,
Rheinpfalz.

Gutturnio dei Colli Piacentini
DOC dry or slightly sweet red wine of
Piacenza, **Emilia-Romagna.**

Gyöngyös
Some of the best sparkling wines of
Hungary are grown in this region. Also red
and white table wines.

Haardt
Town of the **Meerspinne** district,
Rheinpfalz.

Hacienda
Small high quality **Sonoma** County winery.

Hagnau
Village of the **Bodensee** district of **Baden.**

Hahnheim
Village of the **Nierstein** district,
Rheinhessen.

Hainfeld
Village of the **Südliche Weinstrasse**
district, **Rheinpfalz.**

Halbrot
Swiss *rosé* made from both black and
white grapes; the equivalent of
Schillerwein.

Halbstück
A Rhine wine cask holding 600 litres.

Half-on-half
Brand of Dutch liqueur, half **Curaçao** and
half **Orange Bitters.**

Halkidas
Red Greek wine from Euboea.

Hallau
German-Swiss village of the
Schaffhausen canton, its wines are
considered the best of the table wines
made in the eastern cantons.

Hallgarten
The name of a famous wine shipping
family; and of a town of the
Mehrhölzchen district of the **Rheingau.**

Hambach
Village of the **Mittelhaardt** district of the
Rheinpfalz, and in the **Hessische
Bergstrasse.**

Hambledon
Established estate and the first modern
English vyd. nr. Petersfield, **Hampshire.**

Hamilton's
Large family winery of **Barossa** and
Adelaide producing a full range of wines,
including some light white **Mosel** and
Riesling types.

Hanns Christof
A **Liebfraumilch** brand name of the well-
known shippers **Deinhard.**

Hanzell
Small **Sonoma** County winery, aiming for
excellence.

Hard
When applied to wine it means too much
tannin.

Hardy's
Famous family concern blending from a number of districts in the **Southern Vales, South Australia,**

Harling
English vyd. at East Harling, **Norfolk.**

Haro
Town of northern **Spain;** centre of the **Rioja Alta.**

Hárslevelü
Hungarian white grape used in the production of **Tokay.** *See* **Debroi Hárslevelü.**

Harvey's
British and world famous Bristol-based **Sherry, Port** and table wine shippers.

Harxheim
Important village of the *Gr.* **Sankt Alban** *Ber.,* **Nierstein** district.

Hascombe
English vyd. of Godalming, **Surrey,** producing dry delicate wines.

Hattenheim
Important town of the **Rheingau,** producing full-bodied dry wines such as **Steinberger.**

Haut-Bages-Avéros
Cru bourgeois, **Pauillac** *comm.,* **Haut-Médoc.**

Haut-Bages-Libéral, Ch.
5me cru classé of the **Haut-Médoc, Pauillac** *comm.*

Haut-Bailly, Ch.
Grand cru classé red **Graves, Léognan** district, **Graves de Bordeaux.**

Haut-Batailley
5me cru classé of the **Pauillac** *comm.,* **Haut-Médoc.**

Haut-Brion, Ch.
Premier grand cru classé of the **Pessac** *comm.,* **Graves de Bordeaux.** The top **Graves** vyd. and one of the leading six **Bordeaux chx.**

Haut-Combat
VDQS red or *rosé* produced nr. **Avignon, Côtes du Rhône.**

Hautes-Côtes-de-Beaune
AC red or white **Burgundy** from a small area east of the **Côte de Beaune.**

Hautes-Côtes-de-Nuits, Bourgogne
AC red **Burgundy** from a small area west of **Nuits St. Georges.**

Haut-Madère, Ch.
Principal growth of the **Graves de Bordeaux, Villenave d'Ornon** *comm.*

Haut-Marbuzet, Ch.
Better-known *cru bourgeois* of the **St. Estèphe** *comm.,* **Haut-Médoc.**

Haut-Médoc
See **Médoc.**

Haut-Peyraguey, Clos
Premier cru **Sauternes, Bommes** *comm.*

Haut-Pourret, Ch.
Principal growth of **Saint-Émilion.**

Haut-Simard, Ch.
Principal growth of **Saint-Émilion.**

Hautvillers
Premier cru of canton d'**Ay, Champagne.**

The famous **Dom Pérignon** was cellarer at the Abbey of Hautvillers.

Heady
A wine high in alcohol, or rich enough to 'go to the head'.

Heavy
An official definition for a fortified wine subject to higher rates of excise duty. Also a term used for a wine over-endowed with alcohol and fruitiness.

Hectare
Metric measurement equivalent to 2.471 acres.

Hectolitre
French measure equal to 22 gallons (USA 26.4 gallons).

Heidsieck, Charles
Leading **Champagne** house, **Reims.**

Heidsieck & Co
Leading **Champagne** house, **Reims.** Producers of **Monopole.**

Heilbronn
Important wine town of the **Neckar** valley, **Württemberg.**

Heiligenstock
Gr. of the **Johannisberg** *Ber.,* **Rheingau.**

Heiligenthal
Gr. of the **Mainviereck** *Ber.,* **Franken.**

Heitz
Extremely high quality, privately owned and personally run winery in the **Napa Valley.**

Hemus
Brand name of a dessert wine from **Karlovo, Bulgaria.**

Henriques & Henriques
Well-known **Madeira** shippers based at **Funchal.**

Henschke
Barossa family business, well known for white table wines.

Hérault
Dpt. in the Montpellier-Béziers district of the **Midi.** (*See also* **Aude** *and* **Gard.**) Produces large quantities of *ordinaire.*

Hermitage
Distinguished **Rhône** *AC* from a number of vyds. including **Chante Alouette, La Chappelle** and **La Varogne.** Rich reds and fine fruity whites. *See* **Shiraz.**

Herrenberg
Gr. of the **Rheinburgengau** *Ber.,* **Mittelrhein.**

Herrenberg
Gr. of the **Steigerwald** *Ber.,* **Franken.**

Herrlich (Eschbach)
Gr. of the **Südliche Weinstrasse** *Ber.,* **Rheinpfalz.**

Les Hervelets
Premier cru of the **Fixin** *comm.,* **Côte de Nuits.**

Herxheim
Town of the **Mittelhaardt, Rheinpfalz.**

Herzegovina
Small region of **Yugoslavia** but produces some of the best white wines, including *Mostarska* **Žilavka.**

Hessische-Bergstrasse
Small **QbA** wine region of **Germany.** Districts are: **Starkenburg** and **Umstadt.** Most of the wines are drunk locally including some **Weissherbst.**

Heuchelberg
Gr. of the **Württembergisches Unterland, Württemberg.**

Heurige
The Austrian term for *wine of the year.* Also the name for the taverns where it is sold.

Highball
A long drink of diluted spirits, usually **Whisky,** served with cracked ice.

Highwaymans
Large English estate nr. Bury St. Edmunds, **Suffolk.**

Hill Grove
Vyd. at Swanmore nr. Southampton, **Hampshire.**

Himbeergeist
A dry German colourless, raspberry-flavoured spirit.

Hochfeinste
Now illegal, old German label word for *very finest.*

Hochheim
Wine town of the **Rheingau** that gave its name to, and became the derivation of, the English term **Hock** for the wines of the **Rhine.** One of its most famous vyds. is the *Königin Viktoria-Berg.,* owned by Deinhard, which was visited by Queen Victoria in 1850 and which, with her permission, was renamed in her honour.

Hochmess (Bad Dürkheim)
Gr. of the **Mittelhaardt** *Ber.,* **Rheinpfalz.**

Hock
The English name for Rhine wine which has replaced the older name Rhenish. The bottles are brown and it has been

fashionable to serve Hock in tall brown-stemmed glasses. *See* **Hochheim.** The name covers wines from the **Rheingau** in particular but includes wines from all the other districts except the **Mosel.**

Hofrat (Kitzingen)
Gr. of the **Maindreieck** *Ber.,* **Franken.**

Hofstück (Deidesheim) Gr.
Gr. of the **Mittelhaardt** *Ber.,* **Rheinpfalz.**

Hogshead
Wine and spirit cask which has different capacities in different countries. It is half a **Madeira** and **Marsala pipe** – 422.6 litres; half a **Port pipe** – 250 litres; half a **Sherry butt** – 245.4 litres; a **Brandy cask** – 545.2 litres; an **Armagnac cask** – 272.6 litres; a **Rum measure** – 245.272 litres; in **Australia** and **South Africa** – 295.3 litres; for **US** spirits – 45.80 gallons. *See* **Quarter cask.**

Hohenberg
Gr. **Badische Bergstrasse** *Ber.,* **Baden.**

Hohenneuffen
Gr. of the **Remstal-Stuttgart** *Ber.,* **Württemberg.**

Hollands
The name of a very distinctive type of Dutch **Gin,** more commonly called **Jenever.** Originally the Dutch used to crush the juniper berries and ferment their juice with the grain which was distilled. Now Hollands is distilled from a mash of barley malt mixed with juniper or flavouring and it is distilled to a much lower strength than **London Gin** or American **Gin.**

Höllenpfad (Grünstadt)
Gr. of the **Mittelhaardt** *Ber.,* **Rheinpfalz.**

Honey/Honeyed
Characteristic fragrance of certain fine mature wines such as **Sauternes.**

Honigberg
Gr. of the **Hohannisberg** *Ber.,* **Rheingau.**

Honigberg
Gr. of the **Maindreieck** *Ber.,* **Franken.**

Honigsäckel
Gr. of the **Mittelhaardt** *Ber.,* **Rheinpfalz.**

Horizontal tasting
Tasting wines of the same age but of different origins.

Hospices de Beaune
Charity hospital in **Beaune.** Over the years wine growers have donated their land to the Hospices and the revenue from the wines, which are auctioned, completely subsidizes the hospital. Genuine *Hospices de Beaune* wines bear the name of the **Cuvée,** that is to say the name of the donor of the vyd. from which the wine offered was made, as well as the name of the *comm.*

Hospices de Nuits
Similar to the **Hospices de Beaune** but smaller and less famous.

Houghton
Famous winery of **Western Australia** producing top quality **Burgundy-**type white wines.

Huelva
Demarcated region of **Spain,** producing mainly bulk wines.

Hugel, Père et Fils
Leading producers of fine **Alsace** wines, based at **Riquewihr, France.**

Hungary
Although one of the smaller wine-producing countries of Europe, Hungary is famous for its sweet **Tokay** wines, **Bikavér** *Bull's Blood,* and a range of white varietals. An *i* added to the name of a place is the equivalent of the *er* in German wine names. The mark of authenticity is a label with the words:

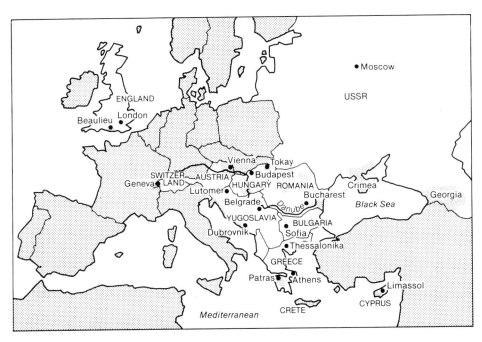

Magyar Állami Export Pincegazdaság in a circle enclosing the word *Budafok. See* **Monimpex.**

Hungerford Hill
Large **Hunter Valley** estate.

Hunter Valley
Famous wine area of **New South Wales,** producing full-bodied reds and **Semillon** and **Chardonnay** whites. The upper Hunter region is newly developed, specializing in white wines.

Huxelrebe
Modern fruity white wine grape from **Germany.** Wines have a slightly **Muscat** bouquet.

Hybrid
In viticulture, a new variety bred by crossing an American variety **(Vitis labrusca)** with a European variety **(Vitis vinifera).** Hybrids are most resistant to disease and may not require grafting. *See* **Seyve-Villard.**

Hymettus
Brand name of red and dry wines of mainland **Greece.**

Ice Wine
See **Eiswein.**

Ihringen
One of the best wine-producing villages of

the **Kaiserstuhl, Baden.**

Ilbesheim
Wine town of the **Südliche Weinstrasse, Rheinpfalz.**

Imbottigliato dal produttore all'origine
Italian for *estate-bottled.*

Impériale
The name of an outsize French bottle for bottling fine **Bordeaux** wines which are intended for keeping. Approximate capacity is 6 litres.

Inferno
One of the better *DOC* red wines of the **Valtellina, Lombardia.**

Ingelheim
A large wine-producing area of the **Bingen** district *Gr.* **Kaiserpfalz.**

Inglenook
Established large **Napa Valley** vyd. producing a good range of quality dessert and table wines.

Institut National des Appellations d'Origine Contrôlées
The French authority responsible for setting and monitoring the classifications of French wines – *see* **AC.**

Iphofen
Village nr. **Würzburg, Franken.**

Irancy
Red or *rosé AC* wines from the village of the same name nr. Auxerre, **Yonne** *Dpt.*

Irish Mist
Proprietary **Irish Whiskey**-based herb liqueur.

Irish Whiskey
Irish Whiskey, most likely the first whisky ever made, is distilled from a mash made of malted and unmalted barley, with small quantities of wheat, oats and rye. The **Pot Still** version is triple distilled (as opposed to two for **Scotch Whisky**), but most Irish Whiskey is now made in a **Continuous Still** for blending with grain whiskey.

Iron
In connection with wine, a faintly metallic, earthy taste derived from the soil.

Irouléguy
A rather heady red table wine from the Basque country, south-west **France**. Also some white and *rosé*.

Irroy
A brand name of **Champagne** well known in Victorian times in England.

Isabella
Old style American grape; similar to **Concord.**

Ischia
A small island in the Bay of Naples producing red and white wines.

Iskra
Brand name of a Bulgarian sparkling wine made by the *méth. champ.*

Isonzo
DOC for ten wines from **Friuli-Venezia Giulia.**

Israel
Most types of wine are made, the most significant being sweet reds and golden **Muscatels.**

d'Issan, Ch.
3me cru classé of the **Haut-Médoc, Cantenac-Margaux** *comm.*

Italian Riesling (or Italico Riesling)
Lower acidity grape than the German **Riesling** grown in northern **Italy** and central and eastern Europe. *See* **Wälschriesling, Olaszriesling.**

Italian Swiss Colony
Established name from **Sonoma** County, now in **San Joaquin.**

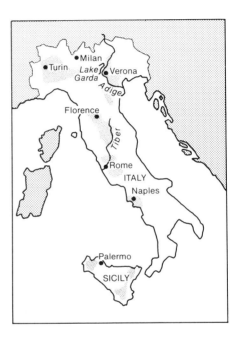

Italy
The largest wine-producing country in the world. Vines are grown in almost every corner of Italy. The main quality-producing areas are **Piedmont, Tuscany, Veneto, South Tyrol** and **Lazio.** The best Italian wines usually carry the **Denominazione di Origine Controllata** *(DOC)* though there are exceptions. Recently the higher 'appellation' *Denominazione di Origine Controllata e Guarantita* has been introduced. In both instances it means the wine is made from approved grapes, grown in a delimited area, and vinified according to certain regulations.

Izarra
A Basque liqueur similar to **Chartreuse**

with an **Armagnac Brandy** basis and flavoured with wild flowers from the **Pyrénées.** It is made in two colours: yellow, which is the sweeter of the two; and green which is the stronger.

Jaboulet, Paul
Old family merchant at Tain, and important growers of *AC* **Hermitage.**

Jaboulet-Vercherre et Cie
Burgundy merchants with cellars at **Pommard.**

des Jacobins, Clos
Well-known small *grand cru classé* of **Saint-Émilion.**

Jadot, Louis
Burgundy merchants with vyds. **Corton Charlemagne** and elsewhere.

Jamaica Rum
Rum distilled from molasses. It is one of the best known and one of the commercially most important of cane rums. It is distilled at a comparatively low strength so that it has a very pungent flavour. Its colour varies with the proportions of caramel used, from a light gold to mahogany.

Japan
Japan grows quantities of table and wine grapes but the wine industry has not yet achieved stable quality production. The traditional drink is **Saké,** but **Whisky**

production is large – much of it is blended with imported Scottish Whiskies.

Jarnac-Champagne
Important **Cognac** *comm.* in the *Dpt.* **Charente-Maritime.**

Jasnières
AC white **Loire** valley wine, **Anjou,** mainly semi-sweet and **moelleux.**

Jaune, vin
See **Vin jaune.**

Jenever
See **Jonge Jenever** and **Oude Jenever.**

Jerez de la Frontera
Centre of the **Sherry** trade.

Jeroboam
In **Champagne** the name is given to a double magnum – in **Bordeaux** five bottles. In **England** it generally refers to the equivalent of four bottles.

Jeropica (Geropica)
Grape juice or syrup, used to sweeten wines, especially **Port** in **Portugal.**

Jerusalem
Famous **Ljutomer** vyd., **Yugoslavia.**

Jesuitengarten
Vyd. at **Forst** which produces some of the best wine of the **Rheinpfalz.**

Jigger
American name for a small measure of spirits: 1½ fluid oz.

Johannisberg
The name of a *Ber.* of the **Rheingau.** *See* **Schloss Johannisberg.** Also the name

given in the **Valais** to the **Sylvaner** grape
and to the white wine made from it.

Johannisberg Riesling
Name given to the true **Rhine-Riesling** in
California.

Joigny
One of the oldest towns of the **Yonne**
Dpt., producing white wines in the style of
Chablis.

Jonge Jenever
Slightly paler, almost white, younger
version of **Oude Jenever.**

Julep
Long drink, formerly a great country
favourite in **England;** as the following lines
from Milton suggest:
> *Behond this cordial Julep here,*
> *That foams and dances in his crystal*
> *bounds,*
> *With spirits of balm and fragrant syrups*
> *mix'd.*

Juliénas
One of the nine *comm.* responsible for
some of the best of the **Beaujolais.**

Juliusspital
Leading producers at **Würzburg,**
Franken, owning over half the famous
Stein vyd. and others.

Jumilla
Demarcated area of the Levante, **Spain,**
producing heavy dark wines strong in
alcohol.

de Jura, Côtes
AC which covers all the lesser wines of
the Jura, including **mousseux** wines, reds,
whites and *rosés.* The characteristic
wines of the region are the **Vins Jaunes.**
The more exclusive *ACs* are **Arbois, Ch.-**
Chalon and **L'Étoile.**

Jurançon
Famous dessert wine high in alcohol from
the French **Pyrénées,** *Pyrénées*
Atlantiques Dpt.

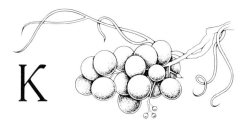

Kabinett
German name for the grade of least ripe
or naturally sweet grapes, producing the
driest of naturally sweet **(QmP)** wines.

Kabinettwein
German term used to identify the special
reserve or selected barrels of the vyd.
owner.

Kadarka
Leading Hungarian red grape. *See* **Egri**
Kadarka.

Kaefferkopf
Famous vyd. of **Ammerschwihr, Alsace.**

Kaffia
One of the best sparkling wines of the
Crimea.

Kahlenberg
Village and vyd. north of Vienna, famous
for **Heurige** wines.

Kahluá
Rum-based proprietary coffee-flavoured
liqueur from Denmark.

Kaiserpfalz
Gr. of the **Bingen** *Ber.,* **Rheinhessen.**

Kaiser Stuhl
Brand name of the **Barossa** Growers' Co-operative, **South Australia.**

Kaiserstuhl-Tuniberg
District of **Baden (QbA),** producing the best wines of the region.

Kallstadt
One of the most important wine towns of the **Mittelhaardt,** *Gr.* **Kobnert, Rheinpfalz.**

Kalterseewein
See **Caldaro.**

Kamp
Tributary of the Danube.

Kanonkop
Stellenbosch estate specializing in full-bodied red wines.

Kanzem
Village of the **Saar** valley, **MSR.**

Kanzlerberg
Vyd. of the **Bergheim** *comm.,* **Haut-Rhin, Alsace,** producing quality white wine.

Kapellenberg
Gr. of the **Steigerwald** *Ber.,* **Franken.**

Kasel
Important town of the **Ruwer** valley, *Gr.* **Römerlay, MSR.**

Kaub
One of the oldest wine villages of the **Mittelrhein.**

Kayserberg
One of the good white wine-producing *comms.* of **Alsace.**

Kecskemét
One of the wine-producing localities of **Hungary** which is noted for its white wines and fruit liqueurs.

Kékfrankos
Hungarian name for the **Gamay** grape.

Kéknyelü
Full-flavoured Hungarian grape.

Keller
German for **cellar.** Thus: *Kellerabfüllung* and *Kellerabzug,* both equivalent of *château-bottled.*

Kelsale
Small but good English vyd. in **Suffolk.** Winner of the *Gore-Browne Trophy* with a wine from the **Madeleine Angevine.**

Keo
Large **Cyprus** wine shippers based at Limassol.

Kerner
Early ripening white wine grape developed in **Germany** by crossing the **Trollinger** and the **Riesling.** Also grown in **South Africa.**

Kesten
Village of the **Mittel-Mosel, MSR.**

Kiedrich
Small town of the **Rheingau** producing quality wines.

Kinheim
One of the smaller wine-producing towns on the left bank of the **Mosel,** in the **Bernkastel** district, **MSR.**

Kir
Popular French **apéritif** made from a

small amount of **Cassis** mixed with dry white wine.

Kirchberg (Volkach)
Gr. of the **Maindreieck, Ber., Franken.**

Kirchenweinberg
Gr. of the **Württembergisches Unterland, Württemberg.**

Kirchhofen
Village of the **Markgräflerland, Baden.**

Kirrweiler
A less important wine-producing area of the **Südliche Weinstrasse, Rheinpfalz.**

Kirsch
Popular spirit distilled chiefly in **Germany, Alsace** and **Switerland** from the fermented juice and stones of small black cherries. It is matured in glass not in wood to ensure its lack of colour.

Kirwan, Ch.
3me cru classé of the **Haut-Médoc, Cantenac-Margaux** *comm.*

Klein Karoo
Demarcated wine district stretching east of **Montagu, Cape Province.**

Klevner
German name for **Pinot Blanc.**

Klöch
Austrian wine district in **Styria.** The soil produces the famous **Traminer** wines of the region.

Klosterberg
Gr. of the **Walporzheim/Ahrtal** *Ber.,* **Ahr.**

Kloster Eberbach
Twelfth century abbey nr. **Hattenheim** in

the **Rheingau,** now State Domain owned and the home of the German Wine Academy, where one of the greatest **Hocks – Steinberger** – is vintaged.

Kloster Liebfrauenberg (Bad Bergzabern)
Gr. of the **Südliche Weinstrasse, Rheinpfalz.**

Klosterneuburg
Famous monastery in Vienna, now a wine cellar, college and research establishment.

Klüsserath
Village of the **Bernkastel** district, **MSR.**

Knipperlé
Alsace white wine **hybrid** grape, now planted in only small quantities.

Kobern-Gondorf
Small town of the **Zell-Mosel** nr. **Koblenz, MSR.**

Koblenz
Important German wine town where the **Mosel** meets the **Rhine.** Headquarters of some of the biggest wine companies like **Sichel et Cie** and Deinhard.

Kocherberg
Gr. of the **Kocher-Jagst-Tauber** *Ber.,* **Württemberg.**

Kocher-Jagst-Tauber
Ber. of **Württemberg.**

Könen
One of the small wine-producing areas of the **Saar** valley, **Scharzberg** *Gr.,* **MSR.**

Königsbach
Wine village of the **Mittelhaardt, Rheinpfalz.**

Königsberg
Important *Gr.* of the **Obermosel** *Ber.,*
MSR.

Königsgarten (Godramstein)
Gr. of the **Südliche Weinstrasse** *Ber.,*
Rheinpfalz.

Ko-öperative Wijnbouwers Vereniging
See **KWV.**

Kopf
Gr. of the **Remstal-Stuttgart** *Ber.,*
Württemberg.

Korbel
Sparkling wine specialists *(meth. champ.)*
of **Sonoma** County, **California.**

Kornell
Important sparkling wine establishment
(méth. champ.), **Napa Valley.**

Krasnodar
Wine region of the **USSR** and one of the
best sparkling wines from the important
Abrau-Dursso collective.

Krems
Important Austrian wine town and district
of the **Wachau.**

Kreuznach
Well-known wine-producing *Ber.* of the
Nahe valley.

Kronenberg
Gr. of the **Kreuznach** *Ber.,* **Nahe.**

Krötenbrunnen
Gr. of the **Nierstein** *Ber., Rheinhessen.*

Kröv
Wine area of the **Mittel-Mosel** nr.
Bernkastel, MSR.

Krug
One of the greatest, if not the greatest,
Champagne houses.

Krug, Charles
Old winery with a good range from the
Napa Valley.

Kümmel
One of the most popular of all liqueurs,
flavoured with caraway seeds which give it
definite digestive properties. It originated
from Holland but is now popular in Russia
and has been made there for many years.
Kümmel has a spirit base distilled mainly
from grain, and is more or less sweetened,
according to the brand.

Kurfürstenstück
Gr. of the **Bingen** *Ber.,* **Rheinhessen.**

Kurfürstlay
Gr. of the **Bernkastel** *Ber.,* **MSR.**

KWV
Ko-öperative Wijnbouwers Vereniging.
The national wine co-operative of **South
Africa** with premises at **Paarl;** it makes a
full range of quality wines and Sherries.

Labarde
One of the *comm.* of the **Haut-Médoc;** its
wines have acquired the right by long use
to be sold with the better-known name of
the nearby *comm.* of **Labarde-Margaux.**

de Labégorce, Ch.
Bourgeois supérieur growth of the **Margaux** *comm.*

Labégorce-Zédé, Ch.
Bourgeois cru of the **Soussans-Margaux** *comm.*, **Haut-Médoc.**

Lacrima Christi del Vesuvio
Red and white wines from the slopes of Mt. Vesuvius, **Campania, Italy.**

Ladoix-Serrigny
AC of the two villages nr. **Beaune** – red and white wine.

Ladouys, Ch.
Minor growth of the **St. Estèphe** *comm.*, **Haut-Médoc.**

Lafaurie-Peyraguey, Ch.
Premier cru **Sauternes, Bommes** *Comm.* Also producing some dry **Bordeaux Supérieur.**

Lafite or Lafite-Rothschild, Ch.
Premier cru classé (first growth) of the **Haut-Médoc,** one of **Bordeaux's** finest vyds. Hugh Johnson calls it a 'perfumed, polished, gentlemanly production'.

Lafite-Carcasset, Ch.
Minor growth of the **St. Estèphe** *comm.*, **Haut-Médoc.**

Lafleur, Ch.
First quality **Pomerol** vyd.

Lafon, Ch.
Unclassified growth of the **Sauternes** district.

Lafon-Rochet, Ch.
4me cru classé, **St. Estèphe** *comm.*, **Haut-Médoc.**

Lagar
Spanish and Portuguese name of the square stone trough in which the ripe grapes are piled at vintage time and crushed underfoot.

Lagosta
Well-known brand of **Vinho Verde.**

Lagrange, Ch.
3me cru classé of the **St. Julien** *comm.*, **Haut-Médoc.** There is also a **Ch. Lagrange** which is a small high quality growth of **Pomerol.**

Lagrein
Tyrolean grape that produces slightly sharp, fruity reds, and *rosés,* in northern **Italy.**

Lagrein del Trentino
DOC dry light and fruity red wine of the **Trentino-Alto Adige.**

La Lagune, Ch.
3me cru classé of the **Haut-Médoc, Ludon** *comm.*

Lahntal
Gr. of the **Rheinburgengau** *Ber.*, **Mittelrhein.**

Lake's Folly
Quality vyd. of the **Hunter Valley.**

Lalande-de-Pomerol
Comm. to the north of **Pomerol**. Not as fine as those of **Pomerol.**

Lamarque
Comm. of the **Haut-Médoc.**

Lamberhurst Priory
Large and award winning English estate and winery nr. Tunbridge Wells, **Kent,** consisting of established **Seyval Blanc, Reichensteiner, Schönburger, Riesling**

and mainly **Müller-Thurgau.** There are new plantings of **Gutedel, Pinot Noir** and **Seibel.** Recent vintages have **EVA** approval.

Lamberti
Producers of **Soave, Valpolicella** and **Bardolino;** east of Lake Garda.

des Lambrays, Clos
One of the *grand cru* vyds. of the **Morey-Saint-Denis,** *AC.*

Lambrusco di Grasparossa
Slightly acid sparkling *DOC* red from **Emilia-Romagna.**

Lambrusco di Sorbara
DOC sparkling dry from **Emilia-Romagna.**

Lambrusco Salamino di Santa Croce
DOC from Emilia-Ramagna similar to **Lambrusco di Grasparossa.**

Lamothe, Ch.
Second growth of **Sauternes.**

Lancers
Sweet carbonated Portuguese *rosé* popular in the **USA.**

Landau
Wine-producing village of the **Rheinpfalz,** *Gr.* **Königsgarten.**

Landgoed
South African for *estate.*

Lanessan, Ch.
Better-known *cru bourgeois* of the **Cussac** *comm.,* **Haut-Médoc.**

Langenbach
Famous wine merchant of **Worms.**

Producer of **Liebfraumilch** under the brand name of **Crown of Crowns.**

Langenlois
Largest wine-producing town of Lower **Austria** which has given its name to the district.

Langenlonsheim
Second largest wine-producing district of the **Nahe** valley.

Langhorne Creek
See **Southern Vales.**

Langoa-Barton, Ch.
3me cru classé **St. Julien** *comm.,* **Haut-Médoc.**

du Languedoc Coteaux
AC district of **Languedoc, Midi.** The district itself includes another fourteen *AC.*

Lanson, Père et Fils
Important **Champagne** growers and merchants at **Reims.**

Larcis-Ducasse, Ch.
Grand cru classé, **St. Laurent des Combes** *comm.,* **Haut-Médoc.**

Larose-Trintaudon, Ch.
Cru bourgeois **St. Laurent,** *comm.,* **Haut-Médoc.**

Laroze, Ch.
Grand cru classé of **Saint-Émilion.** Another of the same name is *cru bourgeois,* **Saint-Émilion,** a third in the **Margaux** *comm.*

Larrivet Haut-Brion, Ch.
Good *bourgeois cru* from the **Léognan** *comm.,* **Graves de Bordeaux.**

Lascombes, Ch.
2me cru classé of the **Haut-Médoc,
Margaux** *comm.*

Laski Rizling
One of the Yugoslavian names for the
Italian Riesling.

Lasserre, Ch.
Grand cru classé of **Saint-Émilion.**

Late-bottled vintage
Port made from the wine of a single year
and bottled when mature.

Latisana
DOC of seven wines from **Friuli-Venezia
Giulia.**

Latium
See **Lazio.**

Latour, Ch.
Premier cru classé of the **Haut-Médoc,
Pauillac** *comm.*, one of the great
Bordeaux clarets. There are seven other
chx. in the **Gironde** *Dpt.* called *Latour, La
Tour* and *de la Tour.*

Latour, Louis
Leading **Burgundy** merchant and grower.

Latour Pomerol, Ch.
Top growth **Pomerol** from the centre of
the district.

Latour-Pourret, Ch.
Principal growth of **Saint-Émilion.**

Latricières-Chambertin
Grand cru vyd. of the **Côte de Nuits.**

Laubenheim
Wine village of the **Nahe** district, *Gr.*
Schlosskapelle.

Laudun
Village of the **Gard** *Dpt.* entitled to the *AC*
Côtes du Rhône, producing white, pink
and red wines.

Laujuc, Ch.
Cru bourgeois of the **Bas-Médoc,
Bégadan** *comm.*

Laurent-Perrier
Well-known **Champagne** house of Tours-
sur-Marne.

Lavaux
The vyds. from Lausanne to Vevey in the
Vaud canton, **Switzerland.**

Laville-Haut-Brion, Ch.
Grand cru classé white **Graves** from the
Talence *comm.*

du Layon, Coteaux
Large *AC* white wine area of **Anjou.** The
best-known wine is the **Quarts de
Chaume** which has its own *app.* **Coteaux
du Layon Chaume** which must be made
of **Chenin Blanc** only.

Lazio (Latium)
Wine region of central **Italy** around Rome.
Famous for **Frascati,** and **Est!-Est!!-Est!!!**

Leacock
Old established **Madeira** shippers.

Leanyka
A Hungarian white grape producing
delicate white wines, especially **Egri
Leanyka.**

de Léchet, Côte
Premier cru **Chablis.**

Lees
The sediment of crystalline matter

(tartrates) left at the bottom of a wine cask after racking from one barrel to another. Red wines throw more sediment than white.

Légèrement doux
Swiss label term for wines with a notable quantity of residual sugar.

Legs
An English term for globules which fall down the sides of the glass after the wine is swirled. It is generally indicative of a rich, naturally sweet wine, e.g. a **Sauternes.** Also known as tears.

Leistadt
Wine town of the **Mittelhardt** district, **Rheinpfalz.**

Leiwen
A white wine town of the **Mittel-Mosel,** which adjoins **Trittenheim.**

Lenz Moser, Dr.
Famous Austrian inventor of the 'high vine' system. Has vyds. at **Krems, Apetlon** and **Mailberg.**

Léognan
One of the finest of the wine-producing *comm.* of the **Graves** district, including **Ch. Haut-Bailly** and **Domaine de Chevalier.**

Léoville-Barton, Ch.
2me cru classé of the **Haut-Médoc, St. Julien** *comm.* with the best reputation of the three *Léovilles.*

Léoville-Las-Cases, Ch.
2me cru classé of the **Haut-Médoc, St. Julien** *comm.* The largest of the three *Léovilles.*

Léoville-Poyferré, Ch.
2me cru classé of the **Haut-Médoc, St. Julien** *comm.* and the least well known of the three *Léovilles.*

Lessona
Soft dry red wine from **Piedmont.**

Lestage, Ch.
Larger *cru bourgeois* estate of the **Médoc, Listrac** *comm.* Also another property in **St. Estèphe** *comm.*

Lexham Hall
Vyd. and winery Kings Lynn, **Norfolk.** Four grape varieties **Müller-Thurgau, Reichensteiner, Scheurebe** and **Madeleine Angevine** produce white, dry, mild and fruity wines.

Liatico
Greek red wine grape; mainly from Crete.

Libertas, Ch. and Oude Libertas
Two wines of *Stellenbosch Farmers' Winery.*

Libourne
An ancient city on the right bank of the Dordogne and once an important market for the wines of **Saint-Émilion, Pomerol** and **Fronsac.**

Liebfrauenmorgen
Gr. of the **Wonnegau** *Ber.,* **Rheinhessen.**

Liebfrauenstift
The historic vyd. in the city of **Worms, Rheinhessen,** said to be the origin of the name **Liebfraumilch.**

Liebfraumilch
A semi-sweet **QbA** wine that can come from the **Rheinhessen, Rheinpfalz, Nache** or **Rheingau** regions of **Germany.**

Lie, sur
Bottling *on the lees* straight from the cask,
e.g. **Muscadet** and **Bourgogne Aligoté.**

Lieser
Small village of the **Bernkastel** district,
Mittel-Mosel, *Gr.* **Kurfürstlay.**

Light
Of wine, one lacking in body or having a
low degree of alcohol. Also an official term
for a natural, unfortified wine.

Liguria
Small, less important and fairly
industrialized wine region of northern **Italy.**
Two *DOC* wines.

Lillet
Semi-dry **apéritif** made from white wine
and **Brandy;** somewhat resembling
Vermouth.

Limberger
Red wine grape grown in **Austria,
Hungary, Yugoslavia,** and **Germany.**

Limoux
Small town nr. **Carcassonne** in the **Aude**
Dpt., noted for a sparkling white wine
known as *Blanquette de Limoux.* The still
version is *Limoux Nature.*

Lindelberg
Gr. of the **Württembergisches Unterland**
Ber., **Württemberg.**

Lindeman
Old established and now large wine
concern owning vyds. in a number of
Australian states. *See* **Ben Ean.**

Lindos
Brand name of a Greek dry white wine
from Rhodes.

Liot, Ch.
Better-known minor **Sauternes** estate,
Barsac.

Liqueur
A sweet strong alcoholic beverage made
from a spirit base with flavourings added.

Liqueur de Tirage
Slightly sweetened still **Champagne** wine
used to top up the bottling vat; always of
the same **Cuvée.**

Liqueur d'expédition
Wine to which cane sugar is added before
topping up the **Champagne** bottles after
dégorgement.

Liquor
American common name for any alcoholic
beverage, usually spirits.

Liquoreux
French term for *rich and sweet.* Italian:
liquoroso.

Lirac
Red, white and *rosé* **Rhône** *AC,* Gard
Dpt.

Listan
Another name for the **Palmino** grape, in
Provence, Algeria, and **South America.**

Listrac
One of the more important wine-producing
comm. of the **Haut-Médoc** although it
cannot boast any of the first five classed
growths. Some of the wines from the
adjoining *comm.* of **Moulis, Lamarque,
Arcins** and **Castelnau** have acquired, by
long usage, the right to be sold under the
better known name of **Listrac.**

Litre
French standard liquid measure of 100
centilitres or 0.22 gallons.

Livadia
A quality **Muscat** wine from the **Crimea.**

Livermore-Alameda
Smallish Californian area across the bay from San Francisco with several wineries including **Concannon,** Stony Ridge, **Weibel** and **Wente** Brothers.

Liversan, Ch.
Good *cru bourgeois of the* **Haut-Médoc, St.-Sauveur** *comm.*

Livran, Ch.
Cru bourgeois estate of the **Bas-Médoc.**

Ljutomer-Ormoz
District of **Slovenia,** producing **Yugoslavia's** finest white wines and famous for its **Riesling.** *See* **Laski Rizling.**

Loché
Comm. of the **Mâconnais.**

Locorotondo
DOC white wine from **Puglia.**

Logroño
Main town of the **Rioja** region.

Loiben
Famous wine district of the **Wachau, Austria.**

du Loire, Coteaux
AC **Anjou** – red, white and *rosé.*

de la Loire Coteaux
AC **Anjou** district producing some sweet wines. *See* **Savennières.** Also dry wines are from the area around **Nantes** in **Muscadet** region.

Lombardia
One of the provinces of northern-central

Italy. It is famous for the **Chiaretto Riviera del Garda,** and the wines of **Valtellina.**

London Gin
Traditionally the driest and strongest type of **Gin** (*see also* **Hollands**), found in **England** and the **USA.**

Longuich
One of the less important white wine-producing areas of the *Ber.* **Bernkastel,** *Gr.* **Probstberg, MSR.**

Lorch
District in the west of the **Rheingau.**

Loreleyfelsen
Gr. of the **Rheinburgengau** *Ber.,* **Mittelrhein.**

Lorettoberg
Gr. of the **Markgräflerland** *Ber.,* **Baden.**

Lorraine
One of the wine-producing provinces of north-eastern **France;** the wines are mostly light and somewhat sharp. They are mainly drunk locally and can be red, white or *rosé.* The area also produces a number of **Vins gris.**

Loudenne, Ch.
Cru bourgeois of the **St. Yzans** *comm.,* **Bas-Médoc,** owned by the British firm Gilbeys. Mainly red but also a good dry white.

Loupiac
Small *AC comm.* of the **Bordeaux** area producing sweet wines of less quality than **Barsac** and **Sauternes.**

La Louvière, Ch.
Mainly white wine vyd. of the **Léognan** *comm.,* **Graves de Bordeaux.**

Louvois
Champagne *cru,* canton d'**Ay,**
Arrondissement de **Reims.**

du Lubéron, Côtes
VDQS of the southern **Côtes du Rhône,**
Dpt. **Vaucluse.**

Ludes
Second class **Champagne** growth of the
canton de **Verzy,** Montagne de **Reims.**

Ludon
Important wine-producing *comm.* of the
Haut-Médoc.

Lugana
DOC dry white from south of Lake Garda,
Lombardia.

Lunel
See **Muscat de Lunel.**

Lupé-Cholet et Cie
Négociants and growers at **Nuits St.**
Georges, including **Ch. Gris.**

Lussac-Saint-Émilion
Comm. and *app.* of **Saint-Émilion.**

Lustau
Independent, family owned **Sherry** house
in **Jerez.**

Lutomer
See **Ljutomer.**

Luxembourg
Wines are similar to those of **Alsace.**
Appellation Complète is the control for
fine wines and labels must give vintage,
locality, vyd. site, grape, name of grower
and the estate.

de Luze, A., et Fils
Bordeaux shipper and owners of chx.
including **Cantenac-Brown.**

Lynch-Bages, Ch
One of the biggest *5me crus classés* of
the **Haut-Médoc, Pauillac** *comm.*

Lynch-Moussas, Ch
Not so well-known *5me cru classé* of the
Haut-Médoc, Pauillac *comm.*

Macau
Important wine-producing *comm.* of the
Haut-Médoc. Its finest estate is **Ch.**
Cantemerle.

Mac-Carthy, Ch.
Minor growth of the **St. Estèphe** *comm.,*
Haut-Médoc.

Macération Carbonique
Wine-making technique where whole
bunches of grapes are fermented in
carbon dioxide. The grape eventually
bursts because of the fermentation and the
resulting wine is very fruity.

Macharnudo
A wine-producing area immediately to the
west of **Jerez,** famous for the excellence
of its **Fino** Sherries.

de Mâconnais, Côte
A large wine-producing district of lower
Burgundy centred on **Mâcon.** The wines

are never of *premier cru* standard but are honest, ordinary wines, both red and white. Some of the best known are the whites from **Pouilly-Fuissé, Pouilly-Loché, Pouilly-Vinzelles** and **St. Véran.**

Mâcon Supérieur
This wine must have an alcoholic strength one degree above a **Mâcon.**

Mâcon-Villages
App. for some excellent white Burgundies, e.g. **Mâcon Viré.**

Madeira
Island off the coast of Africa renowned for its rich dessert wines, which are fortified to leave a residual sugar then 'baked' in an **Estufa** (simulating the old crossing of the Equator in the holds of sailing ships) to give a distinct burnt taste. The four main quality Madeiras (from dry to sweet, and named after the individual grape varieties) are **Sercial, Verdelho, Bual** and **Malmsey.**

La Madeleine, Clos
A tiny *grand cru classé* vyd. of **Saint-Émilion.**

Maderized
Age or poor storage can make white wines lose freshness and fruitiness and become light brown-coloured. In some wines, e.g. **Madeiras** and wines of the **Jura,** it adds to the greatness and gives a taste known as **rancio.**

Madiran
Unusual and established red from the French **Pyrénées.**

Madre, vino
New wine boiled to syrup consistency and used, in Italy, to sweeten dessert wines, as **Geropiga** is made and used in **Portugal.**

Madura
Orange liqueur from Martinique.

Maduro
Portuguese term for *old* or *mature* wine.

Magdeleine
Premier grand cru classé estate, **Côtes Saint-Émilion.**

Magence, Ch.
Lesser **Graves** vyd. **St. Pierre-de-Mous** *comm.*

Magnum
A wine bottle holding the equivalent of two bottles.

Magyar Állami Export Pincegazdaság
See **Hungary.**

Mähler-Besse
Dutch wine merchant of **Bordeaux.** Part-owners of **Ch. Palmer.**

Maikammer
Village of the **Rheinpfalz,** *Gr.* **Mandelhöhe.**

Mailberg
A village which gives its name to a light Austrian wine from the **Weinviertel** district.

Mailly
Grand cru comm. of canton de **Verzy, Champagne.**

Main
A tributary of the Rhine and **(QbA)** town of the **Franken** region. It is also one of the designated **Deutscher Tafelwein** regions.

Maindreieck
Ber. of **Franken.**

Mainviereck
Ber. of **Franken.**

Mainz
Ancient city of the **Rheinhessen.**

Maire, Henri
Merchant and the most important grower
of wines in the **Jura.**

Majorca
A large Spanish island off the coast of
Catalonia; its many vyds. produce a great
deal of *ordinaire* wine and a small quantity
of **Malmsey**-type wine.

Malaga
A demarcated region of **Spain,** noted for
its fortified dessert wines.

Malartic-Lagravière, Ch.
Grand cru classé for red wines, **Léognan**
comm., **Graves de Bordeaux.**

Malbec
A common grape variety of **Bordeaux** and
elsewhere.

Les Malconsorts
One of the outstanding *premier cru* red
wine vyds. of the **Côte de Nuits.** Adjoins
La Tâche.

Malescasse, Ch.
Cru bourgeois of the **Haut-Médoc,**
Lamarque *comm.*

Malescot-St.-Exupéry
3me cru **Margaux, Haut-Médoc.**

Mali Plavać
Native red grape of **Yugoslavia.** (Mali
actually means *small* not red.) The white is
Beli Plavać.

de Malle, Ch.
2me cru **Sauternes, Preignac** *comm.,*
producing sweet and dry white wines. Also
a red **Graves** called **Ch. De Cardaillan.**

Malmesbury
Important centre of the Swartland district
of **South Africa.**

Malmsey
English for the **Malvasia** grape. In **France**
it is *Malvoisie.* Also a sweet dessert wine
made in **Madeira** and **Cyprus.**

Malolactic fermentation
Malic acid converted to lactic acid and
carbon dioxide – malic acid is one of the
most abundant acids in unripe grapes. If
this fermentation is done after bottling, it
decreases acidity in the wine and adds
sparkle.

Malvasia
Italian name for the white grape; also
grown in **Greece, Spain, Madeira, France**
and **Yugoslavia,** responsible for the rich
sweet 'brown' wines of Rhodes.

Malvasia delle Lipari
Sweet dessert *DOC* wine from the Lipari
islands, **Sicily,** made from **Passito** grapes.

Malvasia di Bosa
Strong and aromatic (sometimes dry) white
DOC of **Sardegna.**

Malvasia di Cagliari
Strong, slightly bitter white *DOC* of
Sardegna.

Malvasia di Nus
Dry alpine white with rich 'honey' bouquet,
from the **Valle d'Aosta.**

Malvoisie
Another name for the **Pinot Gris,** and a

sweet tawny unfortified dessert wine from the French **Pyrénées.**

Mancha
Large demarcated wine area of central **Spain.**

Mandarine
Liqueur, the main flavour of which is tangerines.

Mandelhöhe
Gr. of the **Südliche Weinstrasse** *Ber.,* **Rheinpfalz.**

Mandilari
Greek red wine grape, from Crete.

Manduria
Red *DOC* from **Puglia.** Strong and sometimes fortified.

Mannaberg
Gr. of the **Badische Bergstrasse Kraichgau** *Ber.,* **Baden.**

Mantinea
A light dry red wine of Greece.

Manzanilla
A very pale and dry type of **Sherry** from the vyds. of **Sanlucar,** to the west of **Jerez.** It has a peculiar and attractive flavour of its own.

Maraschino
A liqueur distilled from Marasca cherries, in **Dalmatia.** It used to be shipped to all parts of the world from Zadar in very distinctive straw-coloured bottles. It is now manufactured mainly in Padina.

Maraština
Yugoslavian grape producing rich, strong white wine in **Dalmatia.**

Marc
Many wine districts produce a *marc,* the spirit distilled from the residue left after the grapes have been pressed. The best known come from the **Burgundy** regions and the best from the **Hospices de Beaune.** *Marc de Champagne* is particularly fine.

Marches, The
This wine region of **Italy,** on the Adriatic coast, produces some quality red and white wines, the best known being **Verdicchio.**

Marcobrunn
One of the more famous wines of the **Rheingau.**

La Mare
Vyd. of Jersey, **Channel Islands.**

Mareuil-sur-Ay
Champagne *cru* of the **Marne** valley, canton d'**Ay,** Arrondissment de **Reims.**

Marfíl
Brand name of the Alella Co-operative, **Catalonia.**

Margaux
The Margaux *comm.* is in the south of the **Haut-Médoc** and has a concentration of the classified growths. *Ch. Margaux* is a *Premier cru* vyd.

Maribor
Important wine centre of **Slovenia,** and home of the Yugoslavian Institute of Viniculture.

Mariengarten (Forst)
Gr. of the **Mittelhaardt Deutsche Weinstrasse** *Ber.,* **Rheinpfalz.**

Marienthal
A village of the **Ahr** valley. The vyds. of

this region produce some of the good red table wines of **Germany.**

Maring-Noviand
One of the white wine-producing villages of the **Mittel-Mosel.**

Marino
DOC wine of **Lazio,** similar to **Frascati.**

Markgräflerland
Ber. of the **Baden** region.

Marksburg
Gr. of the **Rheinburgengau** *Ber.,* **Mittelrhein.**

du Marmandais, Côtes
VDQS wine district nr. Marmande, Lot et Garonne *Dpt.*

Marne
The *Dpt,* and the r. at the heart of **Champagne.** The r. valley vyds. produce most of the fine wines.

Marque Déposée
French for *trade mark.*

Marquis-d'Alesme-Becker, Ch.
Twin *3me cru classé* with **Ch. Malescot, Margaux** *comm.,* **Haut-Médoc.**

Marquis-de-Terme, Ch.
4me cru classé **Margaux** *comm.,* **Haut-Médoc.**

Marsala
Fortified *DOC* wine from **Sicily,** dry or sweet. Suitable as an **apéritif** or as a dessert wine.

Marsala All'Uovo
A smooth, warming drink made by enriching **Marsala** with egg yolks.

Marsannay
A *comm.* and *app.* of the north of the **Côte de Beaune.** Includes the well-known Clair-Däu domaine. *Bourgogne (Rosé) Marsannay* is a lesser *app.*

Marsanne
Rhône grape. Also grown in **Switzerland, Savoie, Algeria** and **Australia.**

Martillac
See **Ch. Smith-Haut-Lafitte,** and **La Tour-Martillac.**

Martina Franca
DOC from **Puglia.** Used a lot for **Vermouth;** is a pale, dry delicate wine.

Martinens, Ch.
Cru bourgeois of the **Haut-Médoc, Cantenac-Margaux** *comm.*

Martini, Louis
Large family owned, high standard, full range winery of the **Napa Valley.** One of the oldest Californian wineries.

Martini cocktails
The oldest form of a *Martini* is just half **Gin** and half French **Vermouth** well mixed together. Then there is the *dry Martini,* with two-thirds dry **Gin** and one of French **Vermouth,** and a dash of **bitters.** If a very dry *Martini* is required, the proportion of the **Gin** is increased.

Martini & Rossi
Leading brand of Italian **Vermouth.**

Martinsthal
Village in the **Johannisberg** district, **Rheingau.**

La Marzelle
Grand cru classé, **Graves Saint-Émilion,** and a lesser **Saint-Émilion** property also.

Mascara
Centre for the production of some of the best wines of **Algeria.**

Masi, Cantina
Italian producers of fine quality **Veneto** wines including *Campo Fiorin.*

Massandra
Largest district in the **Crimea, USSR,** producing red and dry white wines. Also famous for dessert wine. The name is now used for a large group of collectives. *See* **Saparavi Massandra.**

Masson, Paul
One of the largest and best-known wine-producers in **California.** All types of wine including *Emerald Dry.*

Mastika
An **apéritif** of **Cyprus** and **Greece** made from grape alcohol and gum mastik.

Mateus Rosé
Portugal's biggest selling brand of slightly sweet *rosé.*

Mátraalya
Important wine district in the Matra Hills of northern **Hungary.**

Matras, Ch.
Minor property of **Saint-Émilion.**

Matuschka-Greiffenclau, Graf
Family owners of **Schloss Vollrads.**

Maucaillou, Ch.
Better-known *cru bourgeois* of the **Listrac** *comm.,* **Haut-Médoc.**

Maufoux, Prosper
Family firm of merchants at **Santenay.**

Maury
Wine *comm.* of the French **Pyrénées** producing **Vins doux naturels,** *AC* **Côtes du Roussillon.**

Mauvezin, Ch.
Tiny *grand cru classé* of **Saint-Émilion.**

Mavro Romeiko
Dry full-bodied red wine from Crete.

Mavroudi
Greek red wine grape and wine of that name from the Peloponnese. The label will sometimes say *Can Dia.*

Mavrud
Means *black* in **Bulgaria** – name of a local vine and wine.

Mayacamas
Small high quality vyd., **Napa Valley.**

Mayschoss
Wine village of the **Ahr.**

May wine
Traditional drink made of an infusion of the herb woodruff in Rhine wine.

Mazeyres, Ch.
Larger vyd. of the **Pomerol.**

Mazis-Chambertin
Grand cru neighbour of **Chambertin Clos de Bèze, Côte de Nuits.**

Mazoyères
See **Charmes-Chambertin.**

Mazuelo
Red Spanish grape, grown in the **Rioja** and elsewhere.

McLaren Vale
Wine region of **South Australia,** south of
Adelaide. *See* **Southern Vales.**

McWilliam
New South Wales wine firm of the **Hunter
Valley** and **Rivernia** producing a large
quantity of a full range of quality wines.
Also in **New Zealand.**

Mead
A mildly alcoholic beverage of great
antiquity which was fermented from
honeyed water, and flavoured with various
strongly scented herbs.

Mecsek
District of southern **Hungary** producing
good white wines.

Meddersheim
One of the villages in the **Schloss
Böckelheim** *Ber.,* **Nahe.**

Médoc
The narrow strip of land along the left
bank of the **Gironde** from outside
Bordeaux to the tip of the mouth of the r.
It is divided into the **Haut-Médoc** and the
Bas-Médoc, the former fine vyds. that
have world renown. The **Haut-Médoc,**
ending at **Saint-Seurin-de-Cadourne,**
includes nearly all the sixty-five vyds.
classified as the finest of **Bordeaux** in
1855. From its gravelly soils come some of
the world's finest red wines, based on the
Cabernet Sauvignon, and some
interesting dry whites. It is divided into six
comm.: **Margaux,** closest to **Bordeaux,
St. Julien, St. Estèphe, Pauillac,
Moulis,** and **Listrac,** and the best wines of
these *comm.* will show their area of origin
on the label. Others will carry the lesser
app. Médoc. The 1855 classification
recognized the first five growths of the
Médoc and the other **Bordeaux** wines are
broadly measured in terms of quality
against these.

Médoc Noir
Hungarian name for the **Merlot** grape.

Meersburg
Town of the **Bodensee** *Ber.,* **Baden.**

**Meerspinne (Neustadt, Ortsteil
Gimmeldingen)**
Gr. of the **Mittelhaardt Deutsche
Weinstrasse** *Ber.,* **Rheinpfalz.**

Mehrhölzchen
Gr. of the **Johannisberg** *Ber.,* **Rheingau.**

Mehring
Village of the **Bernkastel** *Ber.,* **MSR.**

Meisenheim
A wine-producing village of the **Nahe**
region, **Schloss Böckelheim** district.

Melini
Important **Chianti Classico** producers at
Pontassieve.

Mélinots
Premier cru **Chablis.**

Mělnik
One of the best wine-producing areas of
Bohemia, Czechoslovakia.

Melon d'Arbois
Name for the **Chardonnay** white wine
grape in the **Jura.**

Melon de Bourgogne
Old white wine grape of the **Burgundy**
region no longer grown there. *See*
Muscadet.

Mendocino County
Adjoining the **Sonoma Valley** to the north
of San Francisco, this area has several

important wineries: **Cresta Blanca, Fetzer,** Husch, **Parducci** and **Weibel** who specialize in sparkling wines.

Mendoza
The oldest and most extensive wine-producing centre of the Argentine.

de Menthe, Crème
See **Freezomint.**

Meranese di Collina
Light *DOC* red from the **Trentino-Alto Adige.**

Mercier et Cie
One of the biggest **Champagne** houses at **Épernay.** Now part of the **Moët** group.

Mercurey
One of the best and most extensive vyds. of the **Côte Chalonnaise.** Most of the Mercurey wines are red, and the whites are of better quality than the others of that district.

Mérignac
Minor *comm.* of **Graves de Bordeaux.**

Merlot
Red grape responsible for the soft and full-flavoured wines of **Saint-Émilion** and **Pomerol.** Also grown for lighter red wines in north **Italy, Switzerland, Australia, Yugoslavia,** and **California.**

Merlot di Pramaggiore
Good *DOC* red from **Veneto.**

Merrydown
Well-known cider manufacturer based at Heathfield, **Sussex,** also producing **Müller-Thurgau** under the label *Horam Manor.*

Mertesdorf
Name of the *Maximun Grünhaus* estate in the **Ruwer** district of the **MSR,** producing some outstanding wines.

Mescal
Potent spirit, also known as **Tequila,** distilled in **Mexico** and **South America** from the *Maguey* or American aloe.

Mesland
See **Touraine.**

Le Mesnil
Premier cru **Champagne** area of the **Côte des Blancs,** between Avize and Oger. *Salon le Mesnil* is a quality producing house.

Metaxa
Proprietary Greek **Brandy.**

Méthode Champenoise
Method of making sparkling wine, especially **Champagne.** The second fermentation takes places in the bottle. The carbonic acid gas produced in the fermentation dissolves in the wine. Sediment produced during the fermentation process is removed from the bottle by the technique called **dégorgement.** The bottle is then finally corked and sealed. When the secured cork is removed the gas escapes taking with it small particles of the wine in the bubbles. See **Liqueur de Tirage** and **Liqueur d'expédition.**

Methuselah
A giant bottle, used mainly for show, holding eight bottles.

Mettenheim
Town of the **Nierstein** *Ber.,* **Rheinhessen.**

Meunier
See **Pinot Meunier.**

Meursault
Important and famous district of the **Côte de Beaune**. Its vyds. produce the great white Burgundies **Puligny-Montrachet** and **Meursault** with reds from **Volnay**.

Mexico
One of the oldest wine-producing countries of the Americas, but modern production is small.

Meyney, Ch.
Important *cru bourgeois* of the **St. Estèphe** *comm.*, **Haut-Médoc.**

Michelsberg
Important *Gr.* of the **Bernkastel** *Ber.*, **MSR.**

Midi
The *Vins du Midi* are the table wines from the **Gard, Hérault,** and **Aude** *Dpts.* of southern **France.** Quantities of mainly *ordinaire* wines are produced.

Mildara
Winery of the **Murray** valley also producing **Sherry** and **Brandy.**

Mildew
One of the blights of vines; a fungoid growth which affects leaves and grapes in warm and humid seasons.

Millefiori
An Italian golden liqueur, very sweet, flavoured with many wild flowers of the Alps.

Mille-Secousses, Ch.
Better-known estate of the **Bourg** district.

Millésime
French for the *year of the vintage.*

Minervois
VDQS district of the **Aude** *Dpt.* close to **Corbières.**

Minheim
One of the smaller villages of the **Bernkastel** *Ber.,* **Gross Kurfürtlay, MSR.**

Minho
Coastal region of northern **Portugal** from which come its most distinctive table wines, the **Vinhos Verdes.**

Minösegibor
Hungarian equivalent of the French **Appellation d'Origine Contrôlée.**

Mirabelle de Lorraine
An *eau-de-vie* from small yellow plums from the **Lorraine** district.

Mirassou
Medium-sized quantity-producing winery, **Santa Clara, California.**

Mise dans nos caves
French for *bottled in our cellars.*

Mise en bouteilles
Bottled – *du domaine* or *à la propriété* – at the property where it is made. In **Bordeaux:** *château-bottled.*

Mise par le propriétaire
Bottled by the grower.

Misket
Bulgarian white **Muscat**-style grape.

Mission
A red **Vitis vinifera** now native to **California.**

La Mission Haut-Brion, Ch.
Grand cru classé of **Pessac, Graves de Bordeaux.**

Mistelle
A white wine made chiefly from the vyds. of the French **Pyrénées** by the addition of a comparatively small quantity of **Brandy** to partially fermented grape juice soon after the vintage. It is sometimes sold as cheap dessert wine, but it is mostly used for making **Vermouth** or as a basis for **apéritif** wines. Quantities of this type come from **Algeria.**

Mittelbergheim
Comm. of the **Bas-Rhin, Alsace.**

Mittelhaardt Deutsche Weinstrasse
Important *Ber.* of the **Rheinpfalz,** producing some of the best wines of the region.

Mittelheim
Town of the **Rheingau** *Ber.,* **Johannisberg,** *Gr.* **Honigberg.**

Mittel-Mosel
That part of the **Mosel-Saar-Ruwer** region which is the *Ber.* **Bernkastel.**

Mittelrhein
Small wine-growing region **(Anbaugebiete)** of **Germany,** stretching from **Bingen** to the **Nahe.** Much of the wine is produced for local consumption. District names are **Bacharach** and **Rheinburgengau.**

Mittelwihr
Comm. of the **Haut-Rhin, Alsace.**

de Mocca, Crème
Sweet coffee-based liqueur.

Moelleux
French for a soft, sweet and fruity wine.

Moët et Chandon
The biggest **Champagne** producer,

Épernay. Includes **Mercier** and **Ruinart.** Also with estates in north and south America.

Molinara
Italian grape used principally in the production of **Valpolicella** and **Bardolino.**

Mommessin, J.
Important **Burgundy** grower **(Clos de Tart)** and merchant.

Monbazillac
Sweet wine from the Dordogne, **Bergerac.**

Monbousquet, Ch.
Popular unclassified **Saint-Émilion,** from *St. Sulpice des Faleyrens.*

Monção
One of the best areas of the **Vinhos Verdes.**

Mondavi, Robert
Innovative, famous **Napa Valley** winery. High quality wines.

Monica
Dessert wine grape of **Sardegna.**

Monica di Cagliari
Red *DOC* fortified wine of **Sardegna.** *Monica di Sardegna* is also a *DOC* wine but less quality.

Monimpex
Hungarian state monopoly with cellars nr. Budapest.

Monopole
In **Burgundy** indicates that the whole of the vyd. named belongs to the same proprietor.

Montagne Saint-Émilion
Wine-producing *comm.* and *app.* of **Saint-Émilion.**

Montagny
One of the best white wine villages and *AC* of the **Côte Chalonnaise.**

Montbrun, Ch.
Minor growth of the **Haut-Médoc, Cantenac-Margaux** *comm.*

Mont de Milieu
Premier cru **Chablis.**

Montecarlo
DOC Tuscan white.

Montée de Tonnerre
Premier cru **Chablis.**

Montefiascone
Town of **Lazio** and home of **Est!-Est!!-Est!!!**

Montepulciano d'Abruzzo
One of the better light red *DOC* red wines of the Adriatic coast.

Monterey Vineyard
Big modern winery of **Salinas.**

Monterrey, Valle de
Demarcated Spanish wine area nr. the northern Portuguese border.

Monthélie
One of the *comm.* of the **Côte de Beaune** which produces good sound red wines.

Montilla-Moriles
Demarcated Spanish region, around Cordoba, producing **Sherry**-like wines.

Montlouis
AC white and sparkling area of the **Touraine** district on the opposite bank of the **Loire** from **Vouvray.**

Montmains
Premier cru **Chablis.**

Montmélian
One of the red wines from **Savoie.**

Montmurat
Red wine of the Cantal *Dpt.*, **France.**

Montpeyroux
VDQS of the **Hérault** *Dpt.*, **France.**

Le Montrachet
The *grand cru* vyd. of the **Côte de Beaune, Puligny-Montrachet** *comm.*

Les Montrachets
Grand cru vyds. of the **Côte de Beaune** producing some famous white wines. *See* **Le Chevalier-Montrachet,** and **Le Bâtard-Montrachet.**

Montravel
Mostly dry Dordogne white wines from four co-operatives. The *AC* **Côtes de Montravel** is traditionally for sweet wines.

de Mont-Redon, Domaine
Large and fine **Rhône** estate in **Châteauneuf-du-Pape.**

Montrose, Ch.
Larger *2me cru classé* of the **Haut-Médoc.**

Monts-Luisants, Les
Partly *grand cru* and *premier cru* vyd. of the **Côte de Nuits** on the **Gevrey-Chambertin** edge of the **Morey-Saint-Denis** *comm.*

Montsoreau
One of the good white wines of the
Saumur district, **Anjou.**

Monzingen
White wine-producing village of the
Schloss Böckelheim district of the **Nahe**
region.

Mór
Northern Hungarian town famous for dry
white fragrant **Móri Ezerjó.**

Morandell
Large Viennese wine merchants.

More-Saint-Denis
A *comm.* of the **Côte de Nuits** less well
known by name than two of its *grand
crus:* **Clos de la Roche,** and **Clos-St.-
Denis.**

Morgeot
Premier cru vyd. of the **Côte de Beaune,
Chassagne-Montrachet** *comm.*

Morgon
A good sound wine from the *comm.* of
Villié-Morgon, and one of the named *AC*
of the **Beaujolais-Villages.**

Moriles
See **Montilla.**

Morin, Ch.
Minor growth of the **St. Estèphe** *comm.,*
Haut-Médoc.

Morio-Muscat
German aromatic white **hybrid** grape from
crossing **Sylvaner** and **Pinot Blanc.**

Morocco
Full-bodied red wines are produced, and
some *rosés.* Most used to be exported to

European Common Market countries,
especially **France,** for blending.

Morre's Diamond
American **hybrid** white grape found in
New York State.

Morris
Established winery of north-east **Victoria**
producing the famous Australian brown
liqueur **Muscat** wine.

Morzheim
Village of the **Südliche Weinstrasse**
Ber., **Rheinpfalz.**

Mosaic
Brand name of a **Cyprus Sherry.**

Moscatel de Setúbal
Famous aromatic dessert wine from
Setúbal, a small demarcated region of
Portugal.

Moscato
The Italian **Muscat** grape, producing fruity
fragrant wines; also sparkling.

Moscato di Cagliari
Strong golden *DOC* from **Sardegna.**

Moscato di Siracusa
Amber dessert *DOC* wine from **Syracuse.**

Moscato di Trani
Strong, golden dessert wine from **Puglia.**

Mosel/Moselle
A long twist of a r. which rises in **France,**
then forms the boundary between
Luxembourg and **Germany.** It enters
Germany seven miles from **Trier** then
winds north-easterly to meet the Rhine at
Koblenz. *Mosel* is the name of an official
Deutscher Tafelwein region, and the

name generally attached in Britain to all wines of the region. *See* **MSR.**

Moselblümchen
The **Mosel's** answer to **Liebfraumilch.**

Mosel-Saar-Ruwer
One of the largest and most important of the eleven quality German wine regions. The **Mosel** is a long, narrow r. valley that meets the Rhine nr. **Koblenz.** The **Saar** and **Ruwer** tributaries join it nr. **Trier.** These three valleys produce some of the finest and best-known white wines of **Germany.**

Moser, Lenz
See **Lenz Moser.**

Mostar
Dry white wine from the Yugoslavian city of that name.

Mosto
Italian, Portuguese and Spanish for *must,* or *grape juice;* sometimes it means new wine.

Mosto cotto
Boiled **must** used in **Italy** as a sweetening agent in the making of dessert wine of the **Marsala** type.

Mou
French term meaning *flabby.*

des Mouches, Clos
Premier cru and one of the largest vyds. of **Beaune.**

Moueix, J-P. et Cie
Important **Saint-Émilion** merchant and proprietor; also of **Pomerol.**

Moulin-à-Vent
One of the best and best-known red wines

of **Beaujolais** from vyds. which are geographically partly in the **Mâconnais.** One of the villages responsible for one of the nine named *crus* of the **Beaujolais.**

Moulin-à-Vent, Ch.
Bourgeois growth of the **Médoc, Moulis** *comm.*

du Moulin-à-Vent, Cru
There are three small growths of the **Graves de Bordeaux** of this name in the *comm.* of **Cérons, Landiras** and **St. Pièrre-de-Mons.**

Moulin de la Rose, Ch.
Minor growth of the **Médoc, St. Julien** *comm.*

du Moulin-du-Bourg, Domaine
Minor growth of the **Médoc, Listrac** *comm.*

Moulin-du-Cadet
One of the smaller *grands crus classés,* **Côtes Saint-Émilion.**

Moulinet, Ch.
One of the lesser **Pomerol** estates.

Moulis
Village and *comm.* of the **Haut-Médoc.** Some of the wines of *Moulis* are sold under the name of the adjoining **Listrac** *comm.* Ch. *Moulis* is a *bourgeois* growth.

Mount Veeder
Small new winery of the **Napa Valley.**

Mourvèdre
Red grape mainly grown in the **Midi.**

Mousseux
French for *sparkling.* According to French law any sparkling wine except

Champagne, e.g. *Bourgogne Mousseux.*
A range of South African *Mousseux* wine
is produced by the **KWV** at **Paarl,
Stellenbosch** and **Tulbagh.**

Moussy
Champagne growth, canton d'**Épernay,**
Arrondissement d'**Épernay.**

Mout
French for **must.**

Mouton-Baronne-Phillippe, Ch.
5me cru classé of the **Pauillac** *comm.,*
Haut-Médoc, belonging to the *Mouton-
Rothschilds.*

Mouton Cadet
Well-known fine brand of red and white
Bordeaux wines, produced by *Mouton-
Rothschild* from wines they buy in.

La Moutonne
Grand cru vyd., **Chablis.**

Mouton-Rothschild, Ch.
Premier cru classé **Pauillac** *comm.,* **Haut-
Médoc.** One of the famous **Bordeaux**
wines.

Mudgee
Small wine area of **New South Wales**
producing full-bodied red and white wines.

Mülheim
One of the smaller districts of the *Ber.*
Bernkastel, *Gr.* **Kurfürstlay, Mittel-
Mosel.**

Mülheim
Village of the **Margräflerland** district of
Baden.

Mulled wine
Said to be an ancient prevention or cure
for a cold. Plenty of sugar is dissolved in a
little hot water; then the red wine is put in

and brought to the boil – it must be moved
away from the fire as soon as it reaches
boiling point. It is then served with a little
grated nutmeg.

Müller, Egon
German wine-grower and shipper of the
Saar, MSR.

Mullerebe
German name for the French **Pinot
Meunier** and grown in **Württemberg** for
making light red wines.

Müller-Thurgau
Grape variety said to be a cross between
Riesling and **Sylvaner.** Has been planted
lately in favour of **Riesling** in cooler
climates, as it ripens early. It grows well in
England and **Austria.**

Mumm, G. H. et Cie
Quality **Champagne** grower and merchant.
Also red, *rosé* and *crémant* wines.

Mundelsheim
Village of *Gr.* **Schalkstein** in
Württemberg.

Münster-Sarmsheim
The better of two wine-producing
Münsters of **Nahe** region.

Munzingen
Village of the **Kaiserstuhl-Tuniberg**
district of **Baden.**

Munzlay
Gr. of the **Bernkastel** *Ber.,* **MSR.**

Murets de Sion, Les
A noted **Fendant** white wine of the **Valais.**

Murfatlar
Large vyd. area on the Black Sea,
Rumania.

Murray River
R. which irrigates some important vyds. in northern **Victoria.**

de Murrieta, Marqués
Highly regarded estate of the **Rioja Alta** producing fine red and white wines.

Murrumbidgee
R. which irrigates a large wine-producing area of **New South Wales.**

Muscadel
Common name for any sweet dessert wine made from **Muscat** grapes.

Muscadelle
White wine grape of the **Bordeaux** region used in the production of **Sauternes.** Also a small but delicious grape cultivated extensively in **Cape Province** and responsible for the reputation of the famous **Constantia** wine.

Muscadet
White wine grape (the **Melon de Bourgogne**) and *AC* white for the **Muscadet** district. Finer wines come under the *app. Muscadet des Coteaux de la Loire.*

Muscat
The generic name of many highly scented grape varieties, which produce lightly sweet wines.
  In **Cyprus** it is the *Muscat of Alexandria;* in south-west **France,** *Muscat de Frontignan* (both of which are popular in **California**); and in **Yugoslavia** the *Muscat Ottonel.*
  The dessert wines it makes are sweet, scented and light.

Muscat d'Alsace
One of the **Noble** grape varieties of **Alsace.**

Muscat de Beaumes de Venise
Naturally sweet golden **Muscat** wine from the **Vaucluse** *Dpt.* **Côtes du Rhône.** Wines can be as high as 14° alcohol.

Muscat de Lunel
Sweet fortified wine of the **Midi.**

Muscat de Rivesaltes
Sweet fortified wine from nr. Perpignan, **France.**

Musigny, le
Famous *grand cru* vyds. of the **Chambolle-Musigny, Côte de Nuits.**

Muskotály (Yellow Muscat)
The Hungarian aromatic **Muscat** grape which contributes to the making of **Tokaji** wines. Also in other Eastern European countries.

Mussbach
Town and important co-operative of the **Rheinpfalz, Mittelhaardt.** Red and white wines.

Must
Unfermented grape juice. The freshly pressed juice of wine-making grapes before it has had time to ferment.

Musty
A bad smell which wine can acquire when in contact with a poor cask or bad cork.

Mycoderma vini
Microscopic spores commonly known as **yeast,** the presence of which in grape juice and other liquids is to a large extent responsible for certain wines like **Sherry.**

Myrat, Ch.
2me cru **Sauternes** of the **Barsac** *comm.*

Nackenheim
Village of the **Rheinhessen** in the
Nierstein *Ber., Gr.* **Domherr.**

Nacktarsch
Gr. of the **Bernkastel** *Ber.,* **Mittel-Mosel,
MSR.**

Nagyburgundi
Hungarian variation of the **Pinot Noir.**

Nahe
One of the important recognized German
quality wine areas, the Nahe runs
upstream from the Rhine at **Bingen.** A
sheltered valley, its growers specialize in
white wines from **Müller-Thurgau, Rhine
Riesling** and **Sylvaner.** The Nahe wines
combine some of the characteristics of the
Rhine with those of the **Mosel.**

Nairac, Ch.
2me cru **Sauternes** of the Barsac *comm.*

Napa Gamay
Distinctive Californian red grape variety
now thought to be related to the **Gamay
Noir** of **France.**

Napa Valley
Famous valley north of San Francisco Bay
where the Californian wine industry had its
renaissance in the late 1960s and early
1970s. It is now the home for some of
California's finest and best-known
wineries, among them **Beaulieu,
Beringer,** Burgess, **Carneros Creek,
Chappellet, Chateau Montelena,
Christian Brothers,** Clos du Val,

Cuvaison, sparkling wine producers
Domain Chandon, Franciscan, **Freemark
Abbey, Heitz, Inglenook, Hanns Kornell,
Charles Krug, Louis Martini,
Mayacamas, Robert Mondavi, Joseph
Phelps, Schramsberg, Spring Mountain,
Stag's Leap, Sterling, Stony Hill,
Trefethen,** and **Villa Mount Eden.**

Nasco di Cagliari
DOC of **Sardegna** – light dry white wines
high in alcohol with a bitter **after-taste.**

Nature, Natur, Naturrein
The French and German words used to
convey the idea of a wine which has not
been sweetened. In **France** it can mean
Champagne without the sparkle. Now
illegal on German wines.

Navarra
Demarcated region of northern **Spain**
producing some dark red table wines high
in alcohol.

Néac
Bordeaux district associated with and
adjoining **Pomerol.**

Nebbiolo
Classic Italian red grape, used for **Barolo,
Barbaresco, Gattinara, Sassella** and
other top Italian red wines.

Nebuchadnezzar
A giant **Champagne** bottle made for show
purposes containing the equivalent of
twenty bottles.

Neckar
R. valley of **Germany** and well-known
district for **Deutscher Tafelwein.**

Nederburg
Famous **Cape Province** estate, now used
as the brand name for a range of wines by
Stellenbosch Farmers' Winery.

Neef
Village of the *Gr.* **Grafschaft,** *Ber.* **Zell-Mosel, MSR,** containing the important Frauenberg vyd.

Négociant-Éléveur
A buyer of wine from the grower, usually in its first year, for maturing and bottling in his own cellars.

Negri
Well-known Italian red wine house of **Valtellina.**

Negus
An old-fashioned hot drink made by adding hot water to **Port** in a 2:1 ratio, and adding sugar, lemon juice and nutmeg.

Nénin, Ch.
An established, important **Pomerol** estate.

Nerveux
French for the idea of vitality in a wine – a wine with body and spirit.

Neuberger
Austrian white grape.

Neuchâtel
One of the smallest red and white wine-producing cantons of **Switzerland.**

Neumagen-Dhron
Wine village of the **Mittel-Mosel,** *Gr.* **Michelsberg, MSR.**

Neustadt
Centre of an important wine-growing area of the **Rheinpfalz,** *Gr.* **Meerspinne.**

Neuville
Village of the Berne canton, **Switzerland.**

Neuweier
Village in the *Gr.* **Schloss Rodeck** of the **Ortenau** district, which produces important **Baden** wines.

New Hall
Established and award winning English vyd. at Purley, **Sussex.** White wines from **Huxelrebe, Müller-Thurgau, Reichensteiner** and some **Pinot Noir** and **Ruländer.**

New South Wales
The main area for the production of premium wines from Cabernet Sauvignon, Chardonnay and Semillon vines is the **Hunter Valley** and Pokolbin, north of Sydney. Other important areas are the Murrumbidgee Irrigation Area and **Riverina,** inland to the south; Rooty Hill, nr. Sydney; Forbes further inland; Mudgee, and Muswellbrook, inland from the **Hunter Valley;** and Corowa mainly for fortified wines.

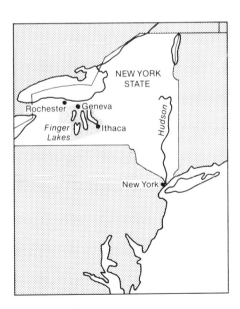

New York State
Second largest (after **California**) wine-producing state of the **USA.** Most of the important wineries are in the **Finger Lakes** district. Much of the wine comes from the

Niagara and **Chautauqua** districts. The Hudson River Valley is the oldest **USA** wine district.

New Zealand
A growing wine industry based mainly on the North Island (with Marlborough on the northern tip of the South Island). Fresh white wines made from **Müller-Thurgau, Riesling, Traminer, Chardonnay, Sauvignon Blanc,** and some quality reds mainly from **Cabernet Sauvignon** and **Pinot Noir.**

Niagara
White American **hybrid** grape from **New York State;** also grown in South America and **Canada.**

Nicolas, Ets.
One of the biggest wine wholesale and retail merchants in **France,** based in Paris.

Niederhausen
Some fine white wines come from this town in the **Schloss Böckelheim** district of the **Nahe** valley.

Niederösterreich
Lower Austria – the region produces most of the country's wine and includes the **Wachau, Retz,** and **Krems** districts.

Niederwalluf
See **Walluf.**

Nierstein
Important wine-producing town and district of the **Rheinhessen.** It produces fine wine known throughout the world as *Niersteiner.*

Nigrara
Italian red grape, used mainly for **Bardolino.**

Nipozzano
Important **Chianti** estate outside the Classico area, nr. Florence, **Italy.**

Nittel
One of the best-known towns of the **Obermosel,** *Gr.* **Gipfel, MSR.**

Noble
Term applied to a grape variety or wine that shows quality.

Noble Rot
See **Botrytis cinerea.**

Noilly Prat
A dry French **Vermouth.**

Noir de Pressac
Pomerol name for the **Malbec** grape.

de Noisette, Crème
Sweet, hazelnut-flavoured liqueur.

Norheim
Village of the *Gr.* **Burgweg,** *Ber.* **Schloss Böckelheim** in the **Nahe** valley.

Nose
The general non-descriptive term used for the bouquet of a wine.

de Nouchet, Clos
Principal growth of the **Castres** *comm.* **Graves de Bordeaux.** Red and white wines.

du Nozet, Ch.
Large and well-known estate of the **Pouilly-Fumé** district of the **Loire.**

Nozzole
Famous Italian estate in the heart of the **Chianti Classico** region.

de Nuits, Côte
The vyds. of the northern half of the **Côte d'Or** – from **Fixin** to south of **Nuits St. Georges.** Includes many great vyds.

Nuits St. Georges
The chief town and **comm.** of the **Côte de Nuits.** It produces a large quantity of red Burgundies.

Nuragus di Cagliari
White *DOC* wine of **Sardegna.**

Nussdorf
Village nr. Vienna famous for **Heurige** wines.

Nutty
A flavour reminiscent of, e.g. hazelnuts, found in some sherries.

Oak
The wood from which the best barrels and casks are made for ageing wine.

Oberemmel
Village of the *Gr.* **Scharzberg,** *Ber.* **Saar-Ruwer, Saar** valley, **MSR.**

Obermosel
District name for the upper **Mosel** above **Trier, MSR.**

Obernai
One of the better-known wine-producing towns of **Alsace.**

Oberrhein
Designated **Deutscher Tafelwein** area.

Ockenheim
Small wine area of the **Rheinhessen, Bingen** *Ber., Gr.* **Sankt Rochuskapelle,** producing red and white wines.

Ockfen
Township producing some of the best wines of the **Saar** valley, *Ber.* **Saar-Ruwer,** *Gr.* **Scharzberg, MSR.**

Oechsle
German term and the scale for expressing the quantity of sugar in a grape before fermentation.

Oeil de Perdrix
Partridge eye – referring to the pink tinge of some white wines.

Oenology
The science of wine.

Oesterreichischer
Another name for the **Sylvaner** grape.

Oestrich
Village of the *Gr.* **Houigberg,** *Ber.* **Johannisberg, Rheingau.**

Offley Forester
Port shippers. Owners of **Quinta Boa Vista.**

Ohio
The largest wine district borders Lake Erie; the most important are on Middle Bass Island and at Kelley. The **Catawba** is the traditional grape.

Oidium
A fungus disease of the vine.

Okolehao or Oke
Spirit distilled in Hawaii from molasses and the roots of taro plants. It is very high in alcohol and has a smoky flavour.

Olasz Riesling
Hungarian for the **Italian Riesling** or **Wälschriesling.**

Olifants River
Northernmost of the demarcated wine regions of **Cape Province.**

Oliver, Ch.
Grand cru classé for white wines of the **Léognan** *Comm.,* **Graves de Bordeaux.**

Oloroso
One of the more popular types of **Sherry,** full and usually rich, often sold sweetened.

Ölspiel
Gr. of the **Maindreieck** *Ber.,* **Franken.**

Oltrepò Pavese
DOC red and white wine area of **Lombardia.**

Oporto
The port of Portugal on the right bank of the r. **Douro** and the centre of the **Port** wine trade. Most **Port** shippers have their offices at Oporto and their cellars at Vila Nova.

Oppenheim
One of the more important townships in the *Gr.* **Krötenbrunnen, Nierstein** region of the **Rheinhessen.**

d'Or, Côte
The 'golden' heart of the **Burgundy** region. It includes the **Côte de Nuits** and the **Côte de Beaune.**

Orange bitters
The most popular form of **bitters** used for flavouring cocktails and other mixed drinks. It is made from the peel of the bitter Seville orange.

Orange Brandy
Brandy with Seville oranges steeped in it with lemons and sugar for three weeks.

L'Oratoire, Clos de
Small *grand cru classé* of **Saint-Émilion.**

Ordensgut (Rhodt)
Gr. of the **Südliche Weinstrasse** *Ber.,* **Rheinpfalz.**

Ordinaire
See **Vin ordinaire.**

Orianda
A dry white wine of the **Crimea.**

Originalabzug and Originalabfüllung
German term for *bottled by the grower,* now no longer permitted on a label. *See* **Erzeugerabfüllung.**

Orlando
See **Gramp.**

Les Ormes-de-Pez, Ch.
Better known *cru bourgeois* of the **St. Estèphe** district, **Haut-Médoc.**

Ortenau
Quality *Ber.* of **Baden** producing red and white wines.

Orvieto
One of the most picturesque cities of Umbria perched on a hilltop and surrounded by vyds., the best wines of which are the white *DOC Orvieto*. There are two varieties: **secco** and **abboccato.**

Osthofen
Village of the **Rheinhessen, Wonnegau**
Ber., Gr. **Gotteshilfe.**

Ostuni
Delicate dry white *DOC* from **Puglia.**

Oude Jenever
The Dutch national matured **Gin** distilled
from fermented grain and flavoured with
juniper. *See* **Hollands.**

Ouzo
The most popular **apéritif** of Greece: it is
a spirit flavoured with aniseed and is
usually served in a tall glass, and mixed
with iced water, when it turns milky and
opalescent.

Oxidized
See **Maderized.**

Paarl
One of the oldest and best demarcated
wine and **Sherry**-producing areas of **Cape
Province.**

Pacherenc du Vic-Bilh
Sweet white *AC* wine of the French
Pyrénées.

País
Originally a Spanish grape, but now a
native of Chile.

Palatinate
See **Rheinpfalz.**

Palestine
The grape vine is indigenous to Palestine
and wine was made for thousands of
years until the vyds. were uprooted by the
Turks. Some of the vyds. were replanted
at the end of the nineteenth century.

Palette
AC wine district nr. **Aix-en-Provence,**
producing mostly for local consumption.

Palma
A type of **Fino Sherry.**

Palmer, Ch.
High quality *3me cru classé* of the **Haut-
Médoc, Margaux** *comm.,* which now
includes **Ch. Desmirail.**

Palo Cortado
Sherry close to an **Oloroso** but with more
the character of a **Fino.**

Palomino
The most important white grape grown in
the **Jerez** district for the making of
Sherry. Now also grown in **Cyprus.** *See*
Listan.

Pamid
Local Bulgarian grape which produces soft
rosé style wines mainly for local
consumption.

de Panisseau, Ch.
Bergerac estate producing good dry white
wine.

Pantelleria
Small island in the Mediterranean between
Sicilia and Tunis, noted for its sweet
muscat wines. There is a separate *DOC*
for the high alcohol version from **Passito**
grapes.

Le Pape, Ch.
Graves de Bordeaux, Léognan *comm.*
producing mainly red wines.

Pape-Clément, Ch.
Red *grand cru classé* of the **Pessac**
comm., **Graves.**

Parducci
Well-established table wine producer of
Mendocino.

Parempuyre
Lesser *comm.* of the **Haut-Médoc.**

Parfait Amour
Sweet, exotic, red- or violet-coloured
liqueur. There are French and Dutch
brands.

Parnay
Comm. of **Saumur** producing fresh fruity
white wine.

Parrina
Light **Toscana** *DOC* red and white wines.

Parsac-Saint-Émilion
Bordeaux *comm.* with its own *app.*

Pasquier-Desvignes
Old established **Beaujolais** merchants at
Brouilly.

Passes
The strips or small labels carrying
information other than that on the neck or
body labels on the bottle.

Passe Tout Grains
A red **Burgundy** made of mixed grapes of
which not less than a third of the total
must be **Pinot Noir.** The rest is usually
Gamay.

Passito
Any sweet Italian dessert wine from
grapes dried – usually by the sun.

da Pasta, Vino
Italian for an ordinary table wine.

Pasteurization
The process named after Louis Pasteur by
which liquids are sterilized by heat. The
temperature of the wine is raised briefly to
approximately 66°C to kill off
contaminating micro-organisms and to
stabilize the wine. It can be done before or
after bottling.

Pastis
French liquorice-flavoured **apéritif**, e.g.
Ricard.

Patache-d'Aux, Ch.
Good quality *cru bourgeois*, **Bégadan**
comm., **Bas-Médoc.**

Patent Still
Continous distilling apparatus invented by
Coffey in 1832 which is more economic
than the **Pot Still** and produces purer but
lesser-flavoured spirits.

Paternina
Well-known **Rioja** bodega.

Patriache
Burgundy merchants of **Beaune.**

Patrimonio
AC of **Corsica** – red or *rosé.*

Pauillac
The biggest town and one of the finest
wine-producing *comm.* of the **Haut-
Médoc.** Its *crus classés* include **Chx.
Lafite, Latour** and **Mouton-Rothschild.**

Paveil-de-Luze, Ch.
Cru bourgeois of the **Soussans** *comm.*
Haut-Médoc.

Pavie, Ch.
Largest *premier grand cru classé* vyd. of
the **Côtes Saint-Émilion.**

Pavillon Blanc de Ch. Margaux
A white wine from the great **Margaux**
comm. entitled only to the *app.* **Bordeaux.**

Pavillon Cadet, Ch.
Grand cru classé, **Côtes Saint-Émilion.**

Paxarete
Small town of the **Jerez** district noted for
Pedro Ximenez grapes. These grapes are
gathered when fully ripe and exposed to
the sun for a week or two before being
pressed, when they yield a very sweet
juice. This is treated with **Brandy** so that it
does not ferment and the *Paxarete* liqueur
is used mostly for sweetening high class
sweet Sherries.

Pays
See **Vins de Pays.**

Peach Brandy
A liqueur made with **Brandy** which is
flavoured with peaches.

Pécharmant
Small *AC* for reds of **Bergerac** in the
Dordogne.

Pécs
Centre of the **Mecsdek** district of **Hungary**
producing good **Rieslings.**

Pédesclaux, Ch.
Small and not well-known *5me cru classé*
of the **Pauillac** *comm.,* **Haut-Médoc.**

Pedroncelli
Family winery of **Alexander Valley,**
California.

Pedro Ximenez
The name of a grape which is particularly
sweet because it is lacking in acidity. The
liqueur wine that is made from this grape
in the south of **Spain** is **Paraxete.** It is
used mainly for blending high-class
Sherries. It is also grown in **California,**
Australia and **South Africa.**

Pelletan, Ch.
Principal growth of **Saint-Émilion, St.-**
Christophe-des-Bardes *comm.*

Pelure d'ognon
Onion skin – a French term used to
describe the peculiar brown sheen which
some old red wines acquire, and also the
tint of some *rosés.*

Penafiel
Full-bodied, red wines from nr. Valladolid,
Old Castile, **Spain.** Also the name of a
sub-region of the **Vinhos Verdes.**

Penedés
Demarcated region of **Catalonia.**
Important for table and sparkling wines.

Penfold's
Large Australian firm with estates in most
of the important districts.

Perelada
Spanish sparkling wines are made in this
district of Ampurdan by both the **Cuve**
Close and *méth. champ.*

Pérignon, Dom
Benedictine monk and cellarmaster at the
monastery of **Hautvillers** in 1668, credited
with being the first to find a way to keep
the bubbles in **Champagne.** Also the
brand name for the *de luxe* **Champagne**
of **Moët et Chandon.**

Periquita
Full-bodied Portuguese red wine, shipped
by Fonseca from the **Setúbal** area.

Perla de Tinnave
White, semi-sweet, blended Rumanian wine.

Perlant
French for *very lightly sparkling.*

Perlwein
German for *sparkling wine* made usually by artificial carbonation.

Pernand-Vergelesses
One of the small *comm.* of the **Côte de Beaune.** Premier cru vyds. but also parts of the great *grand cru* **Corton** and **Corton Charlemagne.**

Pernod
A popular brand of aniseed-flavoured liqueur. *See* **Pastis.**

Perrier
Famous French sparkling table water.

La Perrière
Premier cru vyd. of the **Fixin** *comm.*

Perrier-Jouët
First class **Champagne** growers at **Épernay.** Top label is *Belle Époque.*

Perry
See **Poire, Eau de Vie de.**

Pessac
The *comm.* of the **Graves** district which produces some of the finest clarets, e.g. **Ch. Haut-Brion.**

Petersberg
Gr. which is all of the **Siebengebirge** *Ber.,* **Mittelrhein.**

Petersberg
Gr. of the **Nierstein** *Ber.,* **Rheinhessen.**

Pétillant
French term for wine that is slightly sparkling owing to the fermentation in bottle of small amounts of residual sugar.

Petit Chablis
App. for some of the lesser wines of **Chablis.** Best wines from around Lignorelles, **Maligny** and **Villy.**

Petite Champagne
See **Cognac.**

Petite Syrah
Red Californian grape unrelated to the **Syrah.**

Petit-Faurie de Souchard, Ch.
Grand cru classé, **Saint-Émilion.**

Petit Manseng
Important local white wine grape of **Jurançon.**

Petit Verdot
Grape of **Bordeaux** in the **Haut-Médoc,** and also grown in **Chile.**

Petit Village, Ch.
Pomerol estate and rated one of the best in the area, situated close to **Vieux Ch. Certan.**

Pétrus, Ch.
The great name of the finest of the **Pomerol** wines, and the only one in its class in the region.

de Pez, Ch.
High quality *cru bourgeois* of the **St. Estèphe** *comm.,* **Haut-Médoc.**

Pezinok
Wine-producing area of **Czechoslovakia.**

Pfaffengrund (Nemstadt Ortsteil Diedesfeld)
Gr. of the **Mittelhaardt, Rheinpfalz.**

Pfalz
See **Rheinpfalz.**

Pfarrgarten
Gr. of the **Kreuznach** *Ber.,* **Nahe.**

Phêlan-Ségur, Ch.
Important *cru bourgeois* of the **St. Estèphe** *comm.,* **Haut-Médoc.**

Phelps, Joseph
High quality new winery of the **Napa Valley.** Late harvested wines from **Johannisberg Riesling** are equal to the best from **Germany.**

Phileri
A principal Greek grape variety of the Peloponnese.

Philipponnat
Brand name and established **Champagne** family.

Phylloxera
The American vine louse. It was first recorded in Europe at Kew, nr. London, in 1863 and it has, with few exceptions, spread to every country of the world. The indigenous North American vines, having become partly immune to this pest, are now largely used in European and other vyds. as the stock upon which the various species of **Vitis vinifera,** the European vine, are grafted.

Piada, Ch.
High quality minor growth, **Barsac.**

Le Pian
Lesser wine-producing *comm.* of the **Haut-Médoc,** the wines of which by long usage are sold under the name of the adjoining and better-known *comm.* of **Ludon.**

Piat, Père et Fils
Well-known growers and *négociants* of **Beaujolais.**

Piave
DOC for a number of dry red or white wines of **Veneto.**

Pibran, Ch.
Bourgeois cru of the **Haut-Médoc, Pauillac** *comm.*

Picardan
Rhône grape and one of the thirteen which go to create **Châteauneuf-du-Pape.**

Pichet
A small French earthenware carafe or jug.

Pichon-Lalande, Ch.
Important *2me cru classé* of the **Haut-Médoc,** partly in **St. Julien** and partly in the **Pauillac** *comm.*

Pichon-Longueville Baron, Ch.
2me cru classé of the **Haut-Médoc, Pauillac** *comm.*

Picolit
Rare Italian *DOC* from **Friuli-Venezia Giulia.** Rich and sweet.

Picpoul
The name for the **Folle Blanche** in the south of **France** and the name of a number of light white wines of the **Midi.**

Pièce
French cask: in **Burgundy** 228 litres; in **Beaujolais** 228 or 216 litres; in the **Loire** 220 litres; in **Vouvray** 225 litres; in the **Rhône** and **Mâconnais** 215 litres.

Pied
French for a *single vine stock.*

Piedmont
Not the largest but one of the most important wine-producing regions of **Italy** for quality wines. The best is **Barolo,** the next best are the **Barbera,** and **Nebbiolo.**

de Pierre à Fusil, Gout
See **Flinty.**

Pierry
Second class growth of **Champagne,** from nr. **Épernay,** especially noted for its flinty taste.

Piesport
One of the smallest villages of the **Mittel-Mosel** but the home of some of the famous gently fruity Piesporter wines.

Pilgerfpad
Gr. of the **Wonnegau** *Ber.,* **Rheinhessen.**

Pilton Manor
Small and established English international award winning estate at Shepton Mallet, **Somerset.** Mainly **Müller-Thurgau** and **Seyval Blanc** producing crisp dry delicate wines. The two are blended to produce *de Marsac* sparkling wine by the *méth. champ.*

Pimm's
Proprietary aromatic cordial, **Gin-**based.

Pineau de la Loire
See **Chenin Blanc.**

Pineau des Charentes
Strong, sweet **apéritif** made from white or red grape juice and **Cognac.** Speciality of the **Cognac** region.

Pinotage
South African **hybrid** red wine grape, a cross between **Pinot Noir** and **Hermitage.**

Pinot Blanc
One of the white wine grapes grown in **Burgundy, Champagne, Alsace,** and northern **Italy,** southern **Germany,** Eastern Europe and **California.**

Pinot Chardonnay
See **Chardonnay.**

Pinot Grigio
Italian white wine grape.

Pinot Gris
White grape which produces full-bodied spicy wines. In **Alsace** known as **Tokay; Tocai** in north-east **Italy** and **Yugoslavia,** and **Ruländer** in **Germany.**

Pinot Meunier
Lesser variety of the **Pinot** family.

Pinot Noir
The **Burgundy** grape of the **Côte d'Or** and the black grape variety used in the making of **Champagne.** It is also grown in **California, Germany** (*see* **Spätburgunder**), **Switzerland, Austria** and produces some good wines in **Hungary.** In **Italy** it is known as the *Pinot Nero.*

Pipe
A large cask with tapered ends and of varying capacity, used especially for **Port:** e.g. Lisbon 531.4 litres; standard **Madeira** cask 418 litres; standard **Marsala** cask 422.6 litres; standard **Port** cask 522.5 litres.

Piper-Heidsieck
Old firm of **Champagne** producers in **Reims.**

Piquant
French term meaning the wine is *acid and sharp* – not at all flattering.

Piqué
French for **pricked.**

Piqué-Cailloux, Ch.
Principal growth of **Graves,** from the **Mérignac** *comm.*

Piquetberg or Piketberg
Small demarcated wine area in the north-west of **Cape Province.**

Piquette
The French name for an 'imitation' wine usually made out of the husks of grapes after the juice has been pressed for making wine; they are flooded with water sweetened with the cheapest available sugar and fermented with brewer's yeast.

Pisco
A very potent and usually immature **Brandy** style spirit made from **Muscat** wine in Peru.

Pitching
Adding yeast to a solution to start a fermentation.

Plastering
Plaster of Paris added to low acid **musts** to increase the acidity. It is used in the **Sherry** process.

Plat
French for *flat,* referring to a wine lacking in liveliness and appeal.

Pleasant Valley
New York State winery on the **Finger Lakes** famous for *Great Western* sparkling wines.

Plettenberg, von
Important large estate in the **Nahe** region at **Bad Kreuznach.**

Plince, Ch.
Reliable small **Pomerol** estate nr. Libourne.

Plymouth Gin
A distinctive type of **Gin,** made only by Coates of Plymouth, **England.**

Podensac
One of the *comm.* of the **Gironde** *Dpt.* in the **Graves** region.

La Pointe, Ch.
One of the top quality **Pomerol** estates.

de Poire, Eau de Vie
Pear **Brandy.**

Pol Roger
Top quality **Champagne** house at **Épernay.**

Pomerol
One of the most important red wine districts of **Bordeaux** though the smallest. The vyds. are not classified officially but there is the universally recognized great growth **Ch. Pétrus.**

Pomeys, Ch.
Cru bourgeois **Moulis** *comm.,* **Haut-Médoc.**

Pommard
One of the best-known *comm.* of the **Côte de Beaune** which produces a large quantity of red **Burgundy** much of it of *premier cru* quality.

Pommarède, Ch.
Graves de Bordeaux, Castres *comm.*
Also *Ch. Pommarède-de-Bas.*

Pommery et Greno
Big **Reims Champagne** producers.

Pomys, Ch.
Bourgeois cru of the **Haut-Médoc, St. Estèphe** *comm.*

Ponche
Popular Spanish **digestif** made from **Sherry,** flavoured with herbs. *De Soto* is the best-known brand.

Pontac-Montplaisir, Ch.
Graves de Bordeaux, Villenave-d'Ornon *comm.*

Pontet-Canet, Ch.
Large *5me cru classé* of the **Haut-Médoc, Pauillac** *comm.*

Port
Port is a rich dessert wine made from grapes grown in the valley of the **Alto Douro** and fortified at the vintage time. *See* **Late-bottled, Ruby, Tawny, Vintage, White.**

Portets
Name of the *comm.*, **Graves de Bordeaux.** Also **Graves** *Ch.*

Portugal
The wines of Portugal divide easily into three groups: those table wines produced in certain delimited areas – *see* **Denominação de Origem;** the ordinary wines **Vinho de Consumo;** and **Port** and **Madeira.**

Portugieser (Blauer)
Red wine grape from the Danube region, now widely planted in the **Ahr** and other parts of **Germany** and in **Czechoslovakia.**

Posip
One of the best white wine grapes of **Dalmatia, Yugoslavia.**

Pot
A **Beaujolais** bottle of 50 centilitres.

Potensac, Ch.
Well-known *cru bourgeois* of the **Bas-Médoc.**

Pot Still
The original still, now replaced for many spirits by the **Patent Still** (or **Continuous Still**). Essentially it is a copper kettle in which a fermented mash or a wine base is heated. The alcohol-bearing vapours are collected and condensed to give young spirit. Only the middle part of the distillation, the purest part, is used, and the process is usually repeated twice, sometimes three times to reach the desired purity and flavour. Obligatory in the making of **Cognac,** malt **Whisky,** and also used for some **Irish Whiskies** and **Armagnacs.**

Pouget, Ch.
Lesser-known *4me cru classé* **Margaux** *comm.*, **Haut-Médoc.** Also **Ch. Boyd-Cantenac.**

Pouilly-Fuissé
A district of the **Mâconnais** and a refreshing white wine – the best from the area.

Pouilly-Fumé
This *AC* **Loire** wine is made from **Blanc Fumé,** the local name for the **Sauvignon** grape.

Pouilly-Loché
Individual dry white wine *app.* of the **Mâconnais,** similar but less important than **Pouilly-Fuissé.**

Pouilly-sur-Loire
This *AC* wine is made from the **Chasselas** and is dry.

Pouilly-Vinzelles
App. of a dry white wine of the **Mâconnais** similar to **Pouilly-Fuissé.**

Poujeaux-Theil, Ch.
Cru exceptionnel of the **Moulis** *comm.,* **Haut-Médoc.**

Pourriture Noble
See **Botrytis cinerea.**

Prädikat
Literally *special quality* in **Germany** and **Austria.** *See* **QmP.**

Preignac
Comm. of the **Sauternes** district; its vyds. produce some of the best white wines of the region.

Preiss Zimmer, Jean
Established merchants at **Riquewihr, Alsace.**

Prémeaux
Comm. of the **Côte de Beaune** immediately south of **Nuits St. Georges,** and sells its wines under that name.

Premier cru
Second class of growth below *grand cru* in **Burgundy,** e.g. **Champagne.** The label carries the name of the *comm.* followed by the name of the vyd. and the words *premier cru.* In **Médoc** it is the first of the five *crus classés.* In **Switzerland** any estate-bottled wine can call itself this.

Premières Côtes de Blaye
See **de Blaye, Côtes.**

Premières Côtes de Bordeaux
AC white **Bordeaux** district on the east of the Garonne almost directly opposite the **Graves** and **Sauternes** districts.

Press wine
The wine that is obtained by pressing the residue of the grape **must** after the first fermentation is over.

Les Preuses
Grand cru of **Chablis.**

Pricked
Wine with an excess of acidity – *piqué.*

Prieuré-Lichine, Ch.
4me cru classé **Cantenac** *comm.* with the **Margaux** *app.*

Primeur
See **Beaujolais Primeur.**

Primitivo
Priorato demarcated region nr. Tarragona, known for its **Rancio** wines and strong dark reds.

Prissey
Village in *comm.* of the **Côtes de Nuits-Villages.**

Probstberg
Gr. of the **Bernkastel** *Ber.,* **MSR.**

Prokupac
Important red wine grape of **Yugoslavia.**

Proof spirit
The standard against which beverages are measured for their **alcoholic strength.** Proof spirit is a mixture of alcohol and water which at 16°C contains 49.28 per cent of alcohol by weight (i.e. 100 g of proof spirit contains 49.28 g of alcohol) and 57.10 per cent by volume (i.e. 100 ml of proof spirit contains 57.10 ml alcohol).

The strength of wines is usually described as a percentage of alcohol by volume, so that a 12° wine means that alcohol forms 12 per cent of its volume. For comparison, 70 per cent proof spirit is 40° by volume. *See also* **Sikes.**

Propriétaire-Récoltant
On **Burgundy** labels means *owner-manager.*

Prosecco di Conegliano
DOC sparkling wine from **Veneto.**

Prošek
Naturally sweet and strong white dessert wine much prized in Yugoslavia.

de Provence, Côtes
Wines from **Bouches du Rhône, Var, Alpes Maritime, Vaucluse** *Dpts.* Some have been upgraded from *VDQS* to *AC.* Among best whites are those of **Bellet, Cassis,** and **Bandol.** Also famous for *rosés.*

Prüfungsnummer
See **AP.**

Prunelle
A green French liqueur made from sloe kernels.

Pruning
The cutting back and trimming of the wines to affect life span, quality or quantity of production. In the great vyds. of **France** and **Germany** the methods of pruning are specified by law.

Puerto de Santa Maria
Old port and important town of the **Sherry** area.

Puglia
One of the Italian wine-producing

provinces, nicknamed the 'cellar of Italy'. Ten *DOC* wines.

Puiseaux
Grand cru comm., canton de **Verzy,** of **Champagne.**

Puisseguin-Saint-Émilion
Lesser *comm.* and *app.* of **Saint-Émilion, Bordeaux.**

Pulham
White wine-producing vyd. at Diss, **Norfolk. Müller-Thurgau, Auxerrois** and **Bacchus** are used to produce **Mosel**-style wines. A speciality is a medium dry strawberry 'wine'.

Puligny-Montrachet
A *comm.* of the **Côte de Beaune.** The vyds. with those of the adjoining *comm.* of **Chassagne-Montrachet** produce the finest white wines of **Burgundy.**

Pulque
An intoxicating beverage fermented chiefly in **Mexico** from the Maguey and other kinds of aloes.

Punch
A hot winter drink made by adding spirits, fruit and spices to red wine and heating slowly to the required temperature. It must not boil. Summer punches are also made with a base of cooled white wine.

Puncheon
Cask with various capacities. **Rum** 422.6–518 litres; **Whisky** 431.9–545.5 litres.

Pünderich
Village of the **Bernkastel** *Ber., Gr.* **Vom Heissen Stein, MSR.**

Punsch
Swedish **Rum**-based beverage.

Punt
English term for the indentation in the base of a bottle originally designed to trap the sediment.

Punt e Mes
Proprietary Italian **apéritif.**

Pupitre
French rack for holding sparkling wines with the neck down preparatory to **dégorgement.**

Puttonyos
Buckets used in **Hungary** for measuring the selected grapes which go to make each bottle of **Tokaji Aszú.**

de Puy Blanquet, Domaine
Better-known unclassified **Saint-Émilion** from **St. Christophe des Bardes** *comm.*

Pyrénées
The range of mountains that divides **France** from **Spain.** The *Pyrénées Orientales Dpt.* includes the wine-growing areas of, e.g. **Roussillon, Banyuls** and **Rivesaltes.** *See also* **Jurançon.**

PX
See **Pedro Ximenez.**

Qualitätswein bestimmten Anbaugebiete (QbA)
Quality wine from a specific region, the second rank of German wines. *See* **Anbaugebiete.**

Qualitätswein mit Prädikat (QmP)
Quality wine with special qualities, the highest rank of German wines, i.e. **Kabinett, Spätlese, Auslese, Beerenauslese, Trockenbeerenauslese** and **Eiswein.** *QmP* wines may not have their alcoholic strength increased by the addition of sugar (*see* **Vins Chaptalisés**) – the gradings refer to natural sweetness, and the controls extend from the grapes on the vine to the date of the harvest and the **must** in the cellar.

Quality
General term for wines that are consistently above average in their own class.

Quartaut
Beaujolais, quarter of a **Pièce** – 54 litres. **Bordeaux,** quarter of a **Barrique** – 56 litres. **Burgundy,** quarter of a **Pièce** – 57 litres.

Quarter Cask
Cask name of different sizes, usually half a **Hogshead,** e.g. quarter **Port Pipe** – 127.2 litres; quarter **Sherry** cask – 122.7 litres; for **USA** spirits – 15.30 gallons.

Quarts de Chaume
AC white wine of **Anjou.** *See* **Coteaux du Layon Chaume.**

Quatourze
Small *VDQS* district of the **Midi.**

Quatrième cru (4me)
Fourth growth of the *crus classés* of the **Médoc,** ten chx.

Quelltaler
Old established quality firm at **Clare-Watervale** producing a full range of wines.

Quetsch
A dry, colourless spirit distilled from

Switzen plums, mainly from **Alsace** and **Lorraine.**

Quincy
AC white wine of the **Loire** valley.

Quinta de S. Claudio
High quality **Vinho Verde** estate at **Esposende.**

Quinta do Noval
Famous **Port** estate and shipping house.

Rabaud-Promis, Ch.
Premier cru **Sauternes, Bommes** *comm.*

Rablay-sur-Layon
Comm. of the **Coteaux du Layon, Anjou,** with its own *AC*.

Race
French word used to indicate distinction in a wine.

Racking
See **Pupitre.**

Rainwater Madeira
A pale, light dry to medium **Madeira** – popular in the **USA.**

Raki
Arrack-type spirit distilled from a wine base macerated with figs and other fruit.

Ramonet-Prudhon
Leading **Burgundy** proprietors, **Chassagne-Montrachet.**

Rancio
See **Maderized.**

Randersacker
One of the best wine-producing areas of the *Gr.* **Ewiges Leben, Maindreieck** district of **Franken. Stein** wines.

Ranina
Sweet wine grape of **Yugoslavia.** Known elsewhere as **Bouvier**, it is native to **Austria.**

Raspail
French digestive liqueur.

Rasteau
Village of **Vaucluse** *Dpt.,* celebrated for sweet, lightly fortified red and golden wines, under the *AC* **Côtes du Rhône-Villages.**

Ratafia
French **apéritif** made by adding **Brandy** to unfermented grape juice. Especially *Ratafia de Champagne.*

Ratsch
Wine-producing town of southern **Styria, Austria.**

Rauenthal
Regarded as one of the quality wine-producing villages of the **Rheingau,** producing *Rauenthalers* such as *Langenstück.* Much of the area is State Domain owned.

Rausan-Gassies, Ch.
2me cru classé of the **Margaux** *comm.,* **Haut-Médoc.**

Rausan-Ségla, Ch.
Large of the two *Rausan* estates and a
2me cru classé, **Margaux** *comm.*, **Haut-
Médoc.**

Ravat
The Frenchman who developed the **hybrid**
vines *Ravat 262* and *Ravat 6.*

Ravello
One of the wines of **Campania** – red or
white.

Ravensburg (Thüngersheim)
Gr. of the **Maindreieck** *Ber.,* **Franken.**

Raymond-Lafon, Ch.
Good **Sauternes** estate owned by the
manager of **Yquem.**

de Rayne-Vigneau, Ch.
Large *premier cru* vyd. of **Sauternes,
Bommes** *comm.*

Rczaziteli
Bulgarian white grape.

de Real Tesoro, Marques
Sherry shippers of **Sanlucar.**

Rebello Valente
Brand name of a light vintage **Port** from
Robertson's, themselves owned by
Sandeman.

**Rebstöckel (Neustadt an der
Weinstrasse Ortsteil Diedesfeld)**
Gr. of the **Mittelhaardt, Rheinpfalz.**

Rech
District of the **Ahr** valley, producing chiefly
red wines. Best vyd.: **Herrenberg.**

Recioto
Wine made from the ripest grapes. *Recioto*

di Gambellara, DOC **Veneto;** sweetish
golden wine. – *di Soave,* sweet fruity *DOC*
wine high in alcohol. – *della Valpolicella,*
strong rather sweet *DOC* red. – *Amarone
della Valpolicella,* as above, but dry and
slightly bitter.

Récolte
French term for the *vintage.*

Redman
Small winery making quality wines at
Coonawarra, Australia.

Refosco (Colli Orientali de Friuli)
Full-bodied dry red *DOC* from **Friuli-
Venezia Giulia. Grave del Friuli** – also
DOC but slightly lighter.

Regional wine
See Vins de Pays.

Rehbach
Gr. of the **Nierstein** *Ber.,* **Rheinhessen.**

Rehoboam
A treble **magnum.**

Reichensteiner
White wine **hybrid** grape grown in
England.

Reil
A minor wine village of the **Bernkastel**
Ber., Gr. **Vom Heissen Stein, MSR.**

Reims
The *Montagne de Reims* is the
northernmost of the important **Champagne**
producing areas. Reims itself is the capital
of the area and one of the historically
important cities of **France.** Among the
Champagne houses based there are
**Pommery, Heidsieck, Piper-Heidsieck,
Veuve Cliquot, Roederer** and **Taittinger.**

Remich
Village with the best vyds. of the
Luxembourg stretch of the **Mosel**, with
good **Riesling** soil.

Remoissenet, Père et Fils
Important growers and *négociants* of
Beaune.

Remstal-Stuttgart
Ber. of **Württemberg** region.

Remuage
French term for the turning of **Champagne**
bottles during the months before
dégorgement.

Rémy Martin
Specialists in **fine Champagne Cognac.**

Rémy Pannier
Important wine merchants of **Saumur,
Loire.**

René, Clos
One of the better **Pomerol** estates.

Renski Rizling
Yugoslavian version of the **Rhine
Riesling.**

Reserva
Spanish term for good wine matured for a
longer time in cask.

Réserve
Often seen on **Champagne** labels – it is
not significant.

Reserved for England
On a **Champagne** label it usually means
dry.

Resin/Resinous
Taste particularly associated with Greek

wines **(Retsina)** which have been
flavoured with pine resin.

de Respide, Ch.
One of the most important white wine
estates of the **Graves de Bordeaux** at **St.
Pierre de Mons.**

Reuilly
Small *AC* of the **Loire** valley. Red, white
and *rosé* wines.

Reuschberg
Gr. of the **Mainviereck** *Ber., Franken.*

Reynella
Winery of the **Southern Vales** area
specializing in red wines.

Rheinblick
Gr. of the **Nierstein** *Ber.,* **Rheinhessen.**

Rheinburgengau
Ber. of the **Mittelrhein.**

Rheingau
The wine region on the right bank of the
Rhine which produces some of the finest
German wines, chiefly white. The *Ber.*
name is **Johannisberg.**

Rheingrafenstein
Gr. of the **Bingen** *Ber.,* **Rheinhessen.**

Rheinhessen
The wine region on the left bank of the
Rhine, from **Worms** to **Bingen,** practically
opposite the **Rheingau,** which produces
the second largest quantity of German
mainly white wines of fine quality, and
which are soft and predominantly sweet
and fruity. The main districts are **Bingen,
Nierstein,** and **Oppenheim.**

Rheinpfalz (or Palatinate)
One of Germany's largest wine-producing

regions. The wines are full, soft and predominantly sweet. Districts are: **Mittelhaardt Deutsche-Weinstrasse** and **Südliche Weinstrasse.**

Rhenish
The name by which Rhine wines were known in **England** until the eighteenth century when they began to be called **Hock.**

Rhine Riesling
The name sometimes used for the true **Riesling** grape in Eastern Europe, **Australia, California** and **South Africa.**

Rhône
A fine r. with vyds. more or less the whole of its course. The Rhône vyds. produce white wines in the **Valais** canton of . **Switzerland** and in **Savoie,** and the best red wines are those from vyds. below Lyons and before **Avignon.** The most celebrated are the wines of **Côte Rotie, Hermitage** and **Châteauneuf-du-Pape.**

du Rhône, Côtes
Reds, whites and *rosés* from the **Loire, Rhône, Ardèche, Drôme, Gard** and **Vaucluse.**

du Rhône-Villages, Côtes
A fairly recent *AC* for the *comm.* and villages in the south of the region.

Rhum Negrita
A popular proprietary French **Rum.**

Rhum Saint James
One of the best-known Martinique **Rums.**

Ribeauvillé
Some of the best white wines of **Alsace** come from this *comm.* and important town.

Ribeiro
Demarcated region of north-east **Spain** – a centre for green wines.

Ricard
Proprietary brand of **Pastis,** flavoured with liquorice.

Ricasoli
Tuscan family; originators of **Chianti** at **Brolio.**

Richebourg, Le
A *grand cru* of the **Vosne-Romanée** *comm.,* **Côte de Nuits.**The **Richebourg** and **Romanée-Conti** vyds. are nr. neighbours and their wines are considered by many good judges to be the finest of all red Burgundies.

Ridge
Good quality small winery producing quality red wines on the central coast of **California.**

Ried
Austrian for *vyd.*

Riesling
The grape producing the finest white wines of **Germany.** *Riesling* grapes are now grown in many parts of the world.

Rieussec, Ch.
Large *premier cru* estate of **Sauternes, Farques** *comm.* Neighbour of **Yquem.**

Rilly-la-Montagne
Champagne *cru,* canton de **Verzy,** Arrondissement de **Reims.**

Rioja
This wine region of northern **Spain,** producing the country's best wines, is divided commonly into three major districts: *Rioja Alavesa,* **Rioja Alta** and

Rioja Baja. The first two produce the better quality wines. Rioja is matured in oak casks called **Bordelesas**.

La Rioja Alta, Bodegas
Mature rich Spanish wines, *Ardanza*, *Reserva 904* and dry white *Metropol Extra*.

Ripeau, Ch.
Grand cru classé of the **Graves Saint-Émilion**.

Riquewihr
Major wine-producing town and *comm.* of **Alsace**.

de Riscal, Marques
Top quality bodega of the *Rioja Alavese*.

Riserva
Wine aged for a statutory period in cask, in **Italy**. One year longer than a wine termed **Vecchio**.

Rittersberg
Gr. of the **Badische Bergstrasse Kraichgau** *Ber.,* **Baden**.

La Riva
Sherry shippers and makers of the **Fino** *Tres Palmas*.

Rivaner
Luxembourg name for **Müller-Thurgau**.

Riverina
District of **Murrumbidgee** area, southern **New South Wales**.

Rivesaltes
See **Muscat de Rivesaltes**.

Riviera del Garda
DOC from **Lombardia** – red and *rosé* wines.

Roaix
Village and red wine vyds. of **Vaucluse** with the *AC* **Côtes du Rhône-Villages**.

Roannaises, Côtes
VDQS red of the **Loire**.

Robertson
Small controlled district in the east of **Cape Province**. Red and white table wines but especially **Muscat**.

Robertson
Port shipper; subsidiary of **Sandeman**.

de la Roche, Clos
Grand cru vyd. and *AC* of **Morey-Saint-Denis, Côtes de Nuits**.

Rochecorbon
One of the eight *comm.* of **Touraine,** in the **Vouvray** district.

Rochefort-sur-Loire
Comm. of the **Coteaux du Layon, Anjou**.

Rochegude
One of the **Drôme** villages entitled to the *AC* **Côtes du Rhône-Villages**.

la Roches-aux-Moines
Fruity white wines come from this vyd. of **Savennières, Anjou**.

Rock Lodge
Small but established **Sussex** vyd. producing crisp, dry white wine from **Müller-Thurgau** and **Reichensteiner**.

Rödelsee
One of the smaller wine-producing villages of **Franken, Mainviereck** district.

Roditis
Greek white wine grape of the Peloponnese.

Roederer, Louis
One of the famous **Champagne** growers and merchants at **Rheims.**

Romanèche-Thorins
Beaujolais village contributing to wines of the **Moulin-à-Vent** *app.*

La Romanée
The smallest of the *grand cru* vyds. in the *comm.* of the **Vosne-Romanée, Côte de Nuits,** responsible for some of the finest red Burgundies.

La Romanée-Conti
A small vyd. of the *comm.* **Vosne-Romanée, Côte de Nuits,** producing the best known and most expensive of all red Burgundies. The estate is *Domaine de la Romanée-Conti.*

La Romanée-Saint-Vivant
The largest of the vyds. of the **Vosne-Romanée, Côte de Nuits.**

Romeiko
Greek wine grape, found mainly on Crete.

Romer, Ch.
Lesser-known *2me cru* **Sauternes, Fargues** *comm.*

Römerlay
Gr. of the **Saar-Ruwer** *Ber.,* **MSR.**

Roodeberg
Brand of quality red wine from the **KWV, South Africa.**

Ropiteau
Meursault merchants and growers.

Rosado
Spanish and Portuguese *rosé.*

Rosato
Italian for *pink* and *rosé* wines.

Rosé
Pink wine. The best natural *vin rosé* is that of **Tavel** but *vins rosés* are made elsewhere both still and sparkling, either with red grapes, which are not left long to ferment on their husks, or white wines blended with red wine.

Rosé d'Anjou
AC rosé of **Anjou,** made from **Gamay, Pineau d'Aunis, Cot** and **Groslot** grapes. *See* **Cabernet d'Anjou.**

Rosé de Cabernet
See **Cabernet d'Anjou.**

Rosenbühl (Freinsheim)
Gr. of the **Mittelhaardt** *Ber.,* **Rheinpfalz.**

Rosengarten
Gr. of the **Schloss Böckelheim** *Ber.,* **Nahe.**

Rosenhang
Gr. of the **Zell-Mosel, MSR.**

La Rose-Pauillac
A blended wine from **Pauillac** co-operative.

Rosolio
Italian version of an old French red liqueur which tastes of *roses.*

Rossese di Dolceacqua
Red *DOC* of **Liguria.**

Rosso
Term used generally in **Italy** for *red* wine.

Rosso Conero
DOC red from the **Marches** region.

Rosstal (Karlstadt)
Gr. of the **Maindreieck** *Ber.,* **Franken.**

Rotgipfler
Austrian red wine grape.

Rothbury
Important **Hunter Valley** estate producing quality table wines.

Rotie, Côte
One of the great red wines of the **Côtes du Rhône.** It is best left to mature for some years.

Rotling
In **Germany** the name for a pink wine that has been made by blending red and white grapes or grape **must,** but *not* wine. *See* **Schillerwein.**

Rott
Gr. of the **Starkenburg** *Ber.,* **Hessische Bergstrasse.**

Rotwein
German for *red wine.*

Rouget, Ch.
Lesser-known **Pomerol** estate.

Roumieu, Ch.
Lesser-known *cru bourgeois of* **Sauternes, Barsac** *comm.*

Round
A wine which is harmonious and balanced and is said to give a sense of roundness in the mouth.

Roussanne
Rhône white grape variety.

Rousselet de Béarn
VDQS district of the **Pyrénées** area of **France.**

Rousset-les-Vignes
One of the **Drôme** vyds. of the **Côtes du Rhône-Villages.**

Roussette
The most popular white wine of **Seyssel, Savoie;** also grape variety used in the production of the sparkling **Saint-Peray** from the **Rhône.**

Roxheim
Wine-producing village of the **Nahe, Schloss Böckelheim** district.

Royal Mint Chocolate Liqueur
A recently invented, proprietary liqueur with those flavourings.

Rubesco
See **Torgiano.**

Rubino di Cantavenna
DOC red of **Piedmont** produced by a co-operative.

Ruby
Youngest style of **Port;** full-flavoured and sweet.

Ruby Cabernet
Californian cross-bred grape – **Carignane** and **Cabernet Sauvignon.**

Ruchottes-Chambertin
Small *grand cru* vyd. nr. **Chambertin.**

Rüdesheim
Important town of the **Rheingau.** Its vyds. produce some of the great **Hocks** as well as ordinary wines. Some of the vyds. are State Domain owned. The best have *Berg.* in the name, e.g. *Rüdesheimer Berg. Lay.* Also a village in the *Ber.* **Schloss Böckelheim,** *Gr.* **Rosengarten,** of the **Nahe** district.

Rueda
Spanish town of the Valladolid district, the vyds. of which produce **Sherry**-like golden **flor** growing wines, strong in alcohol.

Ruffino
Large and well-known **Chianti** producer.

Rufinà
Sub-region of **Chianti** in the Florence hills.

Ruinart, Père et Fils
One of the oldest **Champagne** establishments now owned by Moët-Hennessey.

Ruiz Mateos
Sherry bodega producing some of the most expensive and best – the *Don Zoilo* range.

Ruländer
The name for the **Pinot Gris** grown in **Austria** and **Germany.**

Rully
The *comm.* of the **Côte Chalonnaise** including some *premier cru* vyds. Produces some of the most attractive of the white Burgundies of the district.

Rum
Spirit distilled from fermented sugar-cane, or molasses, mostly manufactured in the West Indies.

Rumasa
The biggest **Sherry** conglomerate, one of the largest groups in **Spain,** owners of many bodegas selling under their own names. Also table wines.

Ruppertsberg
An ancient wine town in the *Gr.* **Hofstück** of the **Mittelhaardt, Rheinpfalz.**

Russia
See **USSR.**

Russian River Valley
Important wine-producing area north of San Francisco with major wineries including Dry Creek, **Foppiano,** Geyser Peak, **Italian Swiss Colony.** Sparkling wine producers are **Korbel, Pedroncelli, Simi** and **Souverain.**

Rust
Famous wine centre of **Burgenland, Austria.**

Rustenburg
High quality red wine from **Cape Province** regarded as an **estate wine.**

Rutherford and Miles
Madeira shippers famous for *Old Trinity House.*

Rutherglen
Highly regarded wine district of north-east **Victoria** producing table, dessert and fortified wines.

Ruwer
A small r. which joins the **Mosel** a short distance north of **Trier.** The vyds. of the Ruwer produce some very delicate white wines. *See* **MSR.**

Ruzica
Good dark Yugoslavian *rosé.*

Rye
Type of North American **Whiskey** distilled mainly from rye.

Ryecroft
McLaren Vale estate producing good full-bodied red wines.

S

Saar
A small tributary of the r. **Mosel**. *See* **MSR**.

Saarburg
Town with some of the best vyds. of the *Gr.* **Scharzberg, Saar-Ruwer** district of the **MSR**.

Les Sables-Saint-Émilion
Part of the village of **Libourne** allowed to use the *app.* **Saint-Émilion**.

Saccharomyces cerevisiae
The yeast found on the skins of grapes which ferments the juice of the fruit. *Saccharomyces acidi faciens* can spoil some white wines and in modern wineries undesirable yeasts are destroyed in the **must** and selected cultured yeasts are used.

Sack
A dry, amber wine, originally spelt Seck, occasionally sweetened with honey or sugar, mentioned for the first time in a proclamation fixing retail prices for wine in England in 1532. It came mostly from **Spain** and was sometimes referred to as *Sherris-Sack.*

Saint-Amand, Ch.
Preignac *comm.,* **Sauternes**.

Saint-Amour
The most northerly of the nine *crus* of **Beaujolais,** not far south of **Mâcon**. It is one of the lightest of the *crus.*

Saint-Aubin
Less well-known *comm.* of the **Côte de Beaune** nr. **Chassagne-Montrachet**.

Saint Chinian
Good *VDQS* red, **Hérault** *Dpt.*

Saint-Christoly, Ch.
Minor *cru* of the **Bas-Médoc, Saint-Christoly** *comm.*

Saint Christophe des Bardes
Comm. of **Saint-Émilion** and takes the *AC* **Saint-Émilion**.

Saint-Denis
See **Moray-Saint-Denis.**

Sainte-Croix-du-Mont
AC white **Bordeaux**. Less sweet and less alcoholic than the **Barsacs** and **Sauternes**.

Saint-Émilion
Ancient city of **Bordeaux**. It is surrounded by vyds. which were classified in 1955 and which produce the most consistently full-flavoured wines of the region. There are twelve *premiers grands crus classés* and seventy-three *grands crus classés. See* **Graves Saint-Émilion**.

Saint Estèphe
The northernmost of the four **Haut-Médoc** *comm.* Classified growths are: **Ch. Montrose, Cos d'Estournel, Lafon-Rochet, Cos-Labory,** and **Calon-Ségur.**

Saint Étienne de Lisse
Comm. of **Saint-Émilion,** and takes its *AC.*

Saint-Georges
Large wine-producing *comm.* of **Saint-Émilion** with its own *AC.*

Les Saint-Georges
One of the best **climats** of the *comm.* of **Nuits-St.-Georges.**

Saint-Georges-Côte-Pavie, Ch.
Grand cru classé of **Saint-Émilion.**

Saint Hippolyte
Saint-Émilion *comm.* that takes the *app.* **Saint-Émilion.**

Saint-Jean, Clos
Premier cru vyd. of **Chassagne-Montrachet.**

Saint Josèph
Rhône *AC* red and white, **Ardèche** district.

Saint Julien
Small *comm.* of the great four of the **Haut-Médoc** but with a number of classified growths. There are also *comm.* of this name in the **Rhône** and **Meuse** *Dpt.*

Saint-Julien, Ch.
Part of the yield of the **Ch. Lagrange** is sold under this name, but there is no actual Ch.

Saint-Laurent
Local Austrian red grape, also grown in **Czechoslovakia** and other Eastern European countries.

Saint Laurent des Combes
Comm. of **Saint-Émilion** and takes its *app.*

Saint Martin, Clos
Small *grand cru classé* estate of **Saint-Émilion.**

Saint Maurice
One of the **Drôme** vyds. entitled to the *AC* **Côtes du Rhône-Villages.**

Saint Michael
Gr. of the **Bernkastel** *Ber.*, **MSR.**

Saint-Nicholas-de-Bourgueil
One of the best *AC* red or *rosé* wines of **Touraine** from the **Bourgueil** *comm.*

Saint Pantaleon
A village of **Drôme** entitled to the *AC* **Côtes du Rhône-Villages.**

Saint-Péray
Rhône *AC* from the **Ardèche** district. A sparkling white is produced which has the *AC St. Péray Mousseux,* and also a still white.

Saint Pey d'Armens
Comm. of **Saint-Émilion** and takes its *AC.*

Saint-Pierre-de-Mons
Minor sweet white wine *comm. of* **Bordeaux.**

Saint-Pierre-et-Seviastre-Bontemps, Ch.
Small *4me cru* estate, **St. Julien** *comm.*, **Médoc.**

Saint-Pourçain
A *comm.* of the **Loire** famous for its still white wines.

Saint-Raphaël
Red, bitter-sweet French fortified red wine, flavoured with quinine; drunk as an **apéritif.**

Saint Saphorin
One of the main wine villages of **Lavaux** in the east of the **Vaud, Switzerland.** Dry white wines.

Saint Satur
VDQS of the **Coteaux de Languedoc** in the **Hérault** *Dept.*

Saint Sauveur
One of the lesser wine-producing *comm.* of the **Haut-Médoc.**

Saint Seurin-de-Cadourne
One of the lesser wine-producing *comm.* of the **Haut-Médoc** immediately to the north of **St. Estèphe** and the last entitled to the **Haut-Médoc** *App.*

Saint Sulpice de Faleyrens
Comm. of **Saint-Émilion** and takes its app.

Saint Véran
Recent *app.* for white **Burgundy** from **Pouilly-Fuissé** district.

Saint-Yzans
Comm. of the **Bas-Médoc.**

Saké
A Japanese rice wine obtained by two consecutive processes of fermentation of a brew mostly of rice, but occasionally of other grain.

Salinas
Wine valley south of San Francisco, **California.**

Salmanazar
A large glass bottle, for show more than for use, containing the equivalent of twelve bottles.

Saltram
Southern Vales winery producing good reds.

Salzberg
Gr. of the **Württembergisches Unterland, Württemberg.**

Samshu
The Chinese equivalent of **Saké.**

San Benito
Newly developed wine area of **California.**

Sancerre
A picturesque old city of the **Cher** *Dpt.* in the **Loire** valley. Its vyds. produce chiefly white wines with the *AC* **Sancerre,** but also reds, and *rosés.* The slightly 'green straw'-coloured white is dry and fruity.

Sandeman
Famous major **Port** and **Sherry** shippers.

Sangaree
The name given to long, mixed, iced drinks in some parts of the tropics whether made with wine or spirits as a base.

Sangiovese
Main red grape for **Chianti,** also used for **Montepulciano** and other Italian wines. If it is on the label it is the only grape.

Sangiovese di Romagna
Red *DOC* from **Emilia-Romagna.**

Sangria
Spanish cold red wine cup, made by adding citrus fruits and lemonade.

Sangue di Giuda
Red wine of **Lombardia.**

San Joaquin Valley
America's largest grape growing area, this long valley runs inland, the best part of the length of **California** from well north of San Francisco to nr. Los Angeles. A large production of table grapes and grapes for distilling into **Brandy,** but some mammoth wineries making all grades of quality, including **Gallo,** the world's largest winery, and **Franzia.**

Sankt Alban
Gr. of the **Nierstein** *Ber.,* **Rheinhessen.**

Sankt Margarethen
Wine area of **Burgenland,** producing
mostly white wines.

Sankt Martin
Village of the *Gr.* **Schloss Ludwigshöhe,**
Ber. **Südliche Weinstrasse, Rheinpfalz.**

Sankt Rochuskapelle
Gr. of the **Bingen** *Ber.,* **Rheinhessen.**

Sanlucar de Barrameda
Centre of the **Manzanilla** district, **Spain.**

San Luis Obispo
One of the southern wine-producing
counties of **California, USA.**

San Sadurní de Noya
Large Spanish wine-producing town
making sparkling wines by the *méth.
champ.*

San Severo
Light-weight southern *DOC* wine, **Puglia.**

Sansonnet, Ch.
Grand cru classé estate, **Côtes Saint-
Émilion.**

Santa Clara
Table wine-producing region of **California,**
south of San Francisco Bay. *See* **Central
Coast.**

Santa Maddalena
Good Tyrolean red *DOC* **Trentino-Alto
Adige.**

Santa Ynez Valley
Newer quality **Californian** wine area north
of Los Angeles. Important wineries are
Firestone, Zaca Mesa and Sandford &
Benedict.

Santenay
The southernmost *comm.* of the **Côtes de
Beaune,** producing some light red wines
but also some deeper and fuller. *See* **Les
Gravières, Clos de Tavannes.**

Saperavi
Russian and Bulgarian red wine grape.

Saperavi Massandra
A dry red wine of the **Crimea, USSR.**

Sardegna
Sardinia produces mostly red or sweet
dessert-type wine. Ten *DOC* wines.

Sartene
AC comm. of **Corsica,** producing some of
its quality wines.

Sasbach
Village of the *Gr.,* **Vulkanfelsen,
Kaiserstuhl-Tuniberg** district, **Baden.**

Sassella
Red *DOC* **Valtellina, Lombardia.**

Sassicaia
Red wine and estate of **Toscana.** Possibly
Italy's best red wine.

Saumagen
Gr. of the **Mittelhaardt** *Ber.,* **Rheinpfalz.**

de Saumur, Coteaux
AC district of **Anjou,** producing red and
white wines; the white can be **mousseux**
or **pétillant.**

Saumur-Champigny
Red from **Cabernet Franc** grapes grown
in the **Saumur** region of the **Loire, Anjou,**
and carries its own *app.*

Sauternes
The Sauternes district comprises not only the vyds. of the *comm.* of **Sauternes,** but those of the adjoining **Bommes, Barsac, Preignac** and **Fargues,** and is responsible for the greatest naturally sweet white wines in the world.

Sauvignon Blanc
One of the noblest white grape species responsible together with the **Semillon** for the excellence of the best **Sauternes** and other white wines. It is now grown in **Australia, South Africa, Italy** and the **USA.** Also known as the **Blanc Fumé.**

Sauvignon de St. Bris
Recent white *VDQS* from the **Yonne** *Dpt.* made from the **Sauvignon** grape, unusual for the **Burgundy** region.

Savagnin
Swiss name for the red **Traminer** grape from **Alsace.**

Savatiano
Greek white grape from **Attica** – used in the making of **Retsina.**

Savennières
AC white of the **Coteaux de la Loire, Anjou** and a fine wine, but must be entirely of **Chenin Blanc.**

Savigny-les Beaunes
One of the *comm.* of the **Côte d'Or** which produces much red **Burgundy** of fair quality and some of outstanding merit, similar to the wines of the adjoining *comm.* of **Aloxe-Corton** and **Pernand-Vergelesses.**

Savoie
The French part of the mountainous country bordering southern **Switzerland** and northern **Italy.** Red, white and sparkling wines are produced and mainly drunk locally. *See* **Roussette, Crépy** and **Seyssel.**

Savuto
Rich and full-bodied red *DOC* of **Calabria.**

Schaffhausen
German-Swiss canton of **Switzerland,** producing wines from the **Klevner** grape.

Schalkstein
Gr. of the **Württembergisches Unterland, Württemberg.**

Scharlachberg
Important vyd. of the **Bingen** district, **Rheinhessen.**

Scharzberg
Gr. of the **Saar-Ruwer, MSR.**

Scharzhofberg
Important town of the *Gr.* **Scharzberg, Saar** valley, **MSR.**

Schaumwein
German sparkling wine sold young and of less quality than a **Sekt.**

Schenkenböhl (Wachenheim)
Gr. of the **Mittelhaardt** *Ber.,* **Rheinpfalz.**

Scheurebe
Fruity aromatic German **hybrid** grape, a cross between **Sylvaner** and **Riesling.** Now also grown in **England.**

Schiava
Italian red wine grape from the **Alto-Adige.**

Schiedam
Hollands is sometimes called this as it is distilled in this town in quantity.

Schilcher
An Austrian grape and red wine speciality of **Styria.**

Schild (Abtswind)
Gr. of the **Steigerwald** *Ber.*, **Franken.**

Schillerwein
The name of the pink **QbA** and **QmP**
wines of **Württemberg** made from white
and red grapes. *See* **Weissherbst,
Rotling.**

Schloss
German for *castle* or *château*.

Schlossabzug
German equivalent of *château-bottled.*
The term cannot be used any longer on a
wine label.

Schlossberg
Gr. of the **Starkenburg** *Ber.*, **Hessische
Bergstrasse.**

Schlossberg (Rödelsee)
Gr. of the **Steigerwald, Franken.**

Schloss Böckelheim
Village and also the name of one of the
two districts of the **Nahe**, producing one of
the best-known **Nahe** wines.

Schloss Eltz
Fine estate in the **Rheingau.**

Schloss Grafenegg
Famous wine property of the Metternich
family nr. **Krems.**

Schloss Johannisberg
The district name for the whole of the
Rheingau and probably the most famous
of its estates producing consistently fine
wines.

Schlosskapelle
Gr. of the **Kreuznach** *Ber.*, **Nahe.**

Schloss Ludwigshöhe (Edenkoben)
Gr. of the **Südliche Weinstrasse** *Ber.*,
Rheinpfalz.

Schloss Reichenstein
Gr. of the **Bacharach** *Ber.*, **Mittelrhein.**

Schloss Reinhartshausen
Famous estate of the **Rheingau,**
producing fine **Kabinett** wines.

Schloss Rodeck
Gr. of the **Ortenau** *Ber.*, **Baden.**

Schloss Schönburg
Gr. of the **Rheinburgengau** *Ber.*,
Mittelrhein.

Schloss Stahleck
Gr. of the **Bacharach** *Ber.*, **Mittelrhein.**

Schlosstück (Frankenberg)
Gr. of the **Steigerwald** *Ber.*, **Franken.**

Schloss Vollrads
Famous estate by the town of **Winkel,
Rheingau.** Its *late-picked* grapes produce
some of the best wines of the region.

Schluck
Pleasant Austrian white *ordinaire* from the
Wachau.

Schlumberger et Cie
Growers and merchants of **Guebwiller,**
Alsace.

Schmitt, Franz Karl
Smaller but older producer at **Nierstein.**

Schmitt, Gustav Adolf
Large, old family producer at **Nierstein.**

Schnepfenflug an der Weinstrasse (Forst)
Gr. of the **Mittelhaardt** *Ber.,* **Rheinpfalz.**

Schnepfenflug vom Zellertal
Gr. of the **Mittelhaardt** *Ber.,* **Rheinpfalz.**

Scholtz, Hermanos
Makers of dessert wines at **Malaga, Andalucia, Spain.**

Schönborn, Graf von
One of the best **Rheingau** estates at **Hattenheim.**

Schönburger
New German grape variety. Grown a little in **England.**

Schoongezicht
One of the most beautiful **Cape Province** wine estates manufacturing with **Rustenberg.**

Schozachtal
Gr. of **Württemberg.**

Schramsberg
The best Californian **Champagne** house *(méth. champ.)* in the **Napa Valley.**

Schriesheim
Village of the **Badische Bergstrasse Kraichgau** *Ber.,* **Baden.**

Schröder et Schyler
Bordeaux merchants and owners of **Ch. Kirwan.**

Schubert, von
Owner of Maximin Grünhaus.

Schutterlindenberg
Gr. of the **Breisgau** *Ber.,* **Baden.**

Schwaigern
Württemberg village, *Gr.* **Henchelberg.**

Schwarze Katz
Gr. of the **Zell-Mosel, MSR.**

Schwarzerde (Kirchheim)
Gr. of the **Mittelhaardt** *Ber.,* **Rheinpfalz.**

Schwarzlay
Gr. of the **Bernkastel, Mittel-Mosel, MSR.**

Scotch Whisky
The most popular of all the spirits made from grain. Up to the early 1800s all *Scotch Whisky,* legal or illegal, was made in unsophisticated versions of the **Pot Still.** Then the **Continuous Still** was introduced which allowed the production of large quantities of grain Whisky, and the big, blended brands came into being, part **Pot** or *malt* Whisky, and part grain Whisky from the **Continuous Still.**

Malt Whisky is made in the **Pot Still** from a mash of malted barley. Only the 'heart' of the first distillation goes into the second distillation, and then once again only the 'heart' is retained. This goes into *oak* casks for a legally minimum maturation period of three years. It may then be bottled as a single malt, the product of one distillery; or with other malts in small quantities which go into the make-up of a blend, the different malts contributing their individual characters to the grain Whisky-base.

The vast majority of *malt Whiskies* are distilled in the Scottish Highlands, particularly in the Spey Valley area. However there are malt distilleries in the Lowlands, around Campbeltown, and on the islands, particularly Islay.

Scuppernong
Scented grape found in Virginia. It is a *Vitis rotundifolia* – the grapes grow singly. It makes intensely flavoured wines.

Seaview
Large **McLaren Vale** winery producing
table and dessert wines.

Sebastiani
Large and distinguished old firm, **Sonoma**
County, **California.**

Sec
French for *dry,* but means *sweet* on a
Champagne label. *Sec* is less sweet than
a wine labelled *demi-sec,* which is very
sweet, but it is sweeter than *extra sec,*
which is only slightly sugared.

Secco
Italian for *dry* wine.

Séché
French term used to describe harsh wines
usually suffering from oxidation.

Seco
Spanish for *dry.*

Sêco
Portuguese for *dry.*

Sediment
See **Lees.**

Seeweine
Term meaning lake wines, produced in
the **Bodensee** district of **Baden** by Lake
Constance.

Segonzac
One of the *grand fine* **Champagne** *comm.*
of the **Cognac** region.

Ségur, Ch.
Minor growth of the **Haut-Médoc,**
Parempuyre *comm.*

Séguret
Vyd. of the **Vaucluse** entitled to the *AC*
Côte du Rhône-Villages.

Seibel
French **hybrid** grape grown in **New York**
State and **England.**

Sekt
Quality German sparkling white wine
(QbA). The best is made from **Riesling**
grapes. *See also* **Schaumwein.**

de Selle, Ch.
Well-known **Côtes de Provence** estate,
producing typical local wines.

Selzen
Village of the *Gr.* **Gutes Domtal,**
Nierstein district, **Rheinhessen.**

Sémeillan, Ch.
Minor growth of the **Haut-Médoc, Listrac**
comm.

Sémillon
One of the finest French white grape
varieties. It is also widely grown in
California and **Australia.** *See* **Sauvignon**
Blanc.

Sénancole
Yellow herb-based digestive liqueur from
Provence.

Sénéjac, Ch.
Cru bourgeois, **Haut-Médoc, Le Pian**
comm.

Senheim
Village of the Krampen section of the
Mosel, Zell-Mosel MSR.

Seppelt
Australia's biggest 'Champagne'
producers, with vyds. in a number of major
districts of **South Australia, New South**
Wales and **Victoria.**

Sercial
Grape variety used for dry **Madeiras** of
that name.

Serradayres
Brand of Portuguese table wines.

Serrig
One of the best wine villages of the *Gr.*
Scharzberg, Saar, area of the **MSR.**

Setúbal
See **Moscatel de Setúbal.**

Sève
A French term meaning *sappy* used to
describe a wine which has elegance and
charm.

Sèvre-et-Maine
The *Dpt.* with the best **Muscadet** vyds.

Seyssel
An *AC* white wine of the Haute-Savoie;
also *Seyssel Mousseux.*

Seyval Blanc
Hardy fruity **hybrid** from French and
American vines. Popular in **England.**

Seyval-Villard
Well-known French **hybrid** developer, e.g.
Seyval Blanc.

Sforzato
Strong red *DOC* of **Lombardia,** equivalent
of **Recioto Amarone.**

Sharp
See **Acidity.**

Shebeen
A shop or bar chiefly in Ireland where
excise liquor is sold *without* a licence. A
term also used in **South Africa.**

Sherry
Famous fortified wines made from white

grapes grown in the **Jerez** district in the
south of **Spain.** It is made from the best
wine of each vintage, to which some
Brandy is added, then the **Flor** yeast
converts it to *Sherry,* after which it is
blended with the best wine of other
vintages over a period of years. *See* **Fino,
Amontillado, Amoroso, Manzanilla** and
Oloroso.

Shiraz
The Australian spelling of **Syrah** where it
is one of the most important red wine
grapes. It is also grown in **Cyprus,** and in
South Africa where it is also known as
Hermitage.

Sichel et Cie
Famous merchants in **Bordeaux,
Burgundy, Germany,** London and **New
York.**

Sicilia (Sicily)
Island off the Italian coast producing
classic sweet wines – **Marsala, Malvasia,
Moscato,** and some good table wines, e.g.
Corvo.

Siebengebirge
Gr. of the **Mittelrhein** *Ber.*

Sierre
White wine parish of the **Valais,** the most
renowned wine of which is a **Vin de Paille**
called **Soleil de Sierre.**

Sieveringer
Viennese wine suburb, **Austria.**

Sigalas Rabaud, Ch.
Small *premier cru* estate, **Bommes,**
comm. **Sauternes.**

Sigerrebe
German white wine grape.

Sikes (or Sykes)
Alcoholic strength is measured with a

hydrometer. It was invented in the eighteenth century and that currently in use was developed by Bartholomew Sikes in the early nineteenth century. The hydrometer measures the density of the liquor from which the alcohol strength is calculated.

Siller
Pale red or *rosé* Hungarian wine.

Sillery
Grand cru **Champagne** *comm.* canton de **Verzy**, Arrondissement de **Reims.**

Silvaner
See **Sylvaner.**

Simard, Ch.
Lesser growth of **Saint-Émilion.**

Simard, Clos
Principal growth vyd., **Saint-Émilion.**

Simi
Old winery of **Alexander Valley, California.**

Simmern, von
Old and important family estate at **Hattenheim** in the **Rheingau.**

Simone, Ch.
Well-known property of **Provence**, one of two in the **Palette** vyds.

Sion
Centre of the **Valais** canton of **Switzerland,** famous for **Fendant.**

Sipon
Yugoslavian name for the **Furmint** grape.

Siran, Ch.
Notable *cru bourgeois* of the **Haut-Médoc, Labarde-Margaux** *comm.*

Sitges
Spanish coastal town nr. Barcelona producing some of the country's sweet dessert wines.

Sizzano
Full-bodied *DOC* red of **Piedmont.**

Slings
The name of a number of cold mixed alcoholic beverages more particularly popular in the tropics.

Slivovitz (Slivovitza)
The name of the spirit which is distilled from plums in **Hungary, Yugoslavia** and **Rumania.** It is similar to the Alsatian **Quetsch.**

Sloe Gin
A cordial made by macerating sloes in **Gin** with sugar.

Slovenia
North-west state of **Yugoslavia** famous for **Ljutomer-Riesling.**

Smashes
Mixed iced drinks always with a spirit foundation and some mint flavouring.

Smith-Haut-Lafitte, Ch.
Grand cru classé of the **Graves** region, **Martillac** *comm.*, for red wine. Also white wine.

Smith's Yalumba
Large established family firm of the **Barossa** valley with a full range of wines some marketed with the name **Galway.**

Smoky
The characteristic nose of some **Sauvignon Blanc** or **Chardonnay** wines.

Soave
One of the best-known white wines of **Italy;** *DOC* **Veneto.**

Soberano
Brand of Spanish **Brandy.**

SOGRAPE
Sociedad Commercial dos Vinhos de Mesa de Portugal – **Portugal's** largest wine producer, including **Mateus Rosé** and **Aveleda Vinho Verde.**

Soil
One of the most important natural contributory elements in the quality and flavour of wine from any one grape.

Soleil de Sierra
Noted **Vin de Paille** from **Sierre** in the **Valais.**

Solera
Not a type of **Sherry** but a blending or vatting system used for **Sherry** and **Madeira** production. The barrels of mature wine are topped up progressively with younger wine of the same sort.

La Solitude, Domaine
Graves de Bordeaux of the **Martillac** *comm.*

Solopaca
White or red dry *DOC* from **Campania.**

Solutré-Pouilly
The town of the **Mâconnais** with vyds. in the *comm.* of **St. Veran** and **Pouilly-Fuissé.**

Somló
Outstanding white wine district of **Hungary** famous for **Furmint** wines.

Sommerach
One of the best villages of **Franken,** *Gr.* **Kirchberg,** *Ber.,* **Maindreieck.**

Sonneborn
Gr. of the **Kreuznach** *Ber.,* **Nahe.**

Sonnenbühl
Gr. of the **Remstal-Stuttgart** *Ber.,* **Württemberg.**

Sonnenufer
Gr. of the **Bodensee** *Ber.,* **Baden.**

Sonnenuhr
German for *sundial,* and the name of several vyds.

Sonoma County
Important quality wine area north of the **Napa Valley** by which it is overshadowed. Important vyds. include: **Buena Vista, Chateau St. Jean, Grand Cru,** Gundlach-Bundschu, **Hacienda, Hanzell,** Kenwood and **Sebastiani.**

Sonoma Vineyards
Well regarded **Sonoma County** vyd., **California.**

Sopron
Hungarian *comm.* producing good rich red wines.

Souche
Buying *sur souche* means speculating by buying before the grapes are harvested.

Soussans
Lesser *comm.* of the **Haut-Médoc.**

Soutard, Ch.
Substantial *grand cru classé* estate, **Côtes Saint-Émilion.**

South Africa
The wine industry is based in **Cape Province,** the coolest part of the country, with the best vyds. fanning out from Capetown. There are eleven designated table wine areas: **Constantia, Durbanville, Stellenbosch, Paarl** and **Swartland** (which can also come under

the overall heading *Coastal Region*), **Tulbagh, Worcester, Robertson, Swellendam, Piketberg, Olifants River** and Little Karoo.

Much of the production in the outer areas goes for the making of sweet, fortified wines and **Brandy,** but increasing domestic consumption is seeing more blended and varietal wines being made. The main grape varieties for white wines are **Chenin Blanc** and **Steen** (the most widely planted variety), **Sémillon,** and latterly some **Chardonnay** and **Sauvignon Blanc.** Red varieties are dominated by **Cinsaut, Cabernet Sauvignon, Pinotage** and Tinta Barocca. Much of the production is concentrated in the hands of the *Oude Meester Group, Stellenbosch Farmers' Winery,* the **Ko-öperative Wijnbouwers Vereniging** (to which all grape growers must belong by law), *Gilbeys South Africa* and *Union Wines.* Forty odd estates have the right to sell under their own name.

A *Wine of Origin* system exists to certify the quality of the best wines.

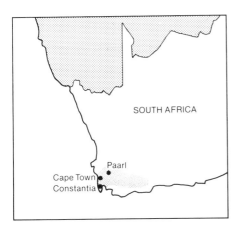

South America
Argentina and **Chile** are the biggest wine producers. A full range of wines is produced, mainly for local consumption.

South Australia
Important vyds. within the **Adelaide** metropolitan area, the **Barossa Valley** and **Clare-Watervale** to the north, the **Southern Vales** including **McLaren Vale**

to the south. Also **Langhorne Creek** and Springton-Eden Valley towards the border with **Victoria. Coonawarra** to the very south-east of the state is considered to be **Australia's** premium area for red wines from **Cabernet Sauvignon** and **Shiraz** vines. Also Keppoch nearby.

Southern Comfort
Proprietary American bourbon **Whiskey**-based fruit and herb-flavoured liqueur.

Southern Vales
Wine area of **South Australia,** south of **Adelaide,** which includes **McLaren Vale** and **Reynella.**

Southfield
Vyd. at Huntley, **Gloucestershire.**

Souverain
Luxurious new establishment at **Alexander Valley, California.**

Spain
One of the largest of the European wine-producing countries with vines grown in almost every part of the country. A large production of *ordinaire* wines in the hinterland, but quality red wines and latterly whites from the **Rioja** region to the north-west and quality red and white wines from the **Penedés** outside Barcelona, also the area producing vast quantities of *méth. champ.* and **Charmat** Spanish sparkling wines.

Andalucia in the south-west is famous for **Sherry,** the area around Cordoba for the **Sherry**-like **Montilla-Moriles,** and **Málaga** for its rich dessert wine of the same name.

The best wines are awarded the **Denominación de Origen,** the Spanish equivalent of **Appellation d' Origine Contrôlée.**

Spanna
See **Gattinara.**

Spirits
Alcoholic liquids obtained by distillation from such base liquids as fermented wine, **molasses,** grain, rice, etc. The differences between them are due to the by-products or impurities, which vary according to the nature of the fermented liquid from which they are distilled, and the method of distillation.

Spitzenwein
Austrian term for *fine wines.*

Sprendlingen
Village of the *Gr.* **Abtey, Bingen** *Ber.* of the **Rheinhessen.**

Sparkling wine
All sparkling wines owe their effervescence to the presence of carbonic acid gas, which, in the act of escaping out of the wine, once the cork has been removed, carry with them fine bubbles of wine beaten up to a 'foam' by the carbon dioxide rushing out. There are two main varieties: those with their own carbonic acid gas in solution due to secondary fermentation in the bottles; and those where carbonic acid gas has been pumped into the bottle. The finest sparkling wine in the world is **Champagne.** See **Méthode Champenoise.**

Spring Mountain Vineyards
Small restored high quality winery of the **Napa Valley.**

Spritzig
Term used to describe a naturally *light sparkle* in wines caused by a slight secondary fermentation in the bottle.

Spumante
Italian for *sparkling.*

Squinzano
Strong red from **Puglia.**

Spätburgunder (Blauer)
Name for the **Pinot Noir** in **Germany** and responsible for its few classic red wines.

Staatliche Weinbaudomäne
The State Domain or estate in **Germany.** Also called *Staatsweingut.*

Spätlese
German for *late-vintaged.* A naturally sweet wine made from the last grapes and the ripest to be picked in bunches in a good year. *See* **Auslese, Beerenauslese, Trockenbeerenauslese.**

Stadecken-Elsheim
Village of the **Nierstein** district, **Rheinhessen.**

Stag's Leap Wine Cellars
New small high quality vyd. in **Napa Valley.**

Spätrot
See **Zierfändler.**

Spiegelberg
Gr. of the **Nierstein** *Ber.,* **Rheinhessen.**

Stalky
Hardness in wine from **tannin** naturally present in the grape stalks.

Stanley Wine Company
Important winery in the **Clare-Watervale** district of **South Australia** with a wide variety of quality red and white wines.

Staple
Young but established estate nr. Canterbury, **Kent,** producing dry fruity wines from **Müller-Thurgau.**

Starkenburg
Gr. of the **Hessische Bergstrasse** *Ber.,* **Rheingau.**

Staufenberg
Gr. of the **Württembergisches Unterland** *Ber.,* **Württemberg.**

Steen
Most widely planted white wine grape of **South Africa,** it is the local name for the **Chenin Blanc.**

Steiermark (Styria)
Important wine-producing region of **Austria.** Famous for **Schilcher.**

Steigerwald
Ber. of **Franken.**

Steil
Gr. of the **Johannisberg** *Ber.,* **Rheingau.**

Stein
Any medium-dry white **South African** wine.

Stein-am-Rhein
Most important district of the **Schaffhausen** canton, **Switzerland.**

Steinberg
A fine **Rheingau** wine from **Hattenheim.** The vyd. is state owned and the grapes are pressed and stored at **Kloster Eberbach.**

Steinhäger
A German **Gin** similar to **Hollands.**

Steinmächer
Gr. of the **Johannisberg** *Ber.,* **Rheingau.**

Steinwein
The white wine of **Würzburg, Franken,** usually sold in **Bocksbeutels.**

Stellenbosch
Wine and university town of **Cape Province** and one of the best of the designated districts for the production of South African table wines. Two of the big three wine producers, the *Stellenbosch Farmers' Winery* and the *Oude Meester Group* are based on Stellenbosch, and around the town are many of the Cape's best wine estates.

Sterling
New, medium-sized **Napa Valley** winery.

Stiegerwald
Eastern district of **Franken.**

Stift
Austrian and German word for *monastery* – monasteries have always been important in the wine-making tradition in many countries.

Stiftsberg
Gr. of the **Badische Bergstrasse Kraichgau** *Ber.,* **Baden.**

Still
Term applied to table wines without sparkle.

Still
The apparatus used to distil spirits, i.e. to separate the alcohol from the water in an alcoholic liquid. *See* **Pot Still** and **Patent Still.**

Stitchcombe
Vyd. of Mildenhall, **Wiltshire.**

Stocks
Large wine estate at Suckley,
Worcestershire.

Stoneyfell
Old established company of **Adelaide,**
famous for *Metala* made from **Cabernet**
and **Shiraz** at **Langhorne Creek.**

Stony Hill
Small pioneer and high quality winery of
the **Napa Valley.**

Stravecchio
Italian word for *very old wine.*

Strega
One of the more popular herb liqueurs
made in **Italy.** It is slightly sweet and used
as a base for mixed drinks as well as on
its own.

Stromberg
Gr. of the **Württembergisches Unterland**
Ber., **Württemberg.**

Stück
German cask containing 1200 litres.

Stuttgart
Chief city of the **Württemberg** region,
producing red and white wines mainly for
local consumption.

Suau, Ch.
Small *2me cru* **Barsac.**

Südliche-Weinstrasse
Ber. of the **Rheinpfalz.**

de Suduiraut, Ch.
Large *premier cru* estate, **Sauternes,**
Preignac *comm.*

Sugared
See **Vins Chaptalisés.**

Supérieur
French wine with one degree of alcohol
above the legal minimum.

Süss Reserve
The unfermented **must** of the same
grapes of the same quality as the wine.
This means for a wine qualified as, e.g. an
Auslese, only that quality of *Süss
Reserve* may be added to bring the wine
to a certain degree of sweetness. *See*
Liqueur de Tirage.

Sutter Home
Small historic winery of the **Napa Valley.**

Suze
French yellowy-green, sweetish gentian
apéritif.

Swan Valley
Important vyd. area nr. Perth, Western
Australia.

Swartland
Demarcated district of **Cape Province.**

Swellendam
Small demarcated area of **Cape Province.**

Switzerland
The most important vyds. are found in the
Vaud and the **Valais.** A few names have a
legal control, e.g. **Dôle.**

Sybillenstein
Gr. of the **Wonnegau** *Ber.,* **Rheinhessen.**

Sylvaner
The white grape responsible for fine
Alsace and **Franken** wine. Also grown in
northern *Italy,* **South Africa** and
California.

Syrah
Important **Rhône** grape, produces rich, purply wine when mature. *See* **Shiraz.**

Szamarodni
Term for any full-fermented Hungarian dry wine.

Szekszárdi Vörós
Dark, strong red Hungarian wine.

Szürkebarát
The **Pinot Gris** in Hungary. *See* **Badacsoni.**

La Tâche
Grand cru vyd. and one of the finest of the **Vosne-Romanée** *comm.* and the **Côte d'Or.**

Tafelwein
See **Deutscher Tafelwein.**

Taillan, Ch. du
Cru bourgeois of the **Haut-Médoc, Le Taillan** *comm.*

Taittinger
Well-known **Champagne** growers and merchants at **Reims.**

Talbot, Ch.
Highly regarded *4me cru classé,* **St. Julien** *comm.,* **Haut-Médoc.**

Tannat
Local grape of Madiran, French **Pyrénées.**

Tannin
An important constituent of wine derived from the skins, pips and stems of grapes. It contributes to the body and keeping quality of a wine.

de Tart, Clos
Grand cru vyd. of the **Vosne-Romanée** *comm.,* **Côte de Nuits.** Some of the finest red Burgundies.

Tartaric acid
One of the most important acids in wine and one found more in association with the grape than any other fruit.

Tartrates
The chemically produced salts (seen as the sediment) which develop from the tartaric acid in a wine. *See* **Lees.**

Tastevin, Confrèrie de
Society for promoting **Burgundy** wines. Some labels indicate their approval. The *Tastevin* is a traditional silver wine-tasting cup.

Tauberberg
Gr. of the **Kocher-Jagst-Tauber** *Ber.,* **Württemberg.**

Tauberklinge
Gr. of the **Badisches Frankenland** *Ber.,* **Baden.**

La Taupine
Premier cru vyd. of the **Monthélie** *comm.,* **Côte de Beaune.**

Taurasi
Good *DOC* red from **Campania.**

Tavel
Acclaimed as one of the best dry *rosés* in
France. *AC* of the **Gard** *Dpt.*

Tawny
A style of **Port** which gains this colour
through being matured in wood. *See*
Vintage Port.

Taylor
Port shippers of full and rich **Vintage** and
Tawny Ports.

Taylor's
The biggest **New York State** winery.

Temperature
White wine is best served cool or cold.
The ideal white wines cellar temperature is
about 48°C; and for most red wines 55°C.
White wines may be cooled quickly in a
refrigerator or an ice bucket, but there is a
chance of ruining red wines by 'heating
them up' to room temperature. If the wine
is left for a few hours in the room in which
it is to be served it will acquire the correct
temperature without damage to the wine.

Tempranillo
Spanish grape used in the making of red
Riojas and other wines.

Tequila
Mexican spirit made from fermented agave
– a cactus-like plant.

Teran
Yugoslavian name for the Italian grape
Refosco – produces a full-bodied dark
red wine.

Terlano (or Terlaner)
DOC from **Trentino-Alto Adige.** White
wines always give the grape name on the
label.

Teroldego Rotaliano
DOC light red to deep red wine of **Trento,
Trentino-Alto Adige.**

Terry (de)
Spanish **Brandy** and **Sherry** producer.

du Tertre, Ch.
5me cru of the **Arsac-Margaux** *comm.,*
Haut-Médoc.

Tertre-Daugay, Ch.
Grand cru classé of **Saint-Émilion.**

Tête de cuvée
French term sometimes used to denote
the best wines of a particular producer,
especially in **Burgundy.**

Teufelstor
Gr. of the **Maindreieck** *Ber.,* **Franken.**

Les Teurons
Premier cru vyd. of the **Beaune** *comm.*

Thann
Town and *comm.* of **Alsace.**

Theuniskraal
Well-known wine estate of the **Tulbagh**
region of **South Africa** specializing in
white wines.

Thin
Of a wine – lacking in body.

Thorin, J.
Beaujolais grower and merchant,
Pontanevaux.

Thorins
See **Romanêche-Thorins.**

Three Choirs
Vyd. at Newent, **Gloucestershire.**

Ticino
One of the more important, Italian-speaking Swiss cantons; red and white wines.

Tiélandry
Premier cru vyd. of the **Beaune** *comm.*

Tinto
Italian, Spanish and Portuguese term for *full-bodied red wine.*

Tio Pepe
Famous **fino Sherry** of **Gonzales Byass.**

Tîrnave
Wine region of **Rumania** famous for **Perla,** a blended white wine.

Tischwein
German for *table wine; vin ordinaire.*

Tocai
North-east Italian white grape. *See* **Pinot Gris.**

Tocai de Lison
DOC **Veneto,** white wine.

Tocai de San Martino della Battaglia
White wine *DOC,* **Lombardia.**

Tokay (Tokaji)
Historically famous rich Hungarian dessert wine from the north-eastern corner of the country. It is made from **Tokay-Furmint** grapes that have been affected by **Botrytis cinerea** which are allowed to shrivel and concentrate the sugar content. These berries are selected and put into buckets called **puttonyos,** and then they are added to ordinary grapes before

fermentation and maturation in small *oak* barrels.
The first quality *Tokaji Aszu* will show the number of puttonyos added to the wine: one puttony is the driest and five the richest. *Tokaji Szamorodni* is a lesser version made by picking shrivelled and non-shrivelled grapes together.

Tokay d'Alsace
See **Pinot Gris.**

Tonneau
Equivalent to 4 **Barriques;** in **Bordeaux:** 900 litres. Other capacities elsewhere.

Tonnerre, Montée de
Premier cru, **Chablis.**

Torgiano
Quality red *DOC* from **Umbria** – small production.

Torres
Well-known Spanish firm making the best wines of **Penedès.**

Toscana (Tuscany)
Fine and important Italian wine region which includes the **Chianti** region.

Touraine
Loire province with a big range of wines. The best are from **Vouvray** (white) and **Bourgueil** (red). Also *rosé.* They can be **mousseux** and **pétillant.**

Touraine-Azay-le-Rideau
App. only applies to wine made from **Chenin Blanc.**

Touraine Mesland
Small district of **Touraine** with its own *AC* red, white and *rosé.*

La Tour-Blanche, Ch.
Premier cru from the **Bommes** *comm.,*
Sauternes.

La Tour-Carnet, Ch.
4me cru classé of the **St. Laurent** *comm.,*
Haut-Médoc.

La Tour de By, Ch.
Large *cru bourgeois* of the **Bas-Médoc,**
Bégadan *comm.,* one of the best vyds. of
the northern **Médoc.**

La Tour-de-Mons, Ch.
Well-known *cru bourgeois* of the **Haut-**
Médoc, Soussans *comm.*

La Tour-du-Pin-Figeac, Ch.
Two *grand cru classés,* **Saint-Émilion.**

La Tour-Figeac, Ch.
Grand cru classé, **Côtes Saint-Émilion.**

La Tour Haut-Brion, Ch.
Grand cru classé for red wines of the
Talence *comm.,* **Graves de Bordeaux.**
Second wine of **La Mission-Haut-Brion.**

La Tour-Martillac, Ch.
Grand cru classé red and white wines
from the **Martillac** *comm.,* **Graves.**

Tournefeuille, Ch.
First class **Pomerol** estate, **Néac.**

Tournus
Historic town of the **Mâconnais.**

La Tour Pibran, Ch.
Cru bourgeois of the **Haut-Médoc,**
Pauillac *comm.*

Traben-Trarbach
Twin village of the *Gr.* **Schwarzlay, Zell-**
Mosel, producing some good light white
wines.

Traminer
White wine grape of **Austria, Alsace,** and
Germany, known commonly as the
Gewürztraminer.

Tramini
The **Traminer** in **Hungary.**

Trappenberg (Hochstadt)
Gr. of the **Südliche Weinstrasse** *Ber.,*
Rheinpfalz.

Trappistine
Greenish **Armagnac**-based herb liqueur.

Trebbianino Val Trebbia
Pale golden *DOC* white from **Emilia-**
Romagna.

Trebbiano
Main white grape of central **Italy.** In
France known as the *Ugni Blanc* and/or
the **Saint-Émilion.**

Trebbiano d'Abruzzo
Dry slightly tannic white wine from
Abruzzo.

Trefethen
Family owned winery of the **Napa Valley.**

Treis-Karden
Village of the *Gr.* **Goldbäumchen, Zell-**
Mosel, MSR.

Trentino-Alto Adige
Small wine region of northern **Italy.** Eleven
DOC areas.

du Tricastin, Coteaux
Red, *rosé* and white *AC* **Rhône** wines
from the **Drôme** district.

Trier
Important German wine city of the **Mosel**
valley, **MSR.**

Trimbach, F. E.
Important grower and merchant in
Ribeauvillé, Alsace.

Trittenheim
Village of the *Gr.* **Michelsberg, Mittel-Mosel** with good light white wines.

Trocken
German term indicating *dry wine.*

Trockenbeerenauslese
The highest grade of naturally sweet wines made from grapes that have dried on the vine from which the finest German white dessert wines are made. *See* **Beerenauslese** and **Edelfäule.**

Troisième cru (3me)
Third growth of the five *crus classés* of the **Haut-Médoc.** Fourteen Chx.

Trois-Moulins, Ch.
Grand cru of **Saint-Émilion.**

Trollinger (Blauer)
German grape which produces some light red wines in the **Württemberg** region.

Tronquoy-Lalande, Ch.
Better-known *cru bourgeois* of the **St. Estèphe** *comm.* of the **Haut-Médoc.**

Troplong Mondot, Ch.
Large *grand cru classé* nr. **Saint-Émilion.**

Trotanoy, Ch.
Leading **Pomerol** vyd.

Trottenvieille
Small *premier grand cru* vyd. of **Saint-Émilion.**

Tsinandali
A quality white wine of Georgia, **USSR.**

Tulbagh
Beautiful demarcated wine region of the **Cape Province** famous for white wines.

Tulloch
Old and reliable **Hunter Valley** concern.

Tuquet, Ch.
Fairly large **Graves, Beautiran** *comm.,* making red and white wines.

Turckheim
Comm. of **Alsace.**

Turkey
Although production and exports to Western Europe were considerable before World War II, Turkey now exports only a small amount of wine.

Twee Jongegezellen
Famous wine estate in **Tulbagh,** producing mainly white wines.

Tyrrell
Traditional **Hunter Valley** estate, producing quality wines.

Ugni Blanc
See **Trebbiano.**

Uitkyk
Historic **Cape Province** wine estate in the **Stellenbosch** district.

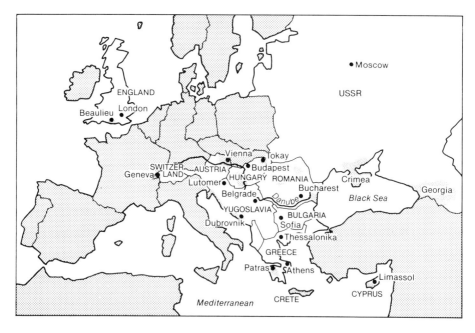

Umbria
Wine region of central **Italy**. Three *DOC* wines, including **Orvieto** and **Torgiano.**

Umstadt
Ber. of **Hessische Bergstrasse.**

Underberg
Brand name of a German digestive **bitter.**

Ungstein
Village of the **Mittelhaardt**, *Gr.* **Hochmess (Bad Dürkheim)** producing consistent wines.

Ürzig
One of the best wine-producing villages of the **Mittel-Mosel**, *Gr.* **Schwarzlay.**

USA
United States of America. *See* **California, New York State, Arkansas, Ohio.**

USSR
One of the world's largest wine-producing areas. The wines are mostly sweet, both red and white, but there are some dry and fortified, and sparkling wine production is increasing. Important areas are Azerbaijan, Georgia, the **Crimea** and the Don Valley.

Vacqueyras
One of the best *comm.* of the **Rhône.** Red, white and *rosé* wines entitled to the *AC* **Côtes du Rhône-Villages.**

Vaillons
Premier cru **Chablis.**

du Val, Clos
Small French owned winery, **Napa Valley.**

Valais
Alpine section of the **Rhône** valley in **Switzerland** producing the famous **Fendant** and **Dôle.**

Val d'Adige
DOC of a large number of *comm.* of **Trentino-Alto Adige.**

Valdepeñas
Small town of La Mancha, **Spain,** producing good red and white wines slightly higher in alcohol than normal table wines. They were traditionally matured in clay jars.

Valdespino
Famous **Sherry bodega** at **Jerez.**

Valencia
Spanish demarcated region of the Levante producing dark red strong wines.

Valencia
Large wine producer of Western **Australia** producing a full range of wines.

Valgella
Good dry red *DOC* from **Lombardia.**

Valle d'Aosta
Small, less important wine region of **Italy** though viniculture is a major activity. Two *DOC* wines.

Valmur
Grand cru vyd. of the **Chablis** region.

Valpolicella
Popular light red *DOC* wines from **Veneto.**

Valtellina
DOC for a range of wines from **Lombardia,** principally from **Nebbiolo** grapes. Also *Valtellina Superiore* which has a higher degree of alcohol.

Valwig
Village of the *Gr.* **Rosenhang, Zell-Mosel** in the **Krampen** stretch of the r.

Van der Hum
A liqueur from **Cape Province, Brandy-** based and flavoured with a fruit similar to a tangerine.

Varela
Sherry shippers; members of the **Rumasa** group.

Varietal
A term sometimes applied to a wine whose name derives from the grape used rather than the place of origin.

Vaucopin
Premier cru **Chablis;** white **Burgundy.**

Vaucrains, Les
Nuits St. Georges vyd., **Côtes de Nuits.**

Vaud
Largest Swiss wine region on the north shore of Lake Geneva.

Vaudésir
Fine *grand cru* **Chablis** vyd.

VDQS
See **Vin Délimite.**

Vecchio
Italian for *old.*

Vega Sicilia
Fine, full-bodied, rare red from Old Castile, **Spain.** Can be up to 16° alcohol.

Veldenz
Picturesque village of the **Bernkastel** *Ber.* of the **MSR.**

Velletri
Dry *DOC* red or white wines from **Lazio.**

Veltliner
See **Grüner Veltliner.**

Vendange
French for the *grape harvest*. The *vintage.*

Vendange tardive
Late vintage. in **Alsace** equivalent to the
German **Auslese.**

Vendemmia
Italian for *vintage.*

Vendimia
Spanish for *vintage.*

Venencia
The silver cup on a long cane, traditionally
used for taking **Sherry** from the cask for
tasting.

Veneto
Important wine-producing region of
northern **Italy. Twelve** *DOC* areas
including **Soave, Valpolicella, Bardolino.**

de Ventoux, Côtes
Red, white and *rosé VDQS,* **Vaucluse,
Côtes du Rhône.**

Verdelho
Madeira grape and the name of the
second driest style.

Verdicchio
White Italian grape.

Verdicchio dei Castelli di Jesi
Famous and historic dry white *DOC,*
Marches wine.

Verdicchio di Mateliac
Similar to the above but not so well
known.

Verdisi
White grape of **Veneto** region, **Italy.**

Verdun
Important estate of **Stellenbosch** well
known for red and white wines.

Verduzzo
DOC from **Friuli-Venezia Giulia.** Full-
bodied semi-sweet white wine.

Vereinigte Hospitien
Hospital in **Trier** owning important vyds. in
a number of districts in the **Mosel** and
Saar districts.

Vergennes, Les
Vyd. of the **Côte de Beaune** with part
entitled to the **Corton** *app.*

Vergenoegd
Old **Cape Province** wine estate at
Stellenbosch.

Vermentino
White Italian table wine from **Liguria.**

Vermentino di Gallura
Strong *DOC* dry white wine of **Sardegna.**

Vermouth
The basis of *Vermouth,* French or Italian,
is white wine, usually a full-flavoured wine
high in alcohol, in which a variety of
aromatic Alpine herbs are macerated. The
result is a light and aromatic **apéritif.**

Vernaccia
Grape of central **Italy** and **Sardegna.** It
produces distinctive wines, e.g. *Vernaccia
di San Gimignano,* a Tuscan white wine.

Vertheuil
One of the lesser wine-producing *comm.*
of the **Haut-Médoc.**

Vertical tasting
Tasting of wines of the same vyd. but of
different vintages.

Vertus
Second level **Champagne** from the canton
de **Vertus, Chälons** Arrondissement.

Verwaltung
German for *property.* Also used to mean
administration e.g. of wine estates.

Verzenay
Important *grand cru* **Champagne** *comm.*
of the **Montagne de Reims.**

Verzy
Premier cru **Champagne** from the
Montagne de Reims.

Veuve-Cliquot
Historically famous and excellent
Champagne house at **Reims.**

Victoria
In the north-east important vyds. nr.
Rutherglen and Milawa, also Tahbilk and
others in the Goulburn Valley, north of
Melbourne. Great Western, west of
Melbourne, is the principal centre for the
production of Australian sparkling wines,
including that named after the district.
Other important vyds. around Mildura in
the very north-west of the state.

Vidal-Fleury, J.
Rhône shippers and growers.

Vieille Cure
A popular French liqueur, distilled at
Bordeaux. It has a **Brandy** base in which
many herbs are macerated.

Vienna
See **Wien.**

Vienot, Charles
Good quality **Burgundy** grower and
merchant at **Nuits St. Georges.**

Viertelstück
Rhine wine cask measure; one-quarter of
a **stück** – 300 litres.

Vieux Château Certan, Ch.
Next to **Ch. Pétrus,** and one of the
leading **Pomerol** growths.

Vignelaure, Ch.
Good red **Provence** estate nr. **Aix-en-
Provence.**

Vignoble
French name for a vyd. area.

Vila Real
Port town of the **Alto Douro.**

Villa Mount Eden
Small estate of the **Napa Valley.**

Villegeorge, Ch.
Small *cru exceptionnel,* **Avensan** *comm.,*
Haut-Médoc.

Villemaurine, Ch.
Grand cru classé of **Saint-Émilion.**

Villenave-d'Ornon
Comm. of the **Graves** region.

Viña
Spanish for *vyd.*

Vin de Garde
A wine suitable for laying down; will
improve with keeping.

Vin de l'année
See **Heurige,** and **Beaujolais de l'année.**

Vin Délimité de Qualité Supérieure (VDQS)
A rank of wines in **France** below *AC* established for traditional local wines of overall quality.

Vin de Paille
A speciality of the **Jura;** the wine is made from fully ripe grapes which are first dried traditionally on beds of straw. It is high in alcohol.

Vin doux naturel
Sweet wine fortified (not natural).

Vin gris
In fact pale *pink* wine not *grey,* from red grapes pressed with a maximum of skin contact before fermentation takes place.

Vinho
Portuguese for *wine. Vinho de meda –* table wine; *Vinho de consumo – ordinaire; Vinho Verde* – green or young wine which may have a slight sparkle.

Vinhos Verdes
Specially demarcated area of **Portugal** for the production of green wines.

VINIMPEX
Bulgarian state wine enterprise.

Vin Jaune
A white wine affected by **Flor** yeast while being aged in barrel. A speciality of Arbois, **Jura.**

Vino
Spanish for *wine,* e.g. *Vino corriente –* ordinary table wine; *Vino generose –* dessert wine.

Vino Nobile di Montepulciano
Traditional and notable Tuscan *DOC* red.

Vin ordinaire
Common French term for inexpensive wine drunk daily in quantity.

Vinosity
The quality or soul of the wine; not just alcoholic strength.

Vin Santo
Strong sweet white wine of **Toscana.**

Vins de pays
The 'third rank' of French wines, below *VDQS,* and *AC,* for wines which have a consistent local or regional character. The rank was created to encourage the improvement of ordinary wines.

Vinsobres
One of the villages of the **Drôme** district entitled to the *AC* **Côtes du Rhône-Villages.**

Vintage
The gathering of the grapes. Also the particular year when the grapes were gathered and the wine made. There is a *Vintage* every year but the quality of the grapes vintaged varies from year to year. There are wines shipped under the date of their vintage and others which are not dated.

Vintage character
A blend of quality **Port** wines matured in wood to have something of the style of **Vintage Port.**

Vintage Port
Port of one vintage, only made in the best years and customarily bottled after two years in cask. Always throws a heavy deposit – decant.

Vin vert
A light acidic white wine, especially from **Roussillon.**

Viognier
Rare **Rhône** valley white grape, used for the fine **Ch. Grillet.**

Viré
Village just north of **Mâcon** producing very good white wines especially in the **Clos du Chapitre.**

Virginia
American state with a small number of vyds. but increasing quality.

Visan
One of the better wine villages of **Vaucluse** – entitled to the *AC* **Côtes du Rhône-Villages.**

Viticulteur
French for *grower of vines.*

Vitis labrusca
American vine stocks, as opposed to the European **Vitris vinifera.**

Vodka
Popular clear spirit produced in many countries by the **Continuous Still** process. It is usually a flavourless and odourless straight, neutral spirit, but in **Russia** and **Poland,** where it is the national drink, a wide variety of flavoured *Vodkas* are available using, e.g. Bison grass or hot red peppers.

Vogelsgärten
Gr. of the **Nierstein** *Ber.,* **Rheinhessen.**

Vogtei Rötteln
Gr. of the **Markgräflerland** *Ber.,* **Baden.**

de Vogüe, Comte
Important red wine domaine in **Le Musigny** *comm.,* **Côte de Nuits.**

Voiura
Local Spanish white grape.

Volatile acidity
The state of wine caused by the presence of **acetic acid** (vinegar) often caused when wine casks are left incompletely filled as the wine evaporates.

Volnay
Important *comm.* and *AC* of the **Côte de Beaune** close to **Meursault,** producing mostly soft, delicate, red wines.

Volnay-Santenots
A red wine *app.* for **Meursault, Côte de Beaune.**

Vom Heissen Stein
Gr. of the **Bernkastel** *Ber.,* **Mittel-Mosel, MSR.**

Vosgros
Premier cru **Chablis.**

Vöslau
Centre of red wine district of Lower **Austria.**

Vosne-Romanée
The small village at the heart of the finest red **Burgundy** vyds. for **Romanée Conti, Richebourg, Romanée St. Vivant, La Tâche.**

Vougeot
Grand cru vyds. in the **Côtes de Nuits** and the home of the celebrated *Clos de Vougeot.*

Vouvray
AC white of **Touraine** – a large range of

fine white wines including sweet styles. Separate *app.* for **mousseux** and **pétillant** wines which are made by the *méth. champ.*

VQPRD
Vini di Qualità Prodotti in Regioni Delimitate. Italian term for quality wines produced in accordance with EEC regulations.

Vulkanfelsen
Gr. of the **Kaiserstuhl-Tuniberg** *Ber.,* **Baden.**

Wachau, The
District around **Dürnstein** producing some of **Austria's** best white wines.

Wacheneim
Village of the **Mittelhaardt,** and *Ber.,* **Bingen, Rheinhessen.**

Waldböckelheim
Village of the *Gr.* **Burgweg, Bad Kreuznach** district of the **Nahe** valley.

Waldrach
Small wine village of the *Gr.* **Romerlay, Ruwer** valley, **MSR,** producing some good wines.

Waldulm
Red wine village of the **Ortenau** district of **Baden.**

Wallhausen
Village of the *Gr.* **Pfarrgarten, Kreuznach** district of the **Nahe.**

Walluf
Village of the **Rheingau,** formerly *Ober-* and *Nieder-Walluf.*

Walporzheim/Ahrtal
The name of the *Ber.* covering the whole of the **Ahr** region.

Wälschriesling
German for the **Italian Riesling.** In **Hungary** the **Olasz Riesling.**

Walsheim
Village of the *Gr.* **Bischofs-Kreuz, Südliche Weinstrasse** district of the **Rheinpfalz.**

Warre
Old established **Port** shippers.

Wartbühl
Gr. of the **Remstal-Stuttgart, Württemberg.**

Wasenweiler
Village of the **Kaiserstuhl-Tuniberg, Baden.**

Wawern
Small village of the *Gr.* **Scharzberg, Saar** valley, **MSR.**

Wehlen
Important wine town of the **Mosel** valley, **Bernkastel** district, **MSR.**

Weibel Champagne Vineyards
Central coast winery producing Californian **Champagne** and table wines.

Weinbaugebiet
A legally defined wine-growing area in
Austria.

Weinbrannt
German for **Brandy.**

Weingut
German for *wine estate.*

Weingutesiegel
The Austrian seal for quality wine indicated
by a red, white and gold disc on the bottle.

Weinhex
Gr. of the **Zell-Mosel, MSR.**

Weinkellerei
German for *wine cellar.*

Weinsberg
Village of the **Württembergisches
Unterland** district of **Württemberg**
producing mainly red wines.

Weinsteige
Gr. of the **Remstal-Stuttgart** *Ber.,*
Württemberg.

Weinstrasse
German for the *road through vyds.,* now
'wine routes' for tourists.

Weinviertel
Name given to quantity-producing district
nr. **Wien.**

Weisser Riesling
Literally *white riesling.* German grape
being used in **South Africa.**

Weissherbst
A German *rosé* from the **Baden** region
made by quickly removing the skins from

the **must.** The wine must be made from
one kind of red grape only, the name of
which must appear on the label.

Well-balanced
Harmony in all aspects of a wine.

Wente Livermore
Large, old estate of **California** noted for its
white wines.

Wertheim
Village of the **Badisches Frankenland**
district of **Baden.**

Westbury
Important English vyd. nr. Reading,
Berkshire, producing both red and white
wines and currently experimenting with
production from **Cabernet** grapes.

Western Australia
Full-bodied red and white wines, plus
fortified styles, from vyds. within the Perth
metropolitan area. New and increasingly
important quality red and white wines from
recently planted vyds. at Margaret River
(which has introduced **Australia's** first
Appellation Contrôlée), Mount Barker,
and Frankland River in the more
temperate southern part of the State.

Westfield
Large vyd. nr. Hastings, **Sussex.**

Westhofen
Large vyd. area of the **Rheinhessen** in the
Wonnegau *Ber.*

Whisky
One of the world's great spirits, it can be
made from a variety of grains: barley,
malted or unmalted, rye, wheat, corn, or
combinations of them. It can be produced
in a **Pot Still** or **Continuous Still,** or be a
blend of the two. It can be single, double
or triple distilled spirit.

The different flavours of the different Whiskies: **Scotch,** *malt* or *blended,* **Irish, Canadian, American, Bourbon,** *corn* or *rye,* derive from the different ingredients used, the method and length of distillation, the type and length of maturation, and in most instances the art of the blender at the end of the cycle.

White Port
Made from white grapes and is golden-coloured. Sweet and dry.

Widmers
Finger Lakes winery selling native varietals: **New York State.**

Wien (Vienna)
Austrian capital surrounded by many suburban vyds. famous for **Heurige** wines.

Williams, Poire
Colourless **eau-de-vie** made from distilled pear juice.

Williams & Humbert
Famous quality **Sherry** house now owned by **Rumasa.**

Wiltingen
Important vyd. area in the **Saar** valley, *Gr.* **Scharzberg,** giving some fine wines.

Wincheringen
One of the more important villages of the **Obermosel, MSR.**

Wine
Wine is the fermented juice of freshly gathered grapes. The colour, bouquet, flavour, strength, and quality of any wine depend on a number of factors, the main ones being: (1) the species of grapes used; (2) the nature of the soil and aspect of the vyd.; (3) the incidence of rain and sunshine; (4) the care given to the cultivation of the vines and to the gathering of the grapes; (5) the manner and degree of pressing and the

fermentation; and (6) the methods adopted for blending and maturing, the time and manner of bottling, packing, despatching, binning, uncorking, decanting and serving.

Fermentation may be slow or rapid, complete or partial, satisfactory or unsatisfactory, but it is as inevitable as it is natural, and it transforms part of the whole of the sugar present in fresh grape juice into alcohol; the sweeter the grapes, the stronger the wine. Fermentation may be checked by the addition of spirit or of chemicals, but there cannot be any such thing as a natural, non-alcoholic wine – it is a contradiction in terms.

Light beverage wines, which are 'natural' wines, contain anything from 8–15° of alcohol by volume; fortified wines are higher; water always is the bulk of the wine but there are also minute quantities of quite a large number of other substances which are responsible for the colour, bouquet, flavour and keeping quality of every wine.

Winkel
One of the better-known villages of the **Johannisberg** *Ber.,* **Rheingau,** with the famous **Schloss Vollrads** estate.

Winniwgen
Village of the *Gr.* **Weinhex, Zell-Mosel, MSR.**

Wintrich
Small vyds. area of the **Bernkastel** district, **MSR.**

Winzergenossenschaft
German for *wine co-operative.* Also **Winzerverein.**

Wolfsmagen
Gr. of the **Starkenburg** *Ber.,* **Hessische Bergstrasse.**

Wollmesheim
Village of the **Südliche Weinstrasse, Rheinpfalz.**

Wonnegau
Southernmost *Ber.* of the **Rheinhessen.**

Wood
Wine is *in the wood* when it is in the cask.

Woody
An undesirable taste imparted to a wine that has been left a little too long in the *oak* cask.

Wootton
Young and well-established award winning English vyd. nr. Wells, **Somerset,** producing crisp fruity wine from **Müller-Thurgau, Seyval Blanc** and a new German variety, **Schönburger.**

Worcester
Demarcated wine region of **South Africa.**

Worms
An important centre of the **Rheinhessen** wine trade with the **Liebfrauenstift** vyd. where **Liebfraumilch** originated.

Wraxall
English vyd. at Shepton Mallet, **Somerset,** producing medium dry fruity wine from the **Müller-Thurgau** and **Sevyal Blanc**

Wunnenstein
Gr. of the **Württembergisches Unterland, Württemberg.**

Württemberg
QbA region of **Germany** producing more red than white, including the local aromatic **Schillerwein.** *Ber.* are *Jagst-Tauber, Remstal-Stuttgart, Württembergisches Unterland.*

Württembergisches Unterland
Ber. of **Württemberg.**

Wurzburg
Centre of the **Franken** wine region, producing **Stein** wines; full-bodied and dry.

Wyndham Estate
Bulk-producing winery of Branxton, **New South Wales.**

Wynns
Large company with wineries in **South Australia** and **New South Wales,** with some outstanding wines, e.g. **Coonawarra, Estate Cabernet,** and sparkling wines by the *méth. champ.*

XO
The oldest **Cognac** found on the ordinary market – a blend of very old Cognacs.

Xynisteri
Main white grape variety of **Cyprus** used with **Mavron** to produce **Commandaria,** the sweet dessert wine.

Yalumba
See **Smith's Yalumba.**

Yeasty
An undesirable taste in some white wines caused mainly by *Saccharomyces acidi faciens.*

Yenda
Brandy distillery in **New South Wales,
Australia,** owned by the **McWilliam**
family. *See* **McWilliam.**

Ygay
See **Castillo Ygay.**

Y Grec
Brand name of a rare dry wine from **Ch.
Yquem.**

Yon-Figeac, Ch.
Large well-known *grand cru classé,*
Graves Saint-Émilion.

Yonne
Wine-producing region and *Dpt.* of **France**
noted for white wines, the best being those
of **Chablis.**

d'Yquem, Ch.
The great *premier grand cru* estate of
Sauternes. It is regarded as the finest of
all naturally sweet white wines of **France.**

Yugoslavia
Produces large quantities of wines of all
types, but is possibly most famous for its
Rieslings produced mainly from the
Italian Riesling and marketed as
Ljutomer.

Yvorne
One of the best white wines of the **Vaud.**

Z

Zell-Mosel
Lower **Mosel** district of the **Mosel-Saar-
Ruwer** stretching from Zell to **Koblenz.**

Zeltingen-Rachtig
Village of the *Gr.* **Münzlay, Bernkastel**
Ber., of **MSR.**

Zgarolo
DOC white, similar to **Frascati,** from
Lazio.

Zierfändler
Austrial flowery white wine grape also
known as the *Spätrot.*

Žilavka
Native Yugoslavian white wine grape.
Produces wines which are full and high in
alcohol.

Zinfandel
Red wine grape, native of **California.**

Zoldszilvani
Green **Sylvaner** – Hungarian grape.